The European Science Foundation (ESF) was established in 1974 to create a common European platform for cross-border cooperation in all aspects of scientific research.

With its emphasis on a multidisciplinary and pan-European approach, the Foundation provides the leadership necessary to open new frontiers in European science.

Its activities include providing science policy advice (Science Strategy); stimulating co-operation between researchers and organisations to explore new directions (Science Synergy); and the administration of externally funded programmes (Science Management). These take place in the following areas: Physical and engineering sciences; Medical sciences; Life, earth and environmental sciences; Humanities; Social sciences; Polar; Marine; Space; Radio astronomy frequencies; Nuclear physics.

Headquartered in Strasbourg with offices in Brussels, the ESF's membership comprises 75 national funding agencies, research performing agencies and academies from 30 European nations.

The Foundation's independence allows the ESF to objectively represent the priorities of all these members.

MEDIA BETWEEN CULTURE AND COMMERCE

CHANGING MEDIA – CHANGING EUROPE SERIES

VOLUME 4

EDITED BY ELS DE BENS

CO-EDITORS: CEES HAMELINK, KAROL JAKUBOWICZ, KAARLE NORDENSTRENG,
JAN VAN CUILENBURG & RICHARD VAN DER WURFF

intellect Bristol, UK / Chicago, USA

First published in the UK in 2007 by
Intellect Books, PO Box 862, Bristol BS99 1DE, UK

First published in the USA in 2007 by
Intellect Books, The University of Chicago Press, 1427 E. 60th Street, Chicago,
IL 60637, USA

A catalogue record for this book is available from the British Library

Cover Design: Gabriel Solomons
Copy Editor: Heather Owen
Typesetting: Mac Style, Nafferton, E. Yorkshire

ISBN 978–1–84150–165–9

Printed and bound by Gutenberg Press, Malta

Contents

Foreword

This volume is the product of a major programme under the title Changing Media – Changing Europe supported by the European Science Foundation (ESF). The ESF is the European association of national organizations responsible for the support of scientific research. Established in 1974, the Foundation currently has seventy-six Member Organisations (research councils, academies and other national scientific institutions) from twenty-nine countries. This programme is the first to be sponsored by both the Social Sciences and the Humanities Standing Committees of the ESF, and this unique cross-disciplinary organization reflects the very broad and central concerns which have shaped the Programme's work. As co-chairpersons of the Programme it has been our great delight to bring together many of the very best scholars from across the continent, but also across the disciplinary divides which so often fragment our work, to enable stimulating, innovative, and profoundly important debates addressed to understanding some of the most fundamental and critical aspects of contemporary social and cultural life.

The study of the media in Europe forces us to try to understand the major institutions which foster understanding and participation in modern societies. At the same time we have to recognize that these societies themselves are undergoing vital changes, as political associations and alliances, demographic structures, the worlds of work, leisure, domestic life, mobility, education, politics and communications themselves are all undergoing important transformations. Part of that understanding, of course, requires us not to be too readily seduced by the magnitude and brilliance of technological changes into assuming that social changes must comprehensively follow. A study of the changing media in Europe, therefore, is indeed a study of changing Europe. Research on media is closely linked to questions of economic and technological growth and expansion, but also to questions of public policy and the state, and more broadly to social, economic and cultural issues.

To investigate these very large debates the Programme is organised around four key questions. The first deals with the tension between citizenship and consumerism, that is the relation between media, the public sphere and the market; the challenges facing the media, cultural policy and the public service media in Europe. The second area of work focuses on the dichotomy and relation between culture and commerce, and the conflict in media policy caught between cultural aspirations and commercial imperatives. The third question deals with the problems of convergence and fragmentation in relation to the development of media technology on a global and European level. This leads to questions about the concepts of the information society, the network society etc., and to a focus on new media such as the internet and multimedia, and the impact of these new media on society, culture, and our work, education and everyday life. The fourth field of inquiry is concerned with media and cultural identities and the relationship between processes of homogenization and diversity. This explores the role of media in everyday life, questions of gender, ethnicity, lifestyle, social differences, and cultural identities in relation to both media audiences and media content.

In each of the books arising from this exciting Programme we expect readers to learn something new, but above all to be provoked into fresh thinking, understanding and inquiry, about how the media and Europe are both changing in novel, profound, and far reaching ways that bring us to the heart of research and discussion about society and culture in the twenty-first century.

Ib Bondebjerg
Peter Golding

1

MEDIA BETWEEN CULTURE AND COMMERCE: AN INTRODUCTION

Els De Bens

An ambitious and ambiguous title

This book addresses the consequences of the profound changes that have affected the media over the last years. Its contributors reflect on the concern and the debate about the role of the media in our rapidly evolving society. They identify and analyse the conflicts and the tensions between cultural policies and market forces at work in the present-day media landscape.

The title 'The Media between Culture and Commerce' may seem rather vague and ambiguous. It is more of a symbolic title that refers to the tensions between the public role of the media and the advancing commercialisation, between the public sphere and the market model, or, in Denis McQuail's succinct phrase, between 'commercialism and non-commercialism' (D. McQuail, 1998, pp. 108–110).

It has not been our intention to explore in depth the concept of culture. As a matter of fact, culture itself is scarcely discussed explicitly in the present book. 'Culture' serves rather as a portmanteau term for anything that connotes the non-commercialism and the idealistic ambitions of the 'public' model. Commercialism refers to the pursuit of profit as a primary goal, while non-commercialism in the media is associated with pluralism, diversity, and all kinds of public interest obligations that are often at odds with the profit motives that are inherent in the market-oriented model.

Privatisation and commercialisation have actually also stimulated creativity and innovation. In the seventies radio was the first medium to be privatised in Europe. For quite some time pirate radio stations anchored outside territorial waters had been challenging the established public broadcasting monopoly. An agreement in the Council of Europe (22 January 1965) allowed for action against these commercial and illegal 'pirates', but not before the latter had acquired a large and enthusiastic following. These stations introduced new music genres and innovative radio styles (including disc jockeys) that were subsequently copied by the public radio broadcasters.

After a second attempt to make illegal the use of the air waves by citizen band (CB) radio amateurs, and then an explosive growth of various types of illegal private radio stations – ranging from small, emancipatory ventures to purely commercial enterprises – the authorities finally decided to legalise private radio broadcasting in the seventies. Again the competitive challenge from the private radio stations incited public broadcasters to make their radio channels more dynamic and, above all, to differentiate them. Together with the new private radio stations, the re-profiled public stations gave a strong boost to the music industry.

The privatisation of television in Europe took place in the mid-eighties and subjected public television broadcasting to shock therapy. Across the board, the public TV stations were denounced for having become outdated, patronising and paternalistic as a consequence of their far-reaching bureaucratisation and politicisation. In several European countries public television broadcasters lost viewers to the newly arrived commercial rivals and their popular, youth-directed, trendy programming. The competition forced the public broadcasters to innovate and to strive for more autonomy, more dynamism, less politicisation, new programmes, and different formats. Thus the various national audio-visual industries were forcefully stimulated when private production companies were allowed to supply the public stations with programmes.

The success enjoyed by the new commercial players in the audio-visual market also affected the printed media. The new audio-visual competitors often appealed to the same advertisers for their funding, and newspapers and magazines were now obliged to reckon with their readers' changing expectations. In the nineties all newspapers underwent facelifts that incorporated more pictures, more colour, eye-catching titles, a fresh layout and a shift in content. They put more emphasis on human interest and on a more narrative style of writing. Newspapers grew 'fatter' and addressed the need for service journalism, including various special interest columns on subjects such as gastronomy, gardening, fitness and health, travel, etc.

It may be safely said that, in the initial stage, the liberalisation and commercialisation of the media market prompted healthy and constructive competition, which enhanced diversity.

By the end of the century, however, it became increasingly clear that the advertising market was not a sufficiently flexible and adequate funding source for the new media players and that the fight for advertising revenues was becoming extremely fierce. To defend their position the large media concerns entered into alliances with various types of media enterprises in order to extend their activities from printed and audio-visual media into the dotcom and the telecom/cable/satellite sectors. Conflict of interest leads to distorted power relations; cutthroat competition is harmful to diversity. In order to maximise profits, the media enterprises have been going to increasingly greater lengths in their quest for as many media consumers, and hence advertising revenues, as possible.

The title of this chapter refers to the media situation in the past five years, in which the tension between commercialism and non-commercialism has sharply increased. It is fairly obvious that between these two extremes, which the title symbolically reflects, there are many shades and different positions. Still, the triumphant rise of commerce and its dominant search for profits has proved to be inexorable.

The fact that during the latest RIPE conference in Copenhagen two colleagues happened to present papers with similar titles can hardly be accidental: A. Murray: Tension Headaches. The Experience of the culture/commerce tension: A study of the social context of scheduling, and J. Steemers: The BBC Balancing Culture and Commerce on the Global Stage. This is clear indication that a wider variety of media researchers have been occupied with the same controversial topic. Their papers refer to the challenges public broadcasting faces when trying to find a balanced position in the tension that exists between culture and commerce. They search for ways in which programme makers and schedulers can 'negotiate the culture/commerce tension by providing a range of programmes that fulfils the two objectives' (A. Murray, 2004).

The market model has been increasingly gaining importance and profit-making has become the central preoccupation of media companies and organisations. Culture has been turned into a commodity that is subject to the laws of the market. Quality is measured by success in the marketplace (Croteau & Hoynes, 2001, p. 34).

Today the 'public' and the 'market' models are blending into one another. Public broadcasters have been copying programming strategies from their commercial counterparts, and vice versa. A number of quality newspapers have not only adopted the tabloid format, but also tabloidised their lay-out and content with the sole purpose of increasing circulation figures.

This book does not present a 'good versus evil' narrative. It steers clear of the classic antithesis between highbrow or elitist, and lowbrow or populist culture, and above all, it avoids the patronising claim to 'know what is best for the people'. In its fullest sense, the term 'culture' in our title stands for diversity, openness, creativity and the non-priority of profit seeking.

Although quality as such may be encountered in all varieties of media, both in the public and in the private sector, it should be obvious that those media that appertain to the public service model (e.g. public broadcasters) or that profess to embrace quality (e.g. quality newspapers) will show a much stronger propensity to preserve culture against gross commercialism.

Commercialism and Hypercommercialism

Apart from describing some major changes in the media industry, this book also detects the causes of these changes and their impact on society as a whole. There is hardly any doubt that the most striking feature of these last years has been the advancing commercialisation, or marketisation, of the media sector.

The liberalisation and the concomitant privatisation of the media markets started in the early eighties as a joint result of political decisions, economic pressures and technological innovations. In most European countries public service monopolies were broken up and a profusion of new commercial TV stations was launched. Indeed, it was commercial television that primarily stimulated the commercialisation of the entire media market. As recently as 1986, McQuail still felt it was justified to write in the Euromedia Research group's policy book that the climate of opinion on commercial broadcasting in most European countries had 'until recently' been unfavourable. In the eighties, the advocates of commercialism in the media, who were at the time considered self-interested, populist and out-and-out liberals, were joined by cultural and economic pragmatists who were firmly convinced that the new media markets were creating new and interesting challenges (McQuail & Siune, 1986, p. 164).

These pragmatists were applauded, with the argument that the new commercial players were going to enhance healthy competition, as they were bound to develop innovative products, programmes and services in order to continue making profits. In the subsequent policy book (1992) the Euromedia Research Group came to the conclusion that the old media order in Western Europe had been swept away and that a new market-driven logic had become the driving force of changes in the European media. Commercialisation was the ineluctable product of the market logic. The academic world remained divided: the advocates of the market-driven model alleged that it would bring refreshing competition and more exciting challenges, while its critics maintained that it was engendering vulgarisation, homogenisation and the gradual breakdown of cultural values (Siune & Treutschler, 1992, pp. 3, 193).

The Euromedia Research Group's last policy book (1998) regarded the advancing commercialisation of the media and its increasingly intensive concentration and internationalisation, as irreversible facts: '... it seems that profit seeking and consumerism have been widely and largely de-demonized in Europe and have acquired respectability' (McQuail & Siune, 1998, p 112).

Denis McQuail envisaged a period of consolidation in which new commercial electronic media and alternative channels of distribution were established. Media groups merged into ever-larger entities, the Internet and the dotcom enterprises expanded steadily, the commercial logic continued to dominate. Public broadcasters also got involved in the process of commercialisation and restructured themselves into market-oriented corporations.

Yet, in spite of all these developments the European media landscape underwent no earth-shattering changes in the nineties. Was it 'the calm before or after the storm' Denis McQuail wondered (McQuail & Siune, 1998, p 18).

The dotcom crash was still to happen. And when it did, it remained to be seen whether it would bring about any fundamental changes for the large media companies. As it turned out, a lot of media companies emerged from the e-crash even stronger, and today they firmly and extensively colonise the content sites on the Internet.

The commercialisation of the media did initially have some innovating effects. The audio-visual sector sought new formats and produced in-house television programmes to meet the viewers' demands; newspapers and weeklies refurbished their lay-out and addressed the new trends in the reading culture; popular music explored new genres; experiments with new online media abounded.

Owing to ruinous competition and the overriding need to accommodate advertisers, the commercialisation of the media eventually produced trivial and standardised content. As McChesney has observed, 'commercial values, when they rule the roost, have proven to be deadly for artistic creativity' (McChesney, 1999, p. 35).

The media's strong tie-in with advertising has quickened its commercialisation. Success with the media consumer is now the primary requirement for the media, as advertisers need to reach the maximum number of consumers. Channel zapping and the fragmentation of the digital television market forced producers to collaborate with advertisers to capture the consumer by means of product placement, bartering, and various merchandising techniques that blur the distinction between content and advertising.

Commercialisation and concentration
Commercialisation has developed hand-in-hand with media concentration. The recent global mega-mergers of traditional media companies, telecom and cable operators and dotcom businesses have been prompted by the economic logic of mass market expansion and been made possible by novel digital communication technologies. These media conglomerates' ultimate goal is to maximise mass consumption and to open up as many new markets as possible. They enjoy the benefits of economics of scale by reducing the production and distribution costs and increasing sales volumes. The global commercial media system is dominated by a small number of, mainly American, transnational media corporations. Where national markets continue to exist, their importance has diminished. The media giants have in recent years been expanding their activities worldwide. For opportunistic reasons they have sometimes adapted to local conditions, but more often than not this 'glocalisation' is merely a veneer. It is confined to low-cost adaptations such as name changes of locations and persons, dubbing into the region's language, etc, while the formats and the narratives remain the same everywhere. Television shows such as Big Brother, Blind Date, or Star Academy, are based on transcultural principles that are applicable anywhere in the world. Big Brother has been shown in 21 countries in the form of local adaptations of the same basic formula: living together in a secluded Spartan environment, panoptic surveillance, obligatory tests and trials, elimination by voting, and above all, the exhibition of ordinary people. The growth of the media conglomerates is facilitated by the fact that media products may be given a longer life cycle by being recycled and transferred from one media form to another. A single film begets a TV series, DVDs, games, radio shows, CDs, books, and further spin-offs and merchandising (from toys and theme parks to clothing, foods, cosmetics, etc). Successful content can now be endlessly milked for revenue. G. Murdock

& P. Golding (1996.) have examined this recycling of content from the political-economical approach.

Digital technology is eminently suitable for this multiplier effect. The Walt Disney Company and Time Warner are experts in developing, re-packaging and re-marketing a single concept or item in different media. The commercial synergy is further boosted by cross-promotion, i.e. promoting a single concept via various media.

On the other hand, digital technology also makes it possible to aim niche products at specific market segments. The media conglomerates will invest in the creation of these niche media markets when they can sell them to advertisers. The special supplements in dailies and weeklies are typical examples. They highlight the products and services (Food, Lifestyle, Home, Travel, etc) offered by particular advertisers.

The expected explosion of digital theme channels is likely to require more flexibility and resources from advertisers than they actually possess, and pay-television will have to be put in place. As TV viewers become spoilt by an abundance of channels offering free viewing, the media companies will have to assess the risks carefully before launching pay-per-view channels. The relative lack of success of pay channels in Europe is significant. Pay-per-view channels offering sports, films and adult programmes may become profitable, but their number will remain limited.

The arrival of digital television also begs the question of whether it will entail any changes in production methods. The time and money needed to make good programmes remain unchanged. The creativity a good script requires does not change either, and the entire production process will remain as time consuming and labour intensive as it has ever been (Jankowski & Fuchs, 1995, p. 157). The multiplication of new channels and the need to fill hundreds of extra programme hours will lead to even more reruns and to even more recycled content. Imports from the US will increase even further and digital technology will serve as the Trojan horse for the American programme industry.

The rise of the media giants also renders them politically more powerful. Politicians are largely dependent on the media for their image-building and for setting the political agenda. Media tycoons such as Robert Hersant, Rupert Murdoch and Silvio Berlusconi have become legendary for combining their media interests with political power. Even when the lobbying is of a more discreet nature, its effect on political decision-making is no less persuasive.

The globalisation of the media conglomerates has been helped along by a number of neo-liberal policy decisions and agreements. Both GATT and the European Commission have smoothed the way for these neo-liberal developments. With its policy of liberalisation the European Commission has aimed to open up the European media markets, arguing that this would render the European media industry more vigorous and decisive in the confrontation with the American media giants. The national governments generally tend to obstruct this European policy because they wish to preserve their own cultural identity, but the neo-liberals argue that cultural quotas and protectionist regulations are disadvantageous to the interests of media consumers, and that subsidies to protect national cultures inhibit the growth and the dynamism of the European media companies.

That mega-mergers are not necessarily successful has been shown by the gigantic loss Time Warner suffered after its merger with AOL, the fateful decision which had been based on the dotcom hype and AOL's artificially high stock market value. Vivendi Universal Media disintegrated as a result of insurmountable debts. The demise of Leo Kirch's empire also shows that media mastodons with an excessively wide range of activities are hard to manage efficiently. Peter Chernin of Fox TV (International News Corporation) declared in an interview that 'in the management of creativity, size is your enemy'. Although all of these giant media concerns are burdened with heavy debts, most of them manage to survive and continue to dominate the international media market.

The Internet dominated by the usual corporate suspects?
Digital technology makes it relatively easy to transfer content from one physical network to another. Interconnectivity of previously separated networks and interoperability of services and applications will lead to the establishment of one single integrated network. This should, at least in principle, enhance the media consumer's freedom of choice and access potential. To take full advantage of the possibilities of digital technology the media corporations have already accomplished mergers between telecom and cable operators and traditional media enterprises that own or control content rights.

Most households today still use separate networks for different services. Only when the costs of switching from one infrastructure to another become negligible, will the competition between infrastructures become a real option. Open access to different physical networks with different content does not support the strategy that is favoured by the large media concerns. Their aim is to bind their clients exclusively to them and to offer not only content but also Internet and e-commerce services. They hold on to their clients by making it difficult for them to switch to another digital provider. To counter the network managers' strategy, the authorities will have to stimulate the 'switching behaviour' with appropriate legislation (Rutten & Poel, 2002, p. 34).

A concrete example of the struggle to retain the media consumer indefinitely is the telecom companies' attempt to offer digital television via the telephone cable network in densely cabled countries, such as the Benelux, where television channels are distributed virtually exclusively via cable. The clients are increasingly faced with considerable switching costs and the cable companies are progressively offering their clients services such as telephone communications, broadband Internet access, as well as various interactive applications. In the fierce competition that will no doubt ensue among network providers, a captivating content will more than likely form the main expedient for attracting and retaining clients. For example, in Belgium, the most densely cabled country in the world with 98% of households connected to the cable network, Belgacom, the major telephone service provider, has launched the idea of offering iDTV together with the public broadcaster, and for this purpose is planning to secure an exclusive contract with the Belgian football league. Flexible switching conditions, moderate prices, and above all, attractive content will stimulate this transfer.

The first stage of this convergence is in fact characterised by 'replacement' among terrestrial, satellite and cable platforms that are offering digital services.

The definite breakthrough in the convergence of the different infrastructures may well be dependent on the further development of the Internet Protocol (IP) and of broadband technology. The IP is a crucial factor in the advance towards complete convergence into the seamlessly integrated and interactive network. The Internet has the capacity to merge computing, telecommunications and broadcasting into a single stream carried on the same physical network. Television channels that are distributed via the World Wide Web are definitely free from further distribution infrastructures. As of now, however, this is still in the future, because 'fibre-to-the-home' is still far from ubiquitous, and the current large network and service providers are trying to bind their clients even more closely with exclusive services through Internet access. The authorities have a very important role to play in these developments. If they prove incapable of implementing access and competition policies to halt the media giants' strategies, 'there will be a real danger that access to and pluriformity of information will turn out to be a joke' (Rutten & Poel, 2002, p. 98).

Also the Internet, which was initially acclaimed as an innovatory and non-commercial medium that could provide the non-profit and civic sectors with a new public open space for debate and discussion, has been occupied by the large media conglomerates. They find it a perfect medium for extending the life cycles of their media products.

For many, the merger of AOL and Time Warner in 2000 signified the definite beginning of the commercialisation of the Internet. 'The merger of AOL and Time Warner is bad news for consumers and citizens. It hammers the last nail in the coffin of the argument that the Internet will democratize the media by giving ordinary citizens the ability to compete in the marketplace against the media giants' (McChesney, 1999, p. 116). This merger embodied the combination of a media, entertainment and cable infrastructure empire with the largest Internet service provider. After the e-crash in 2003 the AOL name was deleted and Time Warner was left holding the financial losses; but the bulk of content sites on the Internet remain in the hands of large media groups. As a matter of fact, it soon became clear that all along the 'old' media partner had been doing much better than AOL and its Internet activities. With Harry Potter, whose different product lines were simultaneously promoted on different media platforms, a lucrative symbiosis was created between media, telecommunications and computers. The promotion of the wide array of Harry Potter products made use of all possible forms of content delivery and merchandising.

It is clear, therefore, that the market is consolidating its hold on the Internet and that the utopian optimism of the early Internet enthusiasts is waning. 'The drive to maximize is the key aspect of convergence since it is the emerging mega corporations that span content and distribution and combine established and emerging media under the same administrative umbrella, who are setting the pace for digitalisation and writing the rules for the emerging marketplace' (Murdock, 2000, p. 38).

The expansion of the newspaper market on the Internet is a further illustration of this trend. In spite of the appearance of some fringe online newspapers and the profusion of web logs, the online user who is looking for news and information principally turns to the websites provided by the established media enterprises. The Internet carries a lot of 'shovelware' that derives from traditional media content.

Here the question presents itself whether media scholars have not overstated the media changes caused by the digital revolution, and whether the economic structures, the established balance of power and the structural inequalities are not going to remain in place for some time to come.

Homogenisation, globalisation and tabloidisation

Aided by the growing concentration in the media industry, commercialisation has also boosted homogenisation, globalisation and tabloidisation. Media conglomerates are averse to taking risks – 'safety first'– and to departing from proven success formulas – 'nothing succeeds like success' (Gitlin, 1983). They have no incentives to innovate for the simple reason that their aim is to meet the demands of the largest possible average audience. Media giants like to market rather similar products, with homogenised content. Audience research turns out to be a circular process, as it asks media consumers to choose from a limited number of hit products. In this regard McChesney refers to the dwindling number of foreign films in American theatres. In the mid-seventies, 10% of films shown in American theatres were foreign, in the eighties only 7%, and in the nineties less than 0.5%. The main cause of this decline was the rise of the mega complex chain theatres, which refuse to show foreign films unless these are guaranteed to please the taste of the American audience and unless the foreign producers are prepared to invest as heavily in the promotion of their films as American producers are willing to do. He comes to the conclusion that the latest generation of American filmgoers has not the faintest idea what the European film industry has to offer (McChesney, 1999, p. 33).

Cultural globalisation that ensues from the dominant position of a limited number of media giants in audiovisual production appears to be inevitable. As early as the seventies several authors (Nordenstreng & Varis, 1974; Schiller, 1976; Mattelart & Dorfman, 1975; Tunstall, 1977; Hamelink, 1978) pointed at American cultural imperialism, in particular its media imperialism, and at its effect on the growing homogenisation of media content. In the late eighties and early nineties a wave of studies examined the impact of imported American programmes when the many new commercial stations were found to prefer filling their television schedules with them, as they were inexpensive to purchase and offered guaranteed success with the viewers, and therefore with the advertisers. All these studies (Pragnell, 1985; Silj, 1988; De Bens, Kelly & Bakke, 1992; Sepstrup, 1990; Blumler, 1992; Biltereyst, 1991) reported growing volumes of imported American films and series. Viewers were found to prefer native productions, but these were relatively costly to produce. One striking conclusion common to all these studies was that European stations imported remarkably little from other European countries. Most European productions were firmly embedded in a particular national or regional culture, and viewers would sooner watch products from the American melting pot. The American commercial media system has always opted for easy success formulas and formats that aim to please as large an audience as possible. From their examination of imported shows broadcast by 36 television channels in six European countries, De Bens & De Smaele concluded that in spite of the European Commission quota system, which imposes a majority of European programmes on European television stations, the import of American fiction programmes had been increasing further (De Bens & De Smaele, 2001). As the European quota system applies to the total broadcasting time, with exclusion of news, sports and advertising, the quota can be easily attained by introducing low-cost domestic productions such as talk shows, quizzes, games and variety shows (the 'quota quickies'). If applied to fiction (films, series, etc) only, the present quota system would be shown to allow massive importation of fiction from the US.

Trends towards globalisation have evidently been strengthened by the worldwide expansion of industrial mega-conglomerates and particularly by multimedia companies that distribute their products and services across the globe. Also, the leading international news agencies – such as Reuters, Associated Press and Agence France Presse – that control almost completely the world's news flow, play an essential role in processes of globalisation.

Hypercommercialism has fostered trivialisation and sensationalism. Croteau & Hoynes (2001, p 157) list an exhaustive series of types of television programmes that are cheap to produce, attract plenty of viewers and thus please advertisers: tabloid gossip shows, fist-fighting dysfunctional families on daytime talk shows, sexual scandals involving politicians, reality shows featuring accidents and police arrests, sensational and bloody crime reports, get-rich-quick game shows, etc. The frontiers of sensation, violence and voyeurism are pushed back unremittingly.

The tabloidising trend has also forced its way into the news broadcasts. Research has convincingly shown that the share of foreign, national, and social and economic news has diminished in favour of trivial sensation, human interest and crime reporting, all of which undermine traditional news values and norms. The news is being dramatised and presented as narrative (Connel, 1998; Djupsund & Carlson, 1998; Esser, 1999 Franklin, 1997; Sparks, 1992). Tabloidisation is 'a downgrading of hard news and upgrading of sex, scandal and infotainment' (Esser, 1999, p. 292).

One of the major causes of this development has doubtless been the commercial pressure on editorial boards. Newspaper circulation figures are falling and the newspapers' advertising revenues are shrinking because of the competition from the numerous new players in the expanding media market. Journalists are obliged to go further and further to score a scoop. It illustrates how content is commercialised by the business logic of lowering costs and accommodating as many advertisers as possible.

It is no coincidence that international news coverage is shrinking, as opposed to service journalism which employs editors and journalists to fill special interest columns such as those on food, fitness, travel, etc. (De Bens, 2001, p. 92).

According to Picard it is the cutthroat competition that is the main menace to quality and diversity. As the media grow increasingly dependent on advertising, they are compelled to compete fiercely for advertising revenues, while there is a limit to the growth of advertising budgets (R. Picard, 2000, p. 186). When many competitors target their products at the same audience niche, they will each have less advertising income to cover the production costs and they will be forced to lower the quality of their products.

The belief that competition increases diversity is being questioned. Richard van der Wurff & Jan van Cuilenburg (2001) have shown that, while moderate competition may increase diversity, excessive competition eventually leads to decreased diversity. From their research into television news broadcasts Hjarvard, (1999) and Hvitfelt (1994) concluded that competition had not improved the quality of television news broadcasts, but rather that TV news had become more dramatised and sensationalist, and less informative.

Rethinking the democratic and cultural role of the media
It is not all sorrow and commercial misery. Europe boasts a long tradition in which cultural institutions such as public broadcasting, museums, libraries, educational institutions, orchestras, arts centres, etc., have been supported financially and guarded from marketisation by purposeful government policies. Winfried Schulz (1997) has forcefully advocated the need for a space in which expression and debate can take place in the public sphere, free from commercial pressure.

The continued existence of a 'public' media model offers proof that society's needs cannot be met by an unfettered media market alone. Media markets sometimes function undemocratically, inducing inequality and failing to meet certain social needs. To make the media take on their democratic and cultural mission, governments will have to intervene through policy measures whenever the market proves to be failing (Bardoel & van Cuilenburg, 2003, p. 31).

This concern calls for various government measures that assist the media sector in performing its public function: public funding of public broadcasters, whose well-defined mission burdens them with major public tasks; measures to support the press sector (zero VAT rate, low postal rates, interest-free loans, support for the development of innovative technologies, support for the training of journalists, direct financial aid to ailing newspapers, financial support of distribution); universal service in the telecommunications sector; frozen prices for cable subscriptions and free Internet access.

Some of these support measures and incentives have already had clear positive effects in a number of countries. In the Scandinavian countries public broadcasters receive adequate public funding, and they have the largest market shares. Because their governments have always maintained benevolent policies towards the printed press, the number of independent newspaper titles and of newspaper readers in these countries is the highest in Europe.

Apart from this material support, some national European governments have taken steps to guarantee media diversity, including antitrust legislation and measures to counter co-ownership. National governments, and to some degree the European Union as well, play a pivotal part in ensuring that the media not only meet the expectations of the market, but also those of the citizens.

Any media policy inevitably suffers from a clash between a concern for the public role of the media and the agenda of the media conglomerates' lobbyists and the neo-liberal politicians. The European Commission has already imposed policies that were inspired by the American free market model, and that boosted the commercialisation of the media. In the introduction to Communication Theory and Research (2005) McQuail points out that '... [T]he fact that there are two levels of communication policy, at national and European level makes for a distinctive pattern of governance and ensures that a variety of principles of the public interest – economic, social and cultural – are continually in play'.

The media themselves have also been reproved for maintaining the status quo and for failing to be receptive to views that transcend the current consensus model. In particular, the reproach that public broadcasters are imitating their commercial competitors is being used by the private broadcasters to question the legitimacy of public funding of public service broadcasting.

This is an ongoing debate that runs through this book. In spite of all these pressures, the European tradition has offered strong resistance to commercialism. The notion of the public sphere remains vital in this debate and the pursuit of 'democratic media' is alive. In some quarters it may be regarded as an old-fashioned notion, but there is no way around the fact that the democratising and cultural role of the media is the backbone of democracy.

Furthermore, there still exist civic movements that mobilise against marketisation and consumerism. G. Murdock sounds hopeful: 'These counter-principles, of reciprocity and public entitlement, offer a powerful ethical alternative to the pay-per regime of marketization and a potential basis for a global cultural commons' (Murdock, 2004, p. 35). He also believes that media and cultural scholarship should play their part in this.

At the end of the ESF Nice Conference the plenary assembly unanimously adopted an important Declaration. This Declaration of the 'Club of Nice' advocates the safeguarding of the public interest. It makes an appeal to the politicians not to choose a neoliberal Darwinist economy that cares predominantly for the private interests of corporations, and seeks to remind them of the historical legacy of the European common good.

This Declaration perfectly illustrates the concerns expressed in this chapter (the text is attached at the end of this book).

Three themes are at the core of this book: media diversity, the future of public broadcasting, and the ways in which policy and governance could provide the conditions for the media to attain a balance 'between culture and commerce'. The maintenance of media diversity and of a strong public broadcasting sector is currently one of the most substantial challenges.

The first part of this book deals with media diversity and concentration. In its opening chapter Jan van Cuilenburg retraces the philosophical background of diversity and surveys the different ways in which the concept of media diversity may be defined.

One of the central questions in this regard is whether diversity and pluriformity are given a fair chance in the present-day heavily concentrated, market-oriented media institutions. A notable distinction is made between reflective and open diversity. The former refers to the way the media address the media consumers' expectations and therefore reflects, as it were, the mind of the people. It is a bottom-up process in which the tone is set by the majority's preferences. Open diversity, on the other hand, is a top-down process in which diversity is viewed normatively and qualitatively. More than reflective diversity, it is likely to lead to innovation and creativity, and a far as news is concerned, to objectivity. Reflective diversity is often the consequence of the commercialisation of the media. Jan van Cuilenburg shows convincingly that all-out competition tends to erode open diversity.

In the next chapter Jan van Cuilenburg and Richard vander Wurff investigate how the different national governments in Europe have developed policies to safeguard and stimulate media diversity through legislation (anti-trust laws and measures against cross-ownership). A primary question here is how diversity is defined and measured in the different countries. In the Netherlands it is measured with a sharply defined method. The initial intention was for the various contributors to this book to apply the same 'easy-to-measure indicators' to their national media systems. Although this method is no doubt an excellent research tool for analysing and assessing media diversity, it turns out that in the different countries the key indicators are different, so that comparative research is all but impossible. Colleagues from Finland, Germany and Belgium present case studies in which media diversity is measured and assessed with other methodologies. In the final chapter of the first part Jan van Cuilenburg & Richard van der Wurff reflect on the divergent ways media diversity is measured in Europe.

The second part of the book looks at the future of public broadcasting and the challenges it faces. Karol Jakubowicz raises the question of whether PSB will continue to exist in a thoroughly commercialised, highly competitive, digital European broadcasting landscape. Public broadcasters will have to justify their public funding ever more expressly through the distinctiveness of their content from that of their commercial counterparts. Looking for evidence as to whether a rationale can be found for the continued existence of PSB, he reviews different schools of thought on how PSB should redefine its tasks and obligations in order to remain relevant at all.

In an addendum to this chapter Marcel Betzel describes the main objectives of the remit, the programme obligations, and the performance and evaluation criteria imposed on most European public service broadcasters. This cross-border comparative overview, which contains a wealth of thought-provoking information, underscores the democratic and cultural function of PSB.

Stylianos Papathanassopoulos gives an overview of the funding of PSB in Europe. The differences between the European countries are striking. Interestingly, it emerges that public broadcasters that receive most public funding (in the Scandinavian countries, the Netherlands, Germany, and the UK), score highest on all criteria and leave their commercial rivals far behind.

During our discussions within the ESF team, the colleagues from eastern and southern Europe sounded quite pessimistic about the position of PSB in their respective countries. They identified various causes: politicisation, insufficient stature, lack of dynamism, meagre public funding and the ensuing intense dependence on advertising, the absence of a robust public tradition. They generally looked on their public broadcasters as 'state' broadcasters.

Trine Syvertsen & Minna Aslama examine how public broadcasting has been preparing for digital applications. Has it been sufficiently financed and how can it justify demanding extra public funding?

In a compelling concluding chapter Karol Jakubowicz looks into how, and to what degree, the public broadcasters in various countries have been fulfilling their remit. He comes to the conclusion that, in spite of the trend towards marketisation and the competition from commercial broadcasting, public service broadcasting has retained a strong position and continues to play a crucial role in safeguarding cultural diversity in Europe. He recommends that PSB should drive media innovation and should receive sufficient financial support when facing the emerging digital challenges.

In the final part Cees Hamelink and Kaarle Noordenstreng investigate how media regulation and policy should be studied within the present-day broader framework of governance. Media governance consists of all the ways in which public authorities together with non-profit and profit organisations can guide policy in the 'right' direction. It is a continuous process in which sensible agreement can only be reached by balancing different, sometimes opposite interests. In today's media landscape governance is growing in significance, and the authors explore this new policy instrument by checking out how different actors 'steer' media governance.

In the book's final chapter Karol Jakubowicz discusses the diverse actors involved in media governance in Europe. He describes the different goals and interests of official organisations such as UN, OSCE, WTO, OECD, EU, ITU, UNESCO, EBU and EPRA, as well as their methods of operation and their impact on international and national media policies and systems.

References

Bardoel, J & J. Van Cuilenburg (2003) *Communicatiebeleid en Communicatiemarkt.* Amsterdam: Otto Cramwinckel.

Biltereyst, D (1991) 'Resisting American Hegemony: a comparative analysis of reception of domestic and US fiction', *European Journal of Communication* ,6: 4, pp. 469–49.

Blumler J. (ed), (1992)*Television and the Public Interest. Vulnerable values in West European Broadcasting.* London: Sage.

Connel, I (1998) 'Mistaken identities: tabloid and broadsheet news discourse', *Javnost,* 5: 3, pp. 11–31

Croteau, D & W. Hoynes (2001) *The Business of Media. Corporate Media and the Public Interest.* Thousand Oaks, California: Pine Forge Press,

Djupsund,G. & T. Carlson (1998) Trivial stories and fancy pictures, *Nordicom Review,* 19:1, pp. 101–113

De Bens, E, M. Kelly, & M. Bakke (1992) 'Television content: Dallasification of Culture?' In K.Siune&W.Treutschler (eds) Dynamics of Media Politics: Broadcast and Electronic media in Western Europe, London: Sage.

De Bens, E (2001) De Pers in Belgie. Tielt: Lannoo.

De Bens E & H. De Smaele (2001) 'The inflow of American television Fiction on European Broadcasting channels revisited', European Journal of communication, vol 16: 1, pp. 51–76.

Esser, F. (1999) 'Tabloidization of news: a comparative analysis of Anglo-American and German press journalism', European Journal of Communication, 14: 3, pp. 291–325.

Franklin, B. (1997) Newszak and Newsmedia. London: Arnold.

Gitlin, T. (1983) Inside Prime Time. New York: Pantheon Books

Hamelink,C, J. (1978) De Mythe van de Vrije Informatie. Baarn: Anthos.

Hjarvard, S. (1999) TV-nyheder i Konkurrence, Frederigsberg, Denmark: Samfundslitteratur.

Hvitfelt, H. (1994) 'The Commercialisation of the Evening News: Changes_in Narrative technique in Swedish TV news' Nordicom Review 2, p. 341

Jankowski, G. F & D. Fuchs (1995) Television today and tomorrow. New York: OUP.

Mattelart A. & A. Dorfman (1975) How to read Donald Duck: Imperialist Ideology in the Disney comic, New York: International General University Press

McChesney, R. (1999) Rich Media, Poor Democracy. Communication Politics in dubious Times, New York: The New Press.

McPhail, T. L. (2002) Global Communication. Theories, Stakeholders and Trends, Boston: Pearson Education Company

McQuail, D. (1998) 'Commercialisation and Beyond', pp107–127 in D.McQuail & K.Siune Media Policy.Convergence Concentration &Commerce. Sage:London.

Mc Quail, D. (2005) 'Introduction' in D. McQuail, E. de Bens & P. Golding (eds) Communication Theory and Research, London: Sage.

McQuail, D. & K. Siune (1986) 'The New media Politics. Comparative Perspectives' in Western Europe, Euromedia Research Group, London: Sage.

McQuail, D & K. Siune (1998) Mediapolicy, Convergence & Commerce Euromedia Research Group, London: Sage,

Murdock, G. (2000) 'Digital Futures:European television in the age of convergence', in J.Wieten,Gr &Murdock& P.Dahlgren (eds) Television across Europe, London: Sage.

Murdock, G. (2004) 'Pasts the Posts. Rethinking Change, Retrieving Critique', European Journal of Communication, 19 (1), p. 19.

Murdock, G. & P. Golding (1996) 'Culture,communications and political economy', in J. Curran &M. Gurevitch (eds) Mass Media and Society, (2nd edition) OUP.

Murray, A.M. (2004) Tension Headaches. The experience of the culture/commerce tension: a study of the social context of scheduling, paper presented at the RIPE Conference, Kopenhague, http://www.yle.fi/keto/ripe/

Nordensrteng, K. & T. Varis (1974) Television Traffic-One –Way Street? Paris: Unesco.

Picard, R. (2000) 'Audience Fragmentation and structural limits on media innovation and diversity', pp. 180–191 in Jan Van Cuilenburg & Richard vander Wurff Media & Open Societies. Amsterdam:het Spinhuis.

Picard, R. (2002) 'Delusions of Grandeur: The Real Problems of Concentration in Media', pp 33–48 in D. Demers (ed) Global Media News Reader. Spokane, Washington: Marquette Books

Pragnell, A. (1985) Television in Europe. Manchester: European Institute for the Media

Rutten, P. & M. Poel (2002) *Marktontwikkelingen in de digitale infrastructuur. Knelpunten bij de toegangkelijkheid en de pluriformiteit van de digitale snelweg,* Werkdocument 86, den Haag: Rathenau Instituut,

Schiller, H. (1976) *Communication and Cultural Domination.* New York: International Arts and Science Press.

Schulz, W. (1997) Changes of the mass media and the public sphere, *Javnost,* 4 (2), pp. 57–70

Sepstrup, P. (1990) *Transnationalisation of Television in Western Europe,* London: Libbey.

Silj, A. (1988) *East of Dallas: the European Challenge to American TV.* London: BFI Publishing

Siune, K. & W. Treutschler (1992) *Dynamics of media Politics. Broadcast and Electronic Media in Western Europe,* Euromedia research Group, London: Sage.

Sparks, C. (1992) 'Popular journalism: theories and practice', in P. Dahlgren & C. Sparks (eds) *Journalism and Popular Culture,* London: Sage.

Steemers, J. (2004) *The BBC-Balancing Culture and commerce on the Global Stage,* paper presented at the RIPE Conference , Kopenhague: http://yle.fi/keto/ripe/

Tunstall, J. (1977) *The Media are America.* New York: Columbia Press.

Wurff, R van der & J.van Cuilenburg (2001) 'Impact of Moderate and Ruinous Competition on Diversity: the Dutch Television Market', *Journal of Media Economics,* 14 (4), pp. 213–229.

2

MEDIA DIVERSITY, COMPETITION AND CONCENTRATION: CONCEPTS AND THEORIES

Jan van Cuilenburg

Philosophical background

Why diversity?

'Truth is not manifest'. This famous dictum of Karl Popper (1902–1994) makes clear why, from a philosophical point of view, diversity in information and opinions in democratic societies is of the utmost importance. Because in general it is epistemologically impossible to establish (scientific) truth beyond any doubt, opinions and ideas should always be open to contest and confrontation with opposing opinions and ideas. This applies particularly to the political realm in democracies. According to Popper, the quality of the democratic discourse in society '… depends largely upon the variety of competing views. Had there been no Tower of Babel, we should invent it' (Popper, 1968 [1962], p. 352).

The idea that diversity is a crucial value in establishing truth is far from new. As early as more than 2000 years ago, Socrates (470–490 BC) implicitly gave diversity a central role in his 'thesis – antithesis – synthesis' dialectics of argumentation. Socrates' method of truth finding has been pleaded for ever since by countless numbers of philosophers and other scientists. To mention only two of them:

- John Milton (1644) issued his famous plea for freedom of the press and for diversity: 'Let (truth) and falsehood grapple … in a free and open encounter (Milton, 1644).'
- John Stuart Mill (1806–1873) underlined the value of opinion diversity in his famous *On Liberty*. Mill argues that truth in the great practical concerns of life is a 'question of reconciling and combining of opposites'. Diversity is advantageous because even

for a true opinion ' … a conflict with the opposite error is essential to a clear apprehension and deep feeling its truth.' (Mill, 1972 [1859], p. 107, p. 105).

Not only in philosophy and politics has diversity grown to be a fundamental value, but also in normative media theory, particularly in the libertarian press theory. In the libertarian theory, diversity in opinions is promoted on the basis of the assumption that '… from mutual toleration and comparison of diverse opinions the one that seems most rational will emerge and generally accepted' (Siebert *et al*, 1969 [1956], p. 44).

According to Napoli (1999, p. 7) diversity is a 'foundation principle in communications policy'. This conclusion is corroborated by numerous government documents throughout the western world (e.g., the EU Greenbook *Pluralism and Media Concentration in the Internal Market*, 1992).

Competition and diversity
In conventional economic and political theory, there is a strong link between competition and diversity. It is generally accepted that diversity of products and services in society is promoted by competition in the marketplace. Ever since Adam Smith wrote his *Inquiry into the Nature and the Causes of the Wealth of Nations* in 1776, the idea that market rivalry between entrepreneurs yields best quality products and services against the lowest prices possible has been widely accepted in Western economics and political ideology. Competition is not only considered to be a guarantee of quality of products, but also as *the* agent of innovation and pluralism in society. This makes economic, political and social competition to a central notion in Western societies. That goes for media too. As an aside, the twentieth century economist Schumpeter did put forward the opposite thesis, that monopoly enhances innovation because monopolists can easily recoup their innovation investments (cf. Faull and Nikpay (eds.), 1999, p. 40; Sánchez-Taberno & Carvajal, 2002, p. 22). However that may be, generally any breakdown of media monopoly is welcomed and competition between newspapers, radio and television stations is applauded. However, as can be shown from economic life, competition is not always fruitful as it might degenerate into ruinous competition, that is, intense, short-term competition on price between enterprises, leading to an overall loss in product quality. Media competition is probably no exception to that. That is why, in analysing the effects of media competition on diversity, we have to address the question of whether there is an optimal point in media markets between media monopoly and ruinous media competition to promote media diversity.

Defining 'media diversity'

The normative Diversity Chain: social diversity, media diversity, opinion diversity
In its most general form, *diversity* may be defined as: the heterogeneity of subjects (people) and/or of objects (material and immaterial things) in terms of one or more specified characteristics.

Accordingly, the keyword is *heterogeneity* in the sense of *variety* or *plurality*.

In operationalising this general definition of 'diversity' three questions have to be answered. First, what are the subjects/objects to be considered? Who/what differs from whom/what: individual people, groups of people, institutions, media (newspapers, broadcasters, magazines)? Second, on the basis of which characteristics do we compare subjects/objects? In case of government policy, characteristics to be chosen should be relevant to the policy pursued. Third, how do we measure differences between subjects/objects?

In media policy literature we come across three different types of diversity. First, social diversity, notably the variety of people in society's political, socio-cultural and socio-economic sphere. Second, media diversity, i.e., the heterogeneity in the supply of media content in society. Third, diversity of information, ideas and opinions in society (in German:'*Meinungsvielvalt*'). Roughly speaking, these three concepts relate to each other in a chain: first, actual *social diversity* in society, next *media diversity* reflecting social diversity, and subsequently *opinion diversity* nurtured by media diversity. The diversity chain ends in democracy, the ultimate purpose that diversity supposedly is serving. In Figure 1 this chain is presented in a more or less teleological, normative way.

A definition of 'media diversity'
Media diversity may be defined as:

> *Media diversity* is the extent to which media content differs according to one or more criteria (Van Cuilenburg and McQuail, 1982; McQuail and Van Cuilenburg, 1983).

To provide an operational definition of *media diversity*, three choices have to be made. First, we need to select one or more relevant dimensions on which media content could and should vary; *e.g.*, political orientation, religious opinions, cultural life styles, media genres, sources of media content. Second, we need to define the level at which diversity

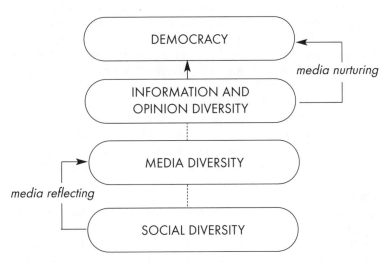

Figure 1 A normative *Diversity Chain*.

may be assessed. And third, we need to formulate a yardstick that we can use to measure whether the variation observed between and within media is somehow sufficient.

Media diversity can be studied at four different levels:

1. at the level of individual *content units* of information (*e.g.*, a television programme, or a newspaper article). Then, we focus on the different preferences and opinions presented in those programmes or articles;
2. at the level of *content bundles* such as a broadcasting channel or a newspaper title. Then, we focus on programme and editorial content supply as a total package by individual media outlets;
3. at the level of a specific *medium type*, radio, television, or the daily newspaper press. Then, analysis focuses on diversity of content supply on the newspaper market or on the television market;
4. the level of society's communications *system* as a whole (broadcasting, newspapers and internet).

The choice of the most appropriate level of analysis should correspond with media consumer behavior, that is, with the full set of content packages that users usually choose, buy or from which they obtain a particular content package. Determining the level of diversity analysis also relates to the notion of *relevant market* common in EU competition policy.

Intra medium and inter medium diversity
Within media markets we can either focus on diversity *within* a specific content package or *between* all content packages in that market (cf. McQuail, 1992, pp. 145–147). The former is *intra medium diversity*, the latter *inter media diversity*. Especially when we study diversity at the level at which users access media markets, intra media diversity is important from a societal point of view. Intra diversity will guarantee that users will be confronted with diverging ideas and opinions. For the individual user, however, inter media diversity is more important. Inter diversity will enable users to choose between different content packages that match their preferences in varying degrees. Intra and inter diversity are complementary and to a certain degree incompatible. The more intra diverse content packages are, the less inter diverse they can be – and vice versa.

Two normative yardsticks for media diversity
There are two normative yardsticks to evaluate empirical media diversity: *reflective diversity* and *open diversity*. According to Hellmann (2001, p. 202) the concept of 'open media diversity' best fits the European public policy model of media policy, whereas 'reflective media diversity' is more central to the American approach of media policy.

Reflective diversity (reflection)
The most common normative approach to the concept of 'media diversity' is in terms of *reflective diversity*, that is, in terms of the actual match between media users' preferences and the reflection of these preferences in media content (Van Cuilenburg and McQuail, 1982, pp. 40–41). *Reflective diversity* is the extent to which existing population preferences are *proportionally* represented in the media.

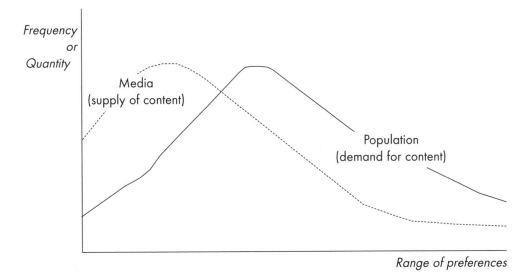

Frequency or Quantity

Media (supply of content)

Population (demand for content)

Range of preferences

Figure 2 Media diversity as reflection of population preferences (a theoretical example).

Reflection in media diversity is depicted in Figure 2. It is a hypothetical example. The population curve represents the distribution of preferences in the population, *e.g.*, political opinions, religious beliefs or interests in particular kinds of news, or any other relevant population characteristic. The other curve, the media curve, represents media supply complementing population preferences and characteristics. Ideally, in the case of maximum media reflection of population preferences and characteristics, both curves fully coincide. The example in Figure 2 shows, however, that media content only partly overlaps with population preferences, indicating media deficiency in population reflection.

Open diversity (openness)
The second yardstick for media diversity originates from a normative point of view that lies outside the realm of actual media use. This approach reflects the notion that media are pervasive social phenomena that may influence people considerably. Thus, to prevent the emergence of biases in public opinion, media content should express different opinions in an equal manner. This type of diversity is *open diversity*: the extent to which divergent preferences and opinions are quantitatively *equally* (*i.e.*, statistically uniformly) represented in the media (Van Cuilenburg and McQuail, 1982, pp. 40–41).

Open diversity is depicted in Figure 3. This Figure portrays actual media supply compared to media supply under the condition of full openness to all conceivable preferences in the population, be they majority or minority preferences or characteristics. Graphically, full openness may be represented by a uniform distribution: the straight horizontal line in Figure 3 indicates that no category of preference or characteristic in the population gets quantitatively more media coverage and attention than any other preference or characteristic category. Consequently, open media diversity mathematically is the maximum diversity any media system can realise.

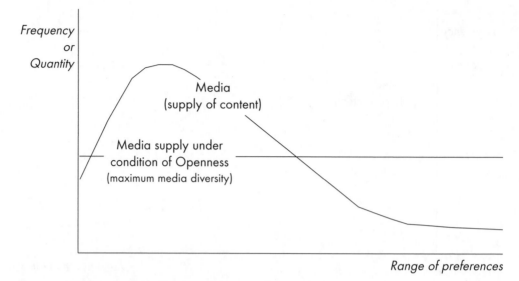

Figure 3 Media diversity as openness (a theoretical example).

The norm of reflective diversity in the media focuses on equal *access for people* to the media, whereas open diversity calls attention to diversity of perspectives and could be labelled as *access for ideas.* There is a dialectic relationship between reflective and open diversity. Media fully reflecting social preferences inevitably ill perform at openness to a great variety of different perspectives, social positions and conditions, whereas perfect media openness harms majority positions in favour of minority perspectives, beliefs, attitudes and conditions.

Two media policy approaches to media diversity

The American approach
The European and the USA approach to media diversity differ. In the USA, according to Napoli (1999, p. 9) the concept of 'media diversity' is best understood from the 'theory of the free marketplace of ideas'. The role diversity plays in American media policy results from two centuries of case law on the First Amendment to the US constitution. American case law stresses 'the widest possible dissemination of information from diverse and antagonistic sources' (Dizard, 1994, pp. 74, 75). In the American perception, the free marketplace of ideas is the most effective vehicle for guaranteeing the freedoms included in the First Amendment. In the free marketplace of ideas people are entitled (1)to *content diversity*, supplied by a great variety of different sources (*source diversity* (2)). From these two, *exposure diversity* (3) in the audience will more or less automatically result. In American media policy, focus consequently is on *source diversity* (competition and antitrust regulation) (see Figure 4).

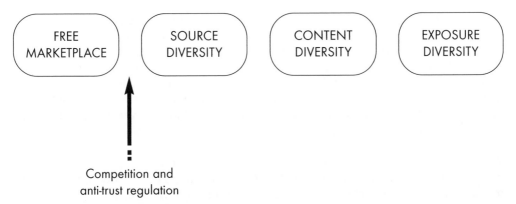

Figure 4 The American approach to media diversity.

The European approach

Although the free marketplace also plays an important role In the European approach to media diversity, access of citizens to pluralistic information gets more emphasis than the freedom of communicators as such, as in the American approach. Notably in the sphere of broadcasting, media diversity in many Western-European countries is actively organised by way of media regulation and the establishment of public service broadcasting (see Figure 5). According to Hoffmann-Riem (1987) and other authors (*e.g.,*

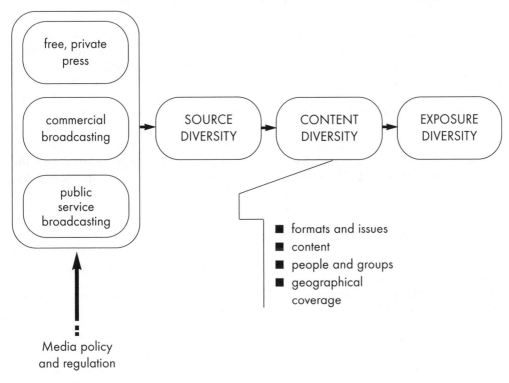

Figure 5 The European approach to media diversity.

McQuail, 1992, p. 144), in the European tradition four empirical dimensions of media diversity are distinguished. First, diversity of *formats and issues,* also in connection with the different functions media may perform (information, education, entertainment). Second, diversity of *content* with the intent of media giving full information on events, opinions and groups in society. Third, diversity of *people and groups* with the intention of giving access and media representation to all constituent groups in society. And fourth, diversity in terms of *geographical coverage and relevance* (local, regional, national and international media content).

Within the European Union, there is currently a policy tendency to rely more than in the past on competition and antitrust regulation to promote access of new competitors to media markets as an effective means of contributing to media diversity.

Media competition and concentration

Media competition
According to classical economic theory, competition in markets in general leads to innovation and diversification in products and services. Applying this assumption to media markets, we may expect media diversity to increase as media market competition increases. Empirical research, however, shows that the relationship between media competition is not linear and positive by definition (not: more competition → more media diversity); we will come back to different types of media competition in the section on the relationship between media competition and diversity.

To study the relationship between media competition and media diversity we may use the well-known *SCP* (structure-conduct-performance) model from industrial organisation theory as adapted for media markets by McQuail (1992, pp. 87–89); (see Figure 6). According to this model, market structure influences market conduct, which in its turn is the main determinant of media performance, and consequently of media diversity. Following Scherer (1996, p. 5; see Table 1), we may distinguish six major market structures, ranging from perfect competition towards monopoly. Each market structure has distinctive characteristics in terms of the number of competitors, the ease of market entry, similarity of goods and services, the control over price by individual firms, and the demand curve facing individual firms (Boone and Kurtz, 1992, p. 640). In general, the

Table 1: Typology of market structures (Scherer, 1996: 5)

number of suppliers	one supplier	few large suppliers	many small suppliers
product differentiation *homogeneous products*	monopoly	homogeneous oligopoly	full ('perfect') competition
heterogeneous products	multi-product monopoly	differentiated oligopoly	monopolistic competition

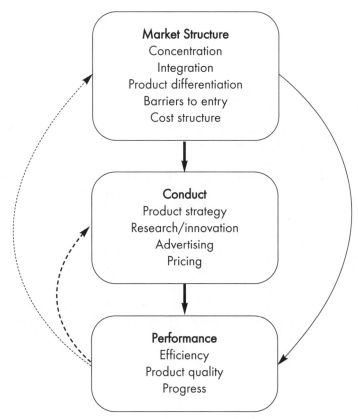

Figure 6 The Structure – Conduct – Performance Model (McQuail, 1992, p. 87).

greater the number of small suppliers and the greater the homogeneity of their products and services, the greater competition in the market, and the other way around.

Competition not only has a structural component, but also a behavioural dimension. Competitive behaviour manifests itself notably in the way media organisations are marketing their products. The type of marketing determines the kind of competitive behaviour one will find in the media market. By and large, marketing handles four strategic variables: *product, distribution, promotion* and *price*, which in one marketing mix or another have to be blended to satisfy chosen consumer segments (Boone and Kurtz, 1992, p. 22; Pride and Ferrell, 1991, p. 5). Competition between media may be based on each of these four distinct types of variables. The prevalent marketing strategies, however, are strategies based on price and strategies based on product.

Media markets tend toward differentiated oligopolies
Media markets have an in-built tendency toward product differentiation. There are two reasons for that. The first reason is that media users' preferences in society are hardly ever fully homogeneous. Strong competition in media markets will consequently yield

product content differentiation that is highly reflective of pluralism and variety in population preferences in society. In addition, an even more important factor leading toward content differentiation is the rather specific cost structure of media products. Media content production, organisation and distribution typically entail high first copy costs of creating or acquiring media content, but often very low or even negligible duplication and distribution costs. Media products and services consequently show increasing returns to scale. This implies that profitability in media industries increases with market share, all other factors held constant. In addition, media products, as cultural products *per se*, show a high risk of market failure. Large companies that can produce or acquire various media products and finance failures out of profits of successful productions, therefore have a strong competitive advantage. In sum, size pays in media industries. That is why we may expect that media markets tend toward heterogeneous oligopolies.

Measuring media competition

To measure the competitiveness of media market structures, we may use the Herfindahl-Hirschman Index, a well established, easy to calculate measure of market competition. It runs between $1/n$ (when a number of n firms of equal size are active in a market) to 1 (monopoly). The HHI index is calculated by summing the squares of the market shares of media owners (see Appendix A, Statistical measures of competition and diversity).

Herfindahl-Hirschman Index

$$HHI = \Sigma\ m_i^2$$

$1/n$ (full competition) $\leq HHI \leq 1$ (monopoly)

where m_i market /audience share of entity i

   n number of media owners, media content producers or media outlets

The HHI index may be presented in terms of number-equivalents, that is, in terms of the equivalent number of equal sized firms (Adelman, 1969; De Ridder, 1984, pp. 47, 48).

HHI in terms of equivalent numbers of equal sized firms (NE)

   HHI in Numbers Equivalents $= 1/HHI$

Media concentration

Media competition is inversely related to media concentration. Generally, 'concentration' may be defined as 'the degree to which the largest companies in the same product / service and geographic market control the economic activities in that market' (Picard, 1989, p. 119). In studying media concentration in a particular geographic media market we have to take into account three different aspects of media concentration, that is:

1. Concentration of media ownership;
2. Concentration of media content production, which is not necessarily the same as concentration of media ownership. This form of concentration may be labelled as *editorial* or *programming concentration*; and
3. Concentration of audiences indicating inequality in audience shares of different media channels and titles (cf. De Ridder, 1984).

Ownership concentration, editorial concentration, and audience concentration are closely related but can, and have to be, independently assessed and measured because there is no full linear and positive relationship between these three phenomena. On some occasions, ownership concentration may result in further editorial and audience concentration, on some other occasions it doesn't. Research from the Netherlands, for example, shows that the present-day Dutch newspaper market is a highly concentrated one, as far as ownership is concerned. The Dutch newspaper market may be characterised as a heterogeneously oligopolistic market in which a very limited number of publishers still caters for a certain level of diversity of editorially independent newspaper products (Commissariaat voor de Media [The Netherlands Media Authority], 2002). There is reason to expect that other European countries currently have newspaper markets with similar market characteristics. De Bens' study on the Belgian newspaper market, for example, does show a fierce decline of newspaper enterprises since 1950 (from 33 enterprises in 1950 to only 6 in 1999), whereas the number of different titles only halved (from 50 titles, to 24) (De Bens, 2000, p. 173).

Horizontal, vertical and diagonal media concentration

In most policy debates on media concentration, focus is on competition and concentration in one particular media market and the effects thereof on media content diversity. Often focus on this type of *horizontal* media concentration suffices for an analysis of factors endangering media diversity. However, other forms of media concentration may negatively influence the quality and diversity of media output as well. In line with authors like Sánchez-Taberno (1993), Meier and Trappel (1998, pp. 41, 42), and McQuail (2000, pp. 200–202), we may make a distinction between:

1. *horizontal media concentration (monomedia concentration)*, that is ownership and/or editorial concentration of control within one particular media market or media industry;
2. *vertical media concentration*, that is concentration of control over two or more different chains (creation, production, packaging, distribution) in the media value chain in a particular media market or media industry;
3. *diagonal media concentration (cross-media concentration)*, that is ownership and/or editorial concentration of control in different types of media markets or media industry.

Whereas horizontal concentration first and foremost requires policy attention because of its potential *immediate* effect on media diversity, vertical and diagonal media concentration deserve attention of politicians, regulators and administrators because these forms of media concentration may result in the accumulation of gatekeeping power (vertical concentration) and in predominant opinion power (as German regulation on media concentration puts it, 'vorhersschende Meinungsmacht') in society.

A Media Monitor Model for Media Concentration and Diversity

To measure media diversity by definition is to measure media ownership and media content in one way or another. Very different approaches can be followed here. One way of analysing the effects of media concentration on media diversity might be the Media Monitor model developed by the Media Authority of the Netherlands. This Media Monitor takes both sides of media markets into account. On the supply side, ownership concentration, editorial/programming concentration, and diversity are measured; on the demand side audience preferences. This design not only allows for a description of the effects of media concentration and competition on editorial concentration and media content diversity, but also for a comparison of media supply to media demand, thus enabling the assessment of the degree of reflective diversity and openness. The Monitor monitors the market of different media types separately, that is, a separate analysis has been made of concentration on the market for newspapers, radio, television and cable distribution (Commissariaat voor de Media [The Netherlands Media Authority], 2002).

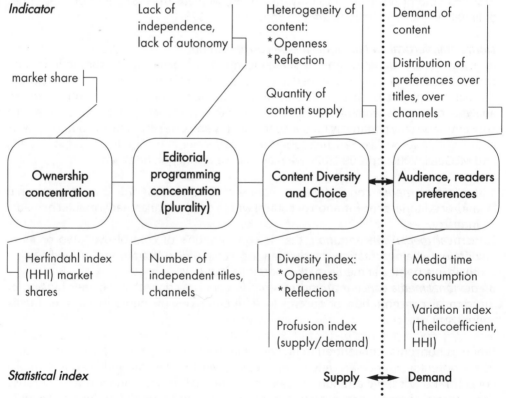

Figure 7 A Media Monitor Model.

In the Media Monitor, four dimensions of media markets are being monitored:

1. *ownership concentration* (and its inverse, ownership competition), that is, the degree to which media owners are able to control media markets;
2. *editorial/programming concentration* (also labelled as *plurality*, and its inverse, editorial competition), that is, the degree to which journalists, editors and programme makers are able to take editorial and/or programming decisions independently and autonomously from media ownership structures;
3. *diversity and choice*, that is, the quantity and variety of media content supply;
4. *audience, readers preferences.*

Media profusion (abundance, plenty)

Figure 7 depicts the model as it is in essence currently used in Dutch media policy to monitor media concentration and diversity. To the original model, however, we have incorporated the dimension of *choice* next to *diversity*, to indicate that a sheer increase in media supply in itself enhances the possibility for media consumers to choose from a variety of products and services. Doing so, we are in line with McQuail (1992, pp. 144–145) who makes a distinction between three standards of media diversity performance: (1) diversity as reflection, (2) diversity as access (that may be compared with 'openness'), and (3) diversity as more channels and choice for the audience.

If we add *choice* to the Monitor model, then it makes sense to develop a kind of *supply/demand* index next to diversity indices for reflection and openness. We may label such an index as the *profusion index*, the term *profusion* referring to rich or lavish supply, abundance (Oxford English Dictionary, Webster's New World Dictionary).[1] Profusion as an abundance index may easily be inferred from the degree of excess of media supply relative to media consumption in society. We may define *media profusion* as: the extent to which the supply of media content to a media market exceeds the audience's actual demand and consumption of media content.

Profusion $= Q_S / Q_D$

$0 \leq$ Profusion

where Q_S quantity of media content supplied in a media market

Q_D quantity of media content consumed in a media market

Media performance

Relating media profusion to diversity, we may consider the *performance* of a *media system* to increase if both diversity and profusion of media products and services increases. We may define *media performance* as:

*Media Performance = Quantity of Content Supply * Quality of Content Supply*

*= Profusion * Diversity*

According to this formula definition, media performance in society is lowest in case of homogeneous media supply that is lagging behind media demand; media performance is highest in case of heterogeneous media supply that is far exceeding media demand.

The concept of 'relevant media information and opinion market'

In analysing media diversity, we usually focus on media markets separately, that is, we assess diversity on the newspaper market, the television market, the radio market and so on. To put it in terms of competition policy and regulation, we consider the newspaper market, the television market and the radio market to be distinct *relevant markets*. We may wonder, however, especially considering the future, if this approach to diversity assessment still makes sense (cf. Sánchez-Taberno and Carvajal, 2002, pp. 28–33).

Markets may be defined in terms of products and geography. In the European Union, a relevant product market is defined as follows: 'A relevant product market comprises of all those products and/or services which are regarded as interchangeable or substitutable by the consumer, by reasons of the products' characteristics, their prices and their intended use (CEC Commission of the European Communities, 1997). Demand substitution constitutes the single most important factor to define a market as a market in itself (for an overview of defining markets with the EU see Faull and Nikpay (eds), 1999, pp. 43–52).

According to De Jong (1989, p. 26), the concept of *relevant market* must not be defined in terms of product and place only, but also in terms of time. The time dimension is often left out of consideration. However, notably in rapidly changing media markets, the time dimension may be a crucial factor: what currently constitutes a relevant media market may be out of date next year. Convergence of IC technologies and the rise of the internet may shed a totally different light on the traditional maxim that daily press diversity should be assessed at the level of all newspapers people can choose from in a particular geographic market. The same applies to television: is the appropriate level of analysis still the set of channels broadcast in a particular region? We may question that.

Following this line of argument, in media policy, to choose media markets to be assessed in terms of concentration and diversity it makes sense to start with defining the *relevant media information and opinion market*. This concept may be defined as follows:

> The *relevant media information and opinion market* for information gathering and opinion formation on X in society is the total, collective, substitutable supply of media content from which people in society gather information and form there opinions on X.

Media diversity is promoted by media policy because of its democratic value. Competition of divergent information, news and opinions on the free marketplace of ideas is considered to be the most valuable method to serve political truth and democracy. Remember once again the 19th century libertarian adage: '… from mutual toleration and comparison of diverse opinions the one that seems most rational will emerge and be generally accepted' (Siebert *et al*, 1969 [1956], p. 44). This being said, the issue of the relevant media information and opinion market has to be settled by the question, what currently constitutes the relevant marketplace of information, ideas and opinions? For democracy, does it matter how people gather information and from which media they form their opinions? Maybe for audiences, from the perspective of opinion formation, media content services and products are getting more and more substitutable. In general, one may predict that the free marketplace of ideas, and thus relevant media opinion markets, become more and more multi-media markets that are much larger and more international than present-day nation- or region-bound, media type-specific markets.

What the consequences of this tendency will be for media diversity assessment and media policy cannot yet be predicted precisely. It seems reasonable, however, to expect that in the near future media policy has to search for media neutral definitions of media diversity that allow assessing media diversity in a multi-media environment, which is getting more and more common to the public. By *media neutral definitions* we mean defining the relevant diversity marketplace not in terms of media types (press, broadcasting, internet) but in terms of media genres and media content products, irrespective the type of distribution technology used. So, perhaps in the not too distant

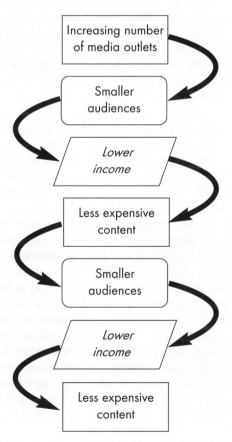

Figure 8 Spiral effect of increasing media outlets and declining content investment (Picard, 2000a: 187).

future, media politicians and regulators will use genre and format definitions of media content, be it press, internet or broadcasting, like: diversity of the *news market*, the *entertainment market*, the *financial news and information market* and the *documentary market*.?

Media competition and diversity: a complex relationship

Competition and media quality

The notion of media competition enhancing media quality is a prevailing opinion of many media practitioners, communication scientists, politicians and administrators in Brussels, Washington and elsewhere. This notion is hardly ever questioned. So, in Lacy and Simon's (1993) overview of economic theory and research into the US daily newspaper press, we find the conclusion that rivalry between media inevitably will result in an increase in quality. Media in competitive markets cannot escape from increasing their editorial budgets just to keep a reasonable market share in order to survive. According to Lacy and Simon, this necessity contributes to quality: 'The increase in quality is necessary for the newspaper to attract readers from its competitors. Newspapers competing for the same readers must match the quality of the competing newspaper in most areas and differentiate themselves in other areas to attract readers.' (1993, p. 102). Even the quantity of media output is stimulated by media competition, as Lacy and Simon argue: 'Two newspapers in a market mean there is more space devoted to news. Even if a majority of the news is somewhat duplicated, having more reporters covering a market increases the possibility of a reporter uncovering information that would be useful in the intellectual market' (1993, p 111).

Editorial quality, however, is not the same as editorial diversity. Here it makes sense to draw the attention once again to an old economic law, Hotelling's Law of 'excessive sameness' of products (1929). According to Hotelling, in many markets it is rational for producers to make their product as similar as possible, because thus they can optimise their market share. Individual rationality here contradicts social desirability that stresses the social importance of product variety. Hotelling's law applied to media markets predicts that *extremely* competitive media markets tend to homogeneity more than monopolistic, oligopolistic or public service media models. Fierce competition enhances *competition on price*. Under conditions of fierce competition, media organisations can only gain reasonable profits by sharply cutting the costs of the production and distribution of their goods and services. Consequently, with fierce competition media markets tend toward reflective diversity, reflecting mainstream, middle of the road preferences and demand. Fierce competition on price in media markets goes with extensive supply of low cost media products 'for the millions' and/or easy to consume media entertainment. Moderate competition on the other hand is *competition on content* rather than on price. Under conditions of moderate competition media markets offer media space to experiment and to serve market niches and minority preferences. Thus, moderate media competition goes with open diversity, in media markets in which each media entrepreneur tries to define his own clientele.

A comparable vision is advocated by Picard:

The increase in media [that is, increase in media competition] cannot be expected to increase diverse views reaching audiences because it constantly reduces the size of audiences and resources available to managers to pursue quality and diversity. ... there is a direct link between the increasing number of media outlets and resources available to content. The fragmentation of the audience requires that the cost of content be reduced. The process compounds itself and transforms into a spiral, however, because cheap content becomes less desirable to audiences (2000a, pp. 186, 187; also, 2002, p. 8).

Some hypotheses on competition and diversity

So, the relationship between media market structure and media performance (quality, diversity) is not by definition linear and positive: some theoretical and empirical arguments do support the proposition that competitive media markets produce high media quality, other arguments lead to the conclusion that even media monopoly or oligopoly may foster media diversity. For an overview of different hypotheses on effects of media market structure on diversity, see Meier and Trappel (1998, pp. 43–47). Available research shows that some forms of media competition are favourable to media diversity and some are not. The distinction between *fierce media competition* and *moderate media competition* might be relevant for analysing the effects of media market structure on content diversity. The relationships between different forms of media competition in a given market and media diversity may be expressed in the three related hypotheses (cf. Van Cuilenburg, 1999).

Hypothesis 1 *Media Competition and Content* Hypothesis (derived from Hotelling)

The more media in a given media market compete for market share, the more they compete on price (= fierce competition), the less they compete on content (= moderate competition).

Hypothesis 2 *Media Diversity* Hypothesis

The more media diversity in a given media market is reflective diversity; the less media diversity is open diversity.

Hypothesis 3 *Media Competition and Diversity* Hypothesis (derived from Hypothesis 1 and Hypothesis 2)

The more media in a given media market compete for market share, the more they compete on price, the less they compete on content, the more media diversity is reflective diversity, and the less media diversity is open diversity.

Specific and more detailed hypotheses derived from these three general propositions were empirically put to test in the Dutch television market (1990–2000) and, in essence, were corroborated (Van der Wurff and Van Cuilenburg, 2001). A comparable empirical analysis for the German television market (Schulz, 2001) also shows that the relationship between media competition and diversity and quality is far from linear and positive. In the nineties in the German market, the programme output increased rapidly as the number of (commercial) programme suppliers and channels increased. However, the dominance of entertainment in programming (*Dominanz der Unterhaltung*), given the economics of television programming, resulted only in 'more of the same' and not in more quality and diversity.

Future trend: more and less competition at the same time

More content providers, more media outlets
In the framework of the foregoing hypotheses, what kind of future competition seems plausible in present-day media markets? There are five trends that currently fundamentally change the media landscape: (1) *digitalisation* of *IC* technology, leading amongst other things to convergence between media (broadcasting) and telecommunications; (2) *exponential growth in media and information supply*, creating media and information abundance (profusion) in society; (3) *exponential diversification* in media products, that is, diversification in content (tailored information), in content-carrying technologies, and in distribution channels and outlets; (4) *stagnation* in media consumption, that is, demand for media products seriously lagging behind supply; and (5) *segmentation* in audiences. These trends together lead to more content providers, more media outlets, and thus more media competition, making media markets increasingly more demand driven.

Some competition on content, most on price
Two of these five trends especially favour competition on content: diversification in supply of media products and segmentation in audiences. *Diversification* in products manifests itself in the production of media products for special interest consumer groups and for niche markets. *Audience segmentation* increases the sales opportunities for different kinds of products and thus promotes monopolistic competition forms between media content providers. One may expect open media diversity to increase as communications technology increases the number of communication channels in society. So, technology promotes *access for ideas*, that is, access for new ideas.

However, the other three trends – digitalisation, growing supply, and stagnation in demand – stimulate media competition on price rather than on content. The *digitalisation* of *IC* technology results in a dramatic fall in prices for electronic transmission of media products. In addition, digitalisation contributes to convergence, that is, to the blurring of boundaries between different modes of electronic communication (broadcasting, internet, telephony). The result from this is twofold: technology reduces media market entry barriers and enables parties to enter media markets that were until recently closed to them. The final result is a striking increase in the number of suppliers and in the volume of supply in nearly every electronic communication market.

Against the exponential growth supply of information and media content we clearly find *stagnation* in media consumption. People are not watching television programmes more than before. Stagnation in consumption is hitting almost every media type, with the exception of the Internet. In many countries the circulation of newspapers, for instance, has stagnated for several decades. From an analysis of the Dutch and American newspaper market, Hendriks concludes: 'The circulation figures suggest that the market for newspapers in economic terms is saturated, in the U.S. one could even speak of a decline since the mid

80s' (Hendriks, 1998, p. 39; see also Picard and Brody, 1997, p. 18). The main characteristic of most media markets nowadays is that demand is lagging far behind supply.

The overproduction of media products inevitably puts pressure on the prices of media products that people are willing to pay. In addition, people also pay less attention to the average media product. Current media markets have to be shared by an ever-increasing number of sellers, all targeting at the same audiences. To still gain a reasonable market share, many media organisations follow a rather conventional product strategy, with hardly any substantial innovation in products. If innovation is still on the media entrepreneur's agenda, it is mostly concerned with process innovation to increase efficiency: by increasing scale of operations to gain economies of scale, and by cutting costs (Hendriks, 1998, pp. 118–119). The end result may be fierce competition on price, and, according to Hotelling's Law and our third hypothesis, an excessive sameness of media products in the form of reflective diversity, serving especially mainstream preferences.

If the number of suppliers of media products in the future keeps on growing, as has been the case during the last decade, there is a chance of ruinous competition. For the television market a situation like this would imply that media organisations do not dare to run the risks inherently related to innovation. Empirical studies show that over the last decade media diversity did not profit from increasing media competition. Here we may refer to Els de Bens' content analysis of the Belgian television market that demonstrated that increasing competition led towards convergence rather than diversity in programme output (De Bens, 2000, p. 172). A Dutch competition/diversity study corroborates the Belgian results for the Dutch market: the more competition intensified over the last decade, the less open diversity and the more excessive sameness in programme types was broadcast (Van der Wurff and Van Cuilenburg, 2001). We may expect that television programming will become more conventional and that the main strategy to attract viewers will be cutting prices, eventually leading to ruinous competition, that is, to a shakeout of marginal and unprofitable broadcasters. The only question then is whether this shakeout will primarily hit the public or the private broadcasters in the television market.

Monopolistic media competition or a homogeneous media oligopoly?
What will happen? Which of the competitive factors in the near future will be decisive, the negative or positive ones? Between the mid 80s and the early 90s there was a breakdown of broadcasting monopolies and the market entry of lots of new commercial and non-commercial (local, regional) parties. Programme output increased rapidly, and so did profits for commercial broadcasters. Current television markets, however, show saturation and market decline. From this, we may predict future profit margins falling and media concentration increasing toward oligopoly once again. Is this new trend toward broadcast oligopoly to be regretted from the perspective of media diversity? It depends, and we have to speculate. It depends on the type of competition that will remain. If the remaining competition between broadcasters is moderate and on content instead of price, then a kind of monopolistic competition will arise and programme output will be of the open-diversity type. However, if the remaining competition in oligopoly is still for market-shares only, then programme output will be very conventional and mainly reflective of majority preferences. Here there is still, at least in

our opinion, a great opportunity for public-service broadcasting, because it does not necessarily depend on large market-shares to perform adequately. Public-service broadcasting can correct market failure due to fierce and ruinous competition. Thus, a plea for public-service broadcasting *and* market might be made, producing optimal conditions for moderate competition and open media diversity (cf. Collins, 1998, p. 374).

Two concluding normative remarks on media policy

To conclude, let me briefly make two normative remarks on media policy in Europe. First, in the last decade, European national and communitarian communications policies have been focusing on privatisation and liberalisation of media markets and on media competition. Certainly, these policies have yielded many positive results such as increasing programme output and falling prices of media products. However, we also find that competition leads to diminishing open diversity and to more sameness and convergence in television programme supply. For the years ahead, this finding should urge media politicians to designing policies that stimulate media product innovation, open diversity and access for new ideas to the media market. This might take the form of European and national subsidies for media productions that improve the quality and diversity of content (cf. Picard, 2000, pp 189,190).

Second, media policies aiming at diversity conventionally focus on the economic basis of media diversity and on the supply side of media markets. So has this chapter. There are, however, also important cultural factors that limit media diversity and innovation. Nordenstreng (2000, p. 43) and Picard (2000a, p. 185) have pointed out that there is a gap between media policy theory on the one hand and audience practice on the other hand. According to Nordenstreng, the idea of responsibilities built into citizenship is present in all reasoning about media and democracy, whereas obviously most citizens hardly pay any attention to, or engage themselves in, the democratic political process. And Picard reminds us that audiences – in spite of all media theorists strongly arguing for media diversity – usually are not interested in diversity. On the contrary: most people have an inherent tendency toward rejecting diversity of opinions and viewpoints through selective attention, perception and recall. This in itself is a strong obstacle to successful policies aimed at more media diversity and innovation. If we want media diversity to contribute effectively to opinion forming in democratic societies (cf. the Diversity Chain in Figure 1), media policies should also aim at enlarging the willingness of citizens to take on their democratic responsibilities, and at enlarging the cultural receptiveness in media audiences to the distinctiveness of different constituent groups, ideologies, religions, and life styles in society. This is a provocative cultural policy task far more difficult than creating a sound competitive economic basis for diversity in media market supply (cf. Van Cuilenburg, 2000, pp. 13–23).

Note

1. I am grateful to Denis McQuail for his linguistic advice on the term 'profusion'. In a recent McKinsey study for the ITC on content regulation (Comparative Review of Content Regulation: A McKinsey Report for the Independent Television Commission, 2002), the term 'content proliferation' is used to denote the same phenomenon. However, the term 'proliferation' semantically has the connotation of diversification and distribution, as in the common phrase 'nuclear proliferation'. That's why we prefer the term 'profusion'

Appendix A: Statistical measures of competition and diversity

Measuring media competition intensity

To measure media concentration, or its inverse competition intensity, there are two indices that are prominent, the Entropy index as introduced for concentration measurement by Theil (1967), and the Herfindahl-Hirschman Index (HHI) (Hannah and Kay, 1977).

The Entropy index measures market uncertainty: the greater the number of competitors, the greater the uncertainty that firms can survive in that market (De Jong, 1989, p. 25). Competition in terms of Entropy is defined as follows (see Formula 1):

Formula 1 Entropy index

$E = - \Sigma m_i {}^2\log m_i$

0 (monopoly) $\leq E \leq {}^2\log n$ (full competition)

in case of monopoly: $m_i = 1$ $\qquad$ $E = 0$

in case of full competition: $m_i = 1/n$ $\quad$ $E = - \Sigma 1/n {}^2\log 1/n = {}^2\log n$

where $\qquad$ ${}^2\log$ $\qquad$ logarithm with base 2

$\qquad\qquad$ m_i $\qquad$ market/audience share of entity i

$\qquad\qquad$ n $\qquad$ number of media owners, media content producers, or media outlets

The Entropy index may be standardised into a relative index (Formula 2).

Formula 2 Relative Entropy index

$E_{relative} = E/ {}^2\log n$

0 (monopoly) $\leq E_{relative} \leq 1$ (full competition)

The Herfindahl-Hirschman Index is also a well established, easy-to-calculate measure of market competition. It runs between $1/n$ (when a number of n firms of equal size are active in a market) to 1 (monopoly). The HHI index is calculated by summing the squares of the market shares of media owners.

Formula 3 Herfindahl-Hirschman Index

$$HHI = \Sigma\, m_i{}^2$$

$1/n$ (full competition) $\leq HHI \leq 1$ (monopoly)

where m_i market /audience share of entity i

           n   number of media owners, media content producers or media outlets

Most often, the entropy and HHI competition/concentration indices are presented in terms of number-equivalents, that is, in terms of the equivalent number of equal sized firms (Adelman, 1969; De Ridder, 1984, pp. 47, 48).

Formula 4 E and HHI in terms of equivalent numbers of equal sized firms (NE)

Entropy in Numbers Equivalents $= 2^E$

HHI in Numbers Equivalents $= 1/HHI$

Statistical diversity measures

Statistically, media diversity can easily be calculated as the coefficient of variability (Fomrula 5). This coefficient can easily be broken down into inter media diversity and intra media diversity (Van Cuilenburg, 1978, p. 14).

Formula 5 Media diversity measured by the coefficient of variability

D (diversity) $= \sigma / \mu$

0 (homogeneity) $\leq D$

where σ standard deviation of media content, in terms of a specific media content dimension (measurement level: interval, ratio)

           μ average of media content, in terms of a specific media content dimension (measurement level: interval, ratio)

The advantage of this coefficient is its intuitive simplicity. Its disadvantage, however, is that the coefficient doesn't have a statistical upper limit. A more sophisticated measure is the entropy coefficient (Formula 6), to be used for measuring diversity along nominal scales (category scales) (Van Cuilenburg and McQuail 1982: 38).

Formula 6 Media diversity measured as entropy

$$D \text{ (diversity)} = (- \Sigma\, p_i\, {}^2\!\log p_i) / \log n$$

$$0 \text{ (homogeneity)} \leq D \leq 1 \text{ (maximum heterogeneity)}$$

where $^2\!\log$ logarithm with base 2

        n number of content type categories

        p_I proportion of items of content type category i

More specific indicators relate actual diversity to the standards of open and reflective diversity. A formula for open diversity is Formula 7:

Formula 7 Open media diversity

$$OD \text{ (open diversity)} = 1 - \Sigma\, |y_i| / 2$$

$$0 \text{ (closeness)} \leq OD \leq 1 \text{ (maximum openness)}$$

where y_I difference between the actual proportion of content type i and the norm for content type i in a situation of maximum openness (i.e., 1 divided by the number of content type categories)

Formula 8 may be used to measure reflective diversity:

Formula 8 Reflective media diversity

$$RD \text{ (reflective diversity)} = 1 - \Sigma\, |z_i| / 2$$

$$0 \text{ (minimum reflection)} \leq RD \leq 1 \text{ (maximum reflection)}$$

where z_i difference between the actual proportion of content type i and the norm for content type i given audience demand

For a recent overview of diversity statistics and their relative (dis)advantages, see: McDonald and Dimmick, 2003.

Appendix B: An overview of Media Monitor concepts

Term	Definition	Measuring standard	Interpretation
Supplier Concentration (Ownership Concentration)	concentration of ownership and control of mass communication means in a certain media market in the hands of one or more suppliers		

Horizontal supplier concentration	supplier concentration within one and the same media market	Herfindahl-Hirschman Index HHI
		
		$HHI = \Sigma\, m_i^2$
		$1/n$ (full competition) $\leq HHI \leq 1$ (monopoly)
		wherein
		m_i market share of supplier i
		n number of suppliers on the market
		
		HHI in *number equivalents* $= 1/HHI$
			the higher the HHI, the higher the level of supplier concentration on the media market
			■ unconcentrated market:
			   $0 \leq HHI < .10$
			■ moderately concentrated market:
			   $.10 \leq HHI < .18$
			■ highly concentrated market:
			   $HHI \geq .18$
			(US Department of Justice, 1997)
			the media market can be classified as a market with … (number of) … equally strong suppliers
			■ unconcentrated market: a market with more than ten equally strong enterprises?
			■ moderately concentrated market: a market with between more than five and ten equally strong enterprises?
			■ highly concentrated market: a market with five or less equally strong enterprises
			(US Department of Justice, 1997)

Vertical supplier concentration	supplier concentration within one and the same media market of different chains in the information chain (*content creation, content packaging, content distribution*)	
Diagonal or cross-media supplier concentration	supplier concentration across media markets or different media types	
Editorial and/or **Programming Concentration**	extent to which editors and/or programme makers lack autonomy in taking decisions on the content of a title and/or programme channel	number of editorially independent press titles and/or number of independent programme channels	the larger the number, the lower the level of editorial and/or programming concentration
Diversity	extent to which media content differs according to one or more criteria	(1) variation coefficient for interval and ratio scales $D \text{ (diversity)} = \sigma / \mu$ where σ standard deviatipm μ mean (2) entropy index for nominal scales $D \text{ (diversity)} = (- \Sigma p_i \, ^2\log p_i) / \log n$ where n number of content type categories p^i proportion of items of content type category i	the greater the variation, the greater the diversity of media content
Reflection, reflective diversity	extent to which the supply of media content matches the preferences of the audience	RD (reflective diversity) = $1 - \Sigma \lvert z_i \rvert \, / \, 2$ 0 (minimum reflection) $\leq RD \leq 1$ (maximum reflection) where z_i difference between the actual proportion of content type i and the norm for content type i given audience demand	the greater RD, the more media reflect the preferences of their audiences

Term	Definition	Measuring standard	Interpretation
Openness, open diversity	extent to which the supply of media content equals a statistically uniform distribution	OD (open diversity) $= 1 - \Sigma \|y_i\| / 2$ 0 (closeness) $\leq OD \leq 1$ (maximum openness) where y_i difference between the actual proportion of content type i and the norm for content type i in a situation of maximum openness (i.e., 1 divided by the number of content type categories)	the greater OD, the more different types of content categories get equal coverage within the media
Media Profusion	extent to which the quantity of media content supply exceeds the quantity of media content demand	$P = Q_S / Q_d$ $0 \leq$ Profusion where Q_S quantity of media content supplied in a media market Q_d quantity of media content consume in a media market	the greater P, the more media supply audiences can choose from to satisfy their media demand
Media Performance	assessment score of the performance of a media system in terms of media diversity and media profusion	Media Performance = Media Diversity * Media Profusion	the higher the Media Performance score, the better a media system performs in terms of both diversity and profusion
Audience Concentration	concentration of audience preferences in a particular media market on one or more media titles or media channels	(1) Herfindahl-Hirschman Index HHI $HHI = \Sigma m_i^2$ $1/n$ (minimum audience concentration) $\leq HHI \leq 1$ (maximum audience concentration) where: m_i market share of media title of channel i n number of media titles or channels on the market	(1) in case HHI: the smaller, the less audience preferences concentrate on one or more titles or channels

(2) Theil's relative entropy index
$$E_{relative} = -\sum m_i \, ^2\log m_i / \, ^2\log n$$
0 (maximum audience concentration) $\leq E_{relative} \leq 1$ (minimum audience concentration)
where m_i market / audience share of media title or channels i
n number of titles or channels

(1) in case HHI:
the smaller, the less audience preferences concentrate on one or more titles or channels
(2) in case of Theils coefficient:
the greater, the less audience preferences concentrate on one or more titles or channels

References

Adelman, M.A. (1969) 'Comment on the 'H' Concentration Measure as a Numbers-Equivalent', *The Review of Economics and Statistics*, Vol. 51, pp. 99–101.

Boone, L.E. & D.L. Kurtz (1992) *Contemporary Marketing*. Fort Worth: The Dryden Press.

CEC Commission of the European Communities (1997) Commission Notice on the Definition of the Relevant Market for the Purposes of Community Competition Law, *Official Journal*, OJ C 372, on 9/12/1997.

Collins, R. (1998) 'Public Service and the Media Economy: European Trends in the Late 1990s', *Gazette*, Vol. 60, No. 5, pp. 363–376.

Commissariaat voor de Media [The Netherlands Media Authority] (2002) *A view on media concentration: concentration and diversity of the Dutch media in 2001*, Hilversum: Commissariaat voor de Media; also available on HYPERLINK "http://www.cvdm.nl/pages/mediaconc.asp" www.cvdm.nl/pages/mediaconc.asp

Commissariaat voor de Media [The Netherlands Media Authority] (2003) *Concentratie en pluriformiteit van de Nederlandse media 2000* [Concentration and diversity of the Dutch media 2002], Hilversum: Commissariaat voor de Media.

De Bens, E. (2000) 'Media Competition: Greater Diversity or Greater Convergence', pp. 158–179 in: J. van Cuilenburg and R. van der Wurff (eds.), *Media & Open Societies: Cultural, Economic and Policy Foundations for Media Openness and Diversity in East and West*, Amsterdam: Het Spinhuis

Dizard, W.P. (1994) *Old Media / New Media: Mass Communication in the Information Age*. White Plains (NY): Longman Publishers.

European Union (1992) Greenbook *Pluralism and Media Concentration in the Internal Market*.

Faull, J. & A. Nikpay (eds.) (1999), *The EC Law of Competition*. Oxford: Oxford University Press.

Hannah, L. & J.A. Kay (1977) *Concentration in Modern Industry*. London: Macmillan.

Hellman, H. (2001) 'Diversity: an End in Itself?' *European Journal of Communication*, 16 (2), pp. 181–208.

Hendriks, P.C.J. (1998) *Newspapers: A Lost Cause? Strategic Management of Newspaper Firms in The United States and The Netherlands*, academic dissertation, Amsterdam: Universiteit van Amsterdam.

Hoffmann-Riem, W. (1987) 'National Identity and Cultural Values: Broadcasting Safeguard', *Journal of Broadcasting*, 31:1, pp. 57–72.

Hotelling, H. (1929) 'Stability in Competition', *Economic Journal*, 34, pp. 41–57.

Jong, H.W. de (1989) *Dynamische Markttheorie* [Dynamic Market Theory]. Leiden: Stenfert Kroese.

Lacy, S. & T.F. Simon (1993) *The Economics and Regulation of United States Newspapers*. Norwood, New Jersey: Ablex Publishing Corporation.

McDonald, D.G. & J.Dimmick (2003) 'The Conceptualization and Measurement of Diversity', *Communication Research*, Vol. 30 (1), pp. 60–79.

McQuail, D. & J. van Cuilenburg (1983) 'Diversity as a media policy goal: A strategy for evaluative research and a Netherlands case study', *Gazette* 31 (3), pp. 145–162.

McQuail, D. (1992) *Media Performance: Mass Communication and the Public Interest*. London: Sage.

McQuail, D. (2000) *Mass Communication Theory* (4th edition). London: Sage.

Meier, W.A. & J. Trappel (1998) 'Media Concentration and the Public Interest', pp. 38–60in: D. McQuail & K. Siune (eds.), *Media Policy: Convergence, Concentration and Commerce*. London: Sage.

Mill, J.S. (1972 [1859]), *On Liberty*. London: Dent and Sons.

Milton,.J. (1997 [1644]) *Areopagitica*. University of Oregon: Renascence Editions.

Napoli, P.M. (1999) 'Deconstructing the Diversity Principle', *Journal of Communication*, 49 (4), pp. 7?34.

Nordenstreng, K. (2000) 'Media and Democracy: What is Really Required', pp. 20–4in J. van Cuilenburg and R. van der Wurff (eds.), *Media & Open Societies: Cultural, Economic and Policy Foundations for Media Openness and Diversity in East and West*. Amsterdam: Het Spinhuis.

Picard, R.G. (1989) *Media Economics: Concepts and Issues*. Newbury Park, California: Sage.

Picard, R.G. (ed.) (2000) *Measuring Media Content, Quality, and Diversity: Approaches and Issues in Content Research*. Turku (Finland): Turku School of Economicsa and Business Administration.

Picard, R.G. (2000a) 'Audience Fragmentation and Structural Limits on Media Innovation and Diversity', pp. 180–191 in J. van Cuilenburg and R. van der Wurff (eds) *Media & Open Societies: Cultural, Economic and Policy Foundations for Media Openness and Diversity in East and West*. Amsterdam: Het Spinhuis.

Picard, R.G. (2002) *The Economics and Financing of Media Companies*. New York: Fordham University Press.

Picard, R.G. & J.H. Brody (1997) *The Newspaper Industry*. Needham Heights, MA: Allyn & Bacon

Popper, K.R. (1968 [1962]) *Conjectures and Refutations: the Growth of Scientific Knowledge*. New York: Harper & Row.

Pride, W.M. & O.C. Ferrell (1991) *Marketing: Concepts and Strategies*. Boston: Houghton Mifflin Company.

Ridder, J.A. de (1984) *Persconcentratie in Nederland* [Press concentration in the Netherlands]. Amsterdam: VU Uitgeverij.

Sánchez-Taberno, A. & M.Carvajal (2002) *Media Concentration in the European Market: Nerw Trends and Challenges*. Pamplona: Universidad de Navarra.

Sánchez-Taberno, A. (1993) *Media Concentration in Europe: Commercial Enterprise and the Public Interest*. Düsseldorf: European Institute for the Media.

Scherer, F.M. (1996) *Industry Structure, Strategy, and Public Policy*. New York: Harper Collins.

Schulz, W. (2001) 'Mehr Wettbewerb, weniger Programmqualität: Was das private Fernsehen gebracht hat [More competition, less programme quality: what private broadcasting has brought us]', in C. Drägert and N. Schneider (eds.), *Medienethik: Freiheit under Verantwortung* [Media Ethics]. Stuttgart: Kreuz Verlag.

Siebert, F.S., T. Peterson & W. Schramm (1969 [1956]) *Four theories of the press*. Urbana: University of Illinois Press.

Theil, H. (1967) *Economics and Information Theory*. Amsterdam: North-Holland Publishing Company.

US Department of Justice and the Federal Trade Commission (1997) *1992 Horizontal Mergers Guidelines, [with April 8, 1997, Revisions to Section 4 on Efficiencies]*. Washington: US Department of Justice.

Van Cuilenburg, J. (1978) 'Measurement of a newspaper's political progressivenes', in *MDN Methoden and Data Nieuwsbrief van de Sociaal Wetenschappelijke Sectie van de Vereniging voor Statistiek*, pp. 4–17.

Van Cuilenburg, J. (1998) 'New Perspectives on Media Diversity: Toward a Critical-Rational Approach to Media Performance', pp. 71–85in Zassoursky andVartanova (eds) *Changing Media and Communications*. Moscow: Faculty of Journalism / ICA.

Van Cuilenburg, J. (1999) 'On Competition, Access and Diversity in Media, Old and New', *New Media & Society*, Vol. 1(2), pp. 183–207.

Van Cuilenburg, J. (2000) 'On Measuring Media Competition and Media Diversity: Concepts, Theories and Methods', pp. 51–84 in R.G. Picard (ed.) *Measuring Media Content, Quality, and Diversity: Approaches and Issues in Content Research*. Turku (Finland): Turku School of Economicsa and Business Administration.

Van der Wurff, R. & J. van Cuilenburg (2001) 'The Impact of Moderate and Ruinous Competition on Diversity: The Dutch Television Market', *Journal of Media Economics*, 14 (4), pp. 213–229.

Van Cuilenburg, J. & D.McQuail, (1982) *Media en Pluriformiteit* [Media and Diversity]. Den Haag: Staatsgeverij.

Van Cuilenburg, J. & R. van der Wurff (eds.) (2000) *Media & Open Societies: Cultural, Economic and Policy Foundations for Media Openness and Diversity in East and West*. Amsterdam: Het Spinhuis.

3

MEASURING AND ASSESSING EMPIRICAL MEDIA DIVERSITY: SOME EUROPEAN CASES

Minna Aslama, Els De Bens, Jan van Cuilenburg, Kaarle Nordenstreng, Winfried Schulz & Richard van der Wurff with contributions from Ildiko Kovats, Gianpietro Mazzoleni and Ralph Negrine
Edited by Jan van Cuilenburg & Richard van der Wurff

Introduction

Freedom of expression and information is one of the fundamental civil rights. It has a prominent position in article 11.1 of the *Charter of Fundamental Rights of the European Union* (2000). The same article states in paragraph 11.2 that 'The freedom and pluralism of the media shall be respected', thus linking freedom of expression and information to media and media pluralism. It is therefore not surprising that throughout Europe media diversity is one of the main goals pursued in media policy. Yet, there is no unified approach, neither in national media policies nor in communication science, to measure and assess media diversity. In this chapter, we present various empirical studies on media diversity done by communication scientists from four different EU member states: Belgium, Finland, Germany and the Netherlands. These studies not only illustrate different approaches to defining, measuring and assessing 'media diversity', but also provide us with building blocks for a unified assessment of media diversity within the European Union.

1. Belgium

by Els De Bens

Belgium is a small, densely populated country with 10 million inhabitants. Through a number of constitutional reforms, Belgium has become a federal state. The Flemish and French communities are fully autonomous to develop their own regulatory framework for broadcast activities, whereas the print and telecom sectors are regulated by Belgian legislation.

Media landscape

The newspaper market in Belgium is a stagnating market with a gradual decline of readership. Since 2001, the advertisement share of television exceeds that of the print sector. Newspaper concentration in Belgium is very high. The national newspaper market (Flemish and French) is dominated by 6 major companies that publish 23 dailies, of which only 12 are independent titles. In Flanders the market leader is the VUM (4 dailies) with a market share of 43%. In the French speaking part the market leader is Rossel (5 dailies) with a market share of 51% (De Bens, 2004, pp. 17–31).

In Flanders the public broadcasting monopoly came to an end in 1989 after the launching of the first commercial television station, VTM. Initially, the government gave VTM a monopoly for commercial television for a period of 18 years. In 1994, however, VTM's monopoly was undermined by the controversial launch of VT4, a new commercial SBS station. As VT4 was officially based in London, and Flemish cable companies were willing to distribute VT4, this station was able to circumvent VTM's 18 years monopoly. To counter VT4, VTM launched a second channel, K2. Meanwhile new thematic channels have been launched (lifestyle, music, business) with moderate audience shares. The public service broadcaster VRT and commercial VTM still dominate the market.

In the French speaking part of Belgium, the public television broadcaster RTBF got a commercial competitor in 1987, RTL-TVi. This new station was less successful than the Flemish VTM, primarily because it did not only compete with the public broadcaster but also with public and commercial channels from France that were popular in French speaking Belgium. Nowadays, competition between RTBF and RTL-TVi is strong.

Public radio in Flanders has a dominant market share to date (85% in 2004). Until 2002 only the public broadcaster had access to frequencies that covered the whole of Flanders. Two new private radio stations that recently got a licence to cover the whole of Flanders still have a small market share. So far they cannot compete with the successful public stations that are allowed to carry advertising (up to 40 million Euros).

In Wallonia, however, the public radio stations have always been heavily challenged by the private stations. The market penetration of the private radio stations is considerably higher than that of the public radio stations.

Regulatory and institutional arrangements

In Belgium, media diversity is only explicitly mentioned in the remit of public service broadcasters. Since the audiovisual sector belongs to the competence of the separate Flemish and French speaking communities, these communities have somewhat different remits. Both remits stress however the crucial role of diversity in the programme supply. In Flanders, Article 8 of the decree of 1995 stipulates that the VRT 'has to reach the widest possible audience with a diversity of programmes that will appeal to the demands of listeners and viewers'. This sounds like reflective diversity! But the decree is more explicit. It underlines that the VRT has to offer 'a qualitative programme, especially in the field of information and culture'. At the same time, they have to offer sport, drama, entertainment as well as education. The programmes also have to support the identity and diversity of Flemish culture. Finally, special attention is claimed for children's programmes and minority groups.

In 1997–2001 and 2002–2006 the VRT received more autonomy as the result of a 'management contract'. The remit as described in the decree of 1995 remained essentially the same. However, from now on VRT had to face performance criteria that imposed audience rating goals. For example, the daily audience reach that was imposed for the information programmes is 1.5 million viewers per day. This is a very high performance figure and many researchers have argued that the VRT information programmes became tabloidised as a result of the high audience goals.

In the French speaking Community, the Decree of 1997 of the PSB also imposes diversity goals.

Article 3 imposes a long list of expectations:

- diversity of programmes with special attention for international, European, federal, and regional information, for culture, education, entertainment and creative performances of authors, composers, theatre of French-speaking Belgian artists;
- through quality and diversity, the RTBF has to reach the widest possible audience but has also to serve minorities;
- the programmes of the RTBF have to stimulate the democratic dialogue.

The RTBF also got 'a management contract' (2002–2005) in which performance criteria were imposed but, unlike the VRT, there are no quotas mentioned, so that the obligation to obtain specific audience ratings remains rather vague.

As far as print media concentration is concerned, Belgium does not possess any specific legislation. Media concentration is implicitly covered by the general competition legislation and cases are brought before the Competition Council as they arise. So far this Council has never acted on any matter of media concentration. Nevertheless, the Belgian newspaper market has become highly concentrated, causing a loss of pluralism and diversity (see next section).

Neither Flanders nor Wallonia possesses any specific legislation on concentration or on cross-ownership. To give an actual example, in Flanders De Persgroep, which has a 34.9% share of the total newspaper market (in 2005), is allowed to have a 50 % participation in the commercial national TV broadcaster VTM, 50% in the regional TV station ATV (Antwerp) as well as 50% in the nation-wide radio station Q-Music, the target audience radio stations Mango and Contact. It has often been argued that these cross ownership activities cause blending of market goals and can damage diversity.

In Belgium the respective Media Authorities are the only controlling and sanctioning bodies in each linguistic community (the Vlaamse Commissariaat voor de Media in Flanders and the Conseil Supérieur de l'Audiovisuel in Wallonia). Each is the sole authority with competence on the audio-visual media. They grant licences and they are responsible for checking whether the broadcasting legislation is adhered to (e.g., offences relating to advertising, sponsoring, and product placement). It is in their power to impose penalties on the broadcasters. As the Flemish Media Authority employs no more than three full-time staff, close monitoring is virtually impossible. The Walloon Media Authority has a more extensive staff and is thus better equipped to exercise control. Also, the French-speaking Community has prepared a draft decree that is aimed at countering cross-ownership and that charges its Media Authority with checking programme diversity in cases of conflict of interest between different stations. However, the debate on the subject is far from being finalised, and there is no legislation in sight.

Competition and diversity in the Flemish newspaper market
A number of studies in Flanders investigate whether intense rivalry on oligopolistic newspaper markets reduces diversity. These studies are reviewed first. Similar studies that analyse the consequences of competition in broadcasting are discussed next.

The introduction to this section already noted that newspaper concentration in Belgium is very high. Since 1950, 25 daily newspapers have disappeared and the number of newspaper enterprises is reduced from 34 to 7. Today these 7 newspaper groups publish 23 newspapers, of which only 16 appear as independent titles (with a full independent editorial staff). The other 7 newspapers appear as parallel editions. In Flanders only 3 major publishers publish 9 titles and the market leader VUM has a market share of 43%. The 4th publisher is an enterprise that publishes one single daily (De Bens, 2004). Concentration meant the end of the strong political opinion press that Belgium once had. The closing down of so many newspapers inevitably resulted in a loss of pluralism, even though some of the larger newspaper enterprises continue publication of an acquired newspaper for some years as a parallel edition before shutting it down.

Table 1: Number of newspaper titles and publishers in Belgium, 1950–2004

	Flanders		Wallonia		Belgium	
	Titles	Publishers	Titles	Publishers	Titles	Publishers
1950	18	14	30	20	48	34
1980	12	7	22	10	34	17
2004	10	4	14	3	24	7

Source: De Bens (2001): 68; updated by author

In one exceptional case a merger safeguarded, rather than ended, the existence of the only existing progressive daily, *De Morgen*. This newspaper was acquired in 1989 by the *Persgroep*, publisher of central liberal newspapers. *De Morgen* could keep its independent editorial staff and its editorial identity and, after a number of difficult years, has now become one of the fastest growing dailies in Flanders. The same story of the only progressive newspaper left in French speaking Belgium, *Le Matin*, has a less successful ending. Like *De Morgen*, *Le Matin* could not survive as a small independent newspaper in an oligopolistic market, but finally no major newspaper group was interested in a takeover and *Le Matin* disappeared in 2001. This resulted in a particular situation: francophone Belgium boasts a strong socialist, progressive majority but all its newspapers are positioned in the centre of the political spectrum.

The merger story of *Het Volk* illustrates how concentration and mergers result in a loss of diversity. The catholic trade union newspaper *Het Volk* was acquired in 1994 by VUM. This caused a lot of consternation because *Het Volk*, which was still selling 115,000 copies a day, enlarged the VUM's share in the Flemish newspaper sector to 45%, which was a critical figure for the Competition and Merger Commission.

The VUM as a publisher of catholic papers probably bought *Het Volk* for defensive considerations, i.e. to eliminate a potential rival. All the same, with *Het Volk* it incorporated a loss-making daily, for which it had to pay a large amount of money.

The VUM group solemnly agreed that the majority of *Het Volk's* staff would be kept on, that the paper would remain in Gent, and above all, that its editorial identity would be guaranteed for at least 5 years. *Het Volk* would thus continue as a full newspaper alongside the other VUM titles. The VUM managing director declared that *Het Volk* would never be downgraded to a parallel edition of its VUM counterpart, *Het Nieuwsblad*.

Yet, it would have been quite naïve to believe that a newspaper group that is mainly owned by banks and financial holdings and whose company director, Andre Leysen, is a captain of industry and an icon of the Flemish employers, would protect and support *Het Volk's* trade union oriented policy. Shortly after the acquisition by the VUM, the management of *Het Volk* was dismissed, and, at first little by little and later at an accelerated rate, congruence arose between the editorial staffs of *Het Nieuwsblad* and *Het Volk*.

A comparison of the two newspapers between 1994 and 2002, when the congruence in editorial staff was complete, shows how and when the newspapers became identical. For each year an artificial week was constructed, and a total of 857 articles were compared (Knockaert, 2004). Advertisements, weather reports, stock market results, cartoons, readers' letters, TV and radio programmes were not included in the study. The results show that between 1994 and 2000 both titles were quite dissimilar. The exchange of articles was limited to the sports pages and regional reporting. This indicates that the VUM initially respected the acquisition contract.

From 2000 onwards, identical articles grew more frequent. The process of congruence accelerated in 2001 and by 2002 the two titles were virtually identical. *Het Volk* thus

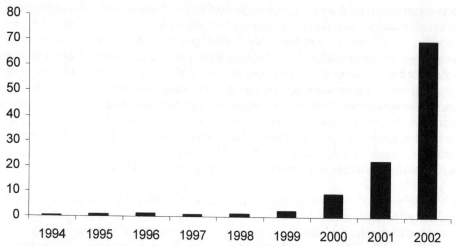

Figure 1 Percentage of identical articles in *Het Nieuwsblad* and *Het Volk*.
Source: Knockaert (2004)

turned into a parallel edition of *Het Nieuwsblad*. In 2002 94% of the articles had the same title, 98% the same text, 95% the same place, and 91% the same illustrations. Apart from the limited regional reporting, the only difference was that the front pages were not identical. And in March 2005, the pages 2 and 3 of *Het Volk* – that still were different from *Het Nieuwsblad* – also were replaced by pages 2 and 3 of *Het Nieuwsblad*, so that both newspapers are now completely identical, except the front page.

Competition and diversity in broadcasting
In Flanders, as elsewhere in Europe, the public broadcaster (VRT) lost its monopoly in the late 1980s when a new commercial broadcaster emerged. However, even before that the public broadcaster faced competition from foreign channels that were available via the very dense cable network. Cable companies offered numerous foreign public stations as early as the 1970s, and from 1982 they also carried a commercial station (RTL). This implies that from the early 1980s the Flemish public was offered 30 to 40 TV channels on their sets. In principle, the availability of more stations means more diversity. But it also implied more competition and a potential loss of viewers for the national public broadcaster.

Impact of foreign competition on public broadcaster programme content
The Flemish remained on the whole faithful to their Flemish public broadcaster, but station loyalty weakened nevertheless. While in 1970 78% watched the VRT (then called the BRT), by 1988 this percentage had dropped to 56% (figures from the BRT's Audience Research Department). About half of the Flemish viewers watching foreign stations tuned in to the Dutch stations – not only because of the language affinity, but also because of the popular appeal of certain programmes on the Dutch channels. The second most successful foreign channel, even though it was in a foreign language, was

the commercial RTL. Flemish viewers were attracted by its entertainment content, especially American fiction.

The public broadcaster looked upon this dwindling number of viewers with disappointment and demanded an appropriate reaction from its programme planners. Its Audience Research Department's 1976 report (BRT, 1979) recommended 'more attractive programmes' to counter the competition. It analysed at which points in time the viewers switched to Dutch channels, and it responded by altering BRT's own programmes. When in 1982, for instance, it was found that on Thursday nights Flemish viewers switched to a popular Dutch TV programme, the public broadcaster countered this by scheduling Dallas in the same time slot, and so regained most of its viewers (De Bens, 1986).

Because of the competition with the Dutch channels and RTL, all of which broadcast for more hours, public broadcasting time also increased. An early analysis of the consequences for diversity showed that between 1970 and 1984 the proportion of broadcasting time devoted to various content categories remained on the whole unchanged, except for an increase in TV fiction. During prime time, however, entertainment and TV fiction increased sharply (De Bens, 1985). These results align with results from similar studies conducted by Souchon (1978 & 1980) in France and Geerts and Thoveron (1979 & 1980) in French-speaking Belgium. These studies also found that diversity diminished during prime time as channels emphasised entertainment and fiction programmes in a competitive environment.

Competition between public and private television

When in 1989 the first Flemish commercial TV station (VTM) was launched, it soon became a success. In a certain sense VTM's position was well protected: it was granted an advertising monopoly for 18 years. The Flemish government took this policy decision on the assumption that the Flemish media market was too small to harbour more than one commercial station. But this commercial TV monopoly was *de facto* broken when VT4 was up-linked from London in a classic U-turn construction, and acquired a place on the Flemish cable network. Eventually Flanders was forced by EU rules to abandon its protectionist policy and licences were accorded to several Flemish commercial channels.

In spite of the commercial newcomers, VTM remained by far the public broadcaster's major opponent. During the first 6 years of competition, the public broadcaster saw its market share drop to 29% (from 57% in 1989 before VTM was launched). This loss of viewers not only hurt the public broadcaster in its pride, but also raised the fear that politicians would use the low ratings to prune the annual grant to public broadcasting. This fear triggered a panicky imitation strategy that no doubt caused the loss of some degree of diversity. This competitive struggle implicated mainly VRT's first channel, TV1, because it was the most widely viewed public channel.

More channels could, in principle, bring more diversity, but competition between the channels was fierce and 'more of the same' was programmed. A longitudinal comparative programme analysis of VRT and VTM for the 1989–1994 period (De Bens, 1997), supplemented by a follow-up study for 1995–1999 (De Bens, 2000), analyses how the first commercial station influences programming on the public broadcaster's channels programming and whether any convergence in programming arose. For each year three months were examined (February, August and September). The various programme categories were divided into three main categories: information, entertainment (shows, talk shows, fiction, game shows, quiz shows, human interest, popular music), and education (broadly defined to include consumer programmes and service programmes). Separate categories were added for children's programmes and arts programmes (on performing arts, literature, classical music, painting and sculpture, film and photography, and architecture). The latter category was included because of the assumption that under fierce competition this category comes under most pressure. Besides, broadcasting arts programmes constitute a challenge for a public broadcaster, not only because it is a part of its remit, but also because a public broadcaster functions as a platform towards a wider audience that cannot often be reached with the 'arts' (McQuail, 1992, p. 284).

The results show that the share of entertainment on the first public channel rose spectacularly: from 48% in 1988 to 74% in 1998, which brought it close to the commercial VTM's figure of 76%. In the same year, K2 (VTM's second channel, which was launched in anticipation of TV4's arrival) and TV4 offered respectively 99% and 98% entertainment. It may be concluded that TV1 and VTM are growing more alike, as are K2 and VT4. Also as far as news programmes shares are concerned, VRT (22% in 1998) and VTM (19.2% in 1998) are quite close. The arts programme category however had completely disappeared from TV1 by 1998.

Meanwhile, the public broadcaster had a revival strategy under way since 1997. A new management contract allowed it more autonomy and power, the complete VRT top management was dismissed, politicisation was curbed, and the channels were reprofiled. The government imposed performance quotas concerning viewing figures: the two channels are required to reach 76% of the population and culture/education has to make up 10% of both channels' activities.

Culture/education is a vague category, however, and we have already pointed out that in 1998 (after the management contract was concluded) the share of 'arts' was nil on TV1. It is fair to state that Canvas, the second public Channel, offers 'only' 42.5% entertainment and in 1998 still devoted 3.3% of its programming to the arts. The question is whether this is sufficient to vouch for the VRT's PSB remit and distinctiveness, as the overwhelming majority of the Flemish public watches TV1 (annual market shares: 26% for TV1, against 9.2% for Canvas in 1998).

The 7o'clock news of TV1 and VTM: different or the same?
The public broadcaster's (VRT) management contracts of 1997–2001 and 2002–2006 impose exceptionally high performance criteria for its television news broadcasts: it is required to reach 1.5 million viewers daily. When the evaluation of the first management contract proved that this requirement had not been met, the public broadcaster decided to make far-reaching alterations to its newscasts so as to attract more viewers. This shows

that it was the government's broadcasting policy itself that prompted the competition between the rival public and private television broadcasters. It has been argued with increasing insistence that the 7 o'clock newscasts on the public (TV1) and on the private (VTM) channel resemble each other ever more closely. The public broadcaster's counterargument that its second channel (Canvas) offers a totally different newscast, with more comment added, proves to be incorrect: the news on Canvas is a shortened version of that on TV1 and the vast majority of Flemish viewers watch the 7 o'clock news on TV1.

A recent study compared the 7 o'clock news on the most widely watched public (TV1) and private (VTM) channels for the periods between the 9th and 15th of February and the 5th and 12th of April 2004. Neither period featured any exceptional or spectacular news events. The main part of the study consisted of a quantitative and qualitative analysis that used 18 content categories. For each content category it was monitored whether the news events were dramatised and presented in an emotional way. The study analysed a total of 586 news items from 14 TV1 newscasts and 300 items from 14 VTM newscasts (De Bens & Paulussen, 2004).

The structural similarities between both newscasts are striking. They include the total time slot of each newscast, the number and the duration of separate news items, the overall structure of the newscast, the use of interviews and reporters. On weekdays the 7 o'clock news lasts an average of 40 minutes on VTM and 42 minutes on TV1. On Saturdays it is shorter on both channels and on Sundays it is longer on TV1, as more sports news is included.

On the public channel the newscast lasts on average 2.5 minutes longer than on the private channel, where it starts 15 seconds earlier than on TV1. On TV1 the 7 o'clock news contains on average of 21 items with an average duration of 113 seconds. VTM's news contains on average 22 items with an average duration of 108 seconds. The differences in the number of items and in duration are not statistically significant. While sports news was not further investigated in our study, we found that TV1 and VTM devote on average 7 and 6 minutes to sport respectively.

Also in terms of formal presentation (reporting, live reports, studio interviews) and geographical news content, the similarities between the two newscasts are striking. Both TV1 and VTM make abundant use of interviews in their 7 o'clock news. Both newscasts interview mainly spokespersons, though experts and politicians are also regularly called upon. Both newscasts also show a majority of domestic news (62% for TV1 and 70% for VTM). International news is spread in a similar way over various international regions. The themes that are most frequently dealt with in the international news on both channels are terrorism and war, disasters, and fires. As far as domestic news is concerned, VTM pays more attention to human interest and crime and corruption, both in terms of the number and the total duration of items. For all other content categories, differences are all but negligible (see Figure 2). Politics receives relatively great attention on both channels; economics and society much less, and arts and culture are hardly given any space at all in the newscasts.

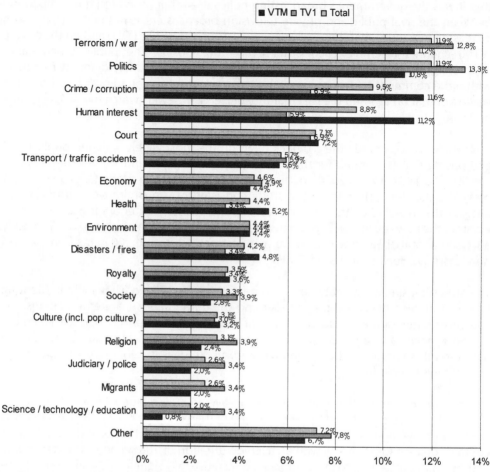

Figure 2 Percentage of items per topic (excluding sports).
Source: De Bens & Paulussen (2004)

Conclusions

The studies reviewed in this section show that both concentration (on newspaper markets) and fierce competition (on television markets) result in a loss of diversity. On the Flemish television market competition had a negative impact on diversity, even before the advent of Flemish commercial TV. Following the market entry of commercial channels, the main public and commercial are growing more alike. Even the 7 o'clock newscasts on the main public and commercial channel are quite similar.

The high performance criteria imposed on the public broadcaster in Flanders contributed to its 'tabloidisation'. In the long run, the permanent pressure to obtain high ratings (1.5 million viewers daily) threatens to undermine its 'distinctiveness', i.e. its difference from the commercial broadcasters. The government therefore may need to revise its policy on performance criteria, while the public broadcaster may have to reflect again on how to emphasise the diversity, pluriformity, and distinctiveness of its main newscast and other programmes in the future.

2. Finland
by Minna Aslama & Kaarle Nordenstreng
Finland has a population of just over 5 million, but its territory is one of the largest in the European Union. Bordering Russia in the East (over 1000 km) and Sweden in the West, it has a distinct language (Finnish), which dominates all media except import-based cinema and record industries, and the media of the Swedish-speaking minority population. Reference data on media is a part of the official statistics on culture and the media, produced by the state bureau of statistics (Statistics Finland, 2005).

Media landscape
The Finnish media landscape is characterised by a high rate of consumption of print media – amongst the highest in the world. There are over 50 daily newspapers (4–7 issues per week), of these nearly 30 are issued literally daily, and over 170 other newspapers (1–3 issues per week) – not counting roughly 100 papers with free circulation (including a local *Metro*). In terms of newspaper circulation per thousand inhabitants, Finland comes third after Japan and Norway.

Newspapers are quite widely dispersed across the territorially large country but they are no longer as local/regional as they used to be. There are two main newspaper chains, Sanoma/WSOY and Alma Media, which together control some 40% of the total newspaper circulation. Besides newspapers, there are nearly 3000 magazine titles, not counting periodic publications with less than 4 issues per year. Two publishers (Yhtyneet Kuvalehdet and Sanoma Magazines Finland) control over 60% of the magazine market that accounts for almost 20% of the total media revenues. The strong position of the print media is also reflected in the breakdown of advertising expenditure by different media categories: in 2001, the print media accounted for some 70% of the total.

The electronic media have seen many major structural changes during the past decades. Both the radio and television markets, traditionally led by public service broadcaster Finnish Broadcasting Company (YLE), were de-regulated. There are over 60 commercial local radio stations in addition to the five national radio networks operated by YLE. A particular feature of the Finnish television markets is that there has never been a broadcasting monopoly based on law and commercial TV in Finland operated for 35 years under the public service (YLE's) licence, with its own time blocs on the two national public service channels. In 1993, commercial television got its own licence and national channel MTV3, and in 1997 the fourth terrestrial channel, the commercial Nelonen began its operations.

In ten years from 1993 to 2002, television viewing increased by approximately 40 minutes per day, while nation-wide terrestrial analogue television supply increased by some 23 hours per day (Aslama & Wallenius, 2003). This, together with a small but growing cable channel supply, has changed the intensity of concentration in the television market. In 1993, the Herfindahl-Hirschman Index (HHI) was .44, but the end of the public service dominated system resulted in a HHI score of .37 by 2002. Yet, both figures still indicate a relatively concentrated market structure, resulting from a mixed system of just a few nation-wide channels.

Regulatory and institutional arrangements

In Finland, the basic objective of media policy is freedom of speech. The principle, designated as 'freedom of expression', is included in the Constitution of Finland (revised in 2000; see Chapter 2, section 12)[1] and in the Act on the Exercise of Freedom of Expression in Mass Media, which provides medium-neutral regulation of freedom of speech (revised in 2004)[2]. The current goals, however, emphasise the support for an efficiently functioning market. The present government programme (June 2003), under the heading 'The policy on information society and communications', sets as goals the boosting of competitiveness and productivity. Another aim is to maintain Finland's position as one of the world's leading producers and users of information and communications technology. More citizen-focused aims are to promote social and regional equality, and to improve citizens' well-being and quality of life through effective utilisation of information and communications technologies. The new Communications Market Act (2003)[3] – covering all communication networks from mobile to terrestrial broadcasting networks – aims at securing that networks and services are available to all telecommunication operators and users throughout the country, and that they are technologically advanced, of high quality, reliable, safe and inexpensive.

Diversity of content is not explicitly expressed in the general policy formulations. However, references are made in specific instances to cultural diversity, particularly regarding access to and content of new communication technologies. Moreover, medium-specific legislation, mainly pertaining to press (subsidies) and to broadcasting, includes more specific references to diversity and operational measures to ensure it. An example is the law on the public service Finnish Broadcasting Company YLE (1993)[4] that states that the Company should provide 'comprehensive television and radio programming … for all citizens under equal conditions' and 'a wide variety of information, opinions and debates on social issues, also for minorities and special groups' (Chapter 3, section 7).

Diversity as media policy goal is not directly related to concentration or competition, except as expressed in the general aim to boost competitiveness and productivity of the communications market and, with communication technologies, of the Information Society as a whole. Concentration as such is not mentioned as a threat to diversity. But concentration and competition are part of media policy. For example, there are subsidies to counter concentration and competition of the press, and market-entry regulations to maintain a 'moderate competitive environment'.

State subsidies to the press are the main instrument to counter the trend of newspapers disappearing from the market, i.e., to maintain pluralism and diversity in the print media. The main forms of subsidy used are classified as selective and non-selective. Non-selective forms include reduced or subsidised transportation rates for all newspapers (subscribed, not free advertising papers), mainly through the public postal service, as well as tax exemptions – applied to all papers regardless of their political orientation or circulation. This form accounted for the majority of the financial subvention to the printed press until the 1980s, but lately it has been reduced to a marginal share. Selective forms, on the other hand, mean direct support to certain papers, typically party organs according to their political weight measured by the number of seats in Parliament. In the cultural field, so-called opinion papers have a separate selective assistance programme through which the state wishes to encourage pluralism, but the financial volume and media policy importance of this form is much smaller that the 'political' form. At present, selective subsidies are used to pay a good deal of costs of the main party organs, but since they are relatively small by size, the state subsidies represent just 1–2% of the total press economy.

The focus in broadcasting is on the structural approach: given the existence of the public service broadcasting, the focus is on the regulation of new commercial and public service entries to the market. Since no sanctions concerning programming are imposed, the system fosters self-regulation. The rationale that has been clear for the past decade (Aslama, Hellman, & Sauri, 2004b) is that if industry structure is kept viable and competition moderate, programme diversity follows as a by-product.

Empirical studies
There is no independent authority to monitor media diversity at large in Finland. The only official move in this direction is an annual project to depict the supply of Finnish nation-wide television channels started by the Ministry of Transport and Communications in 2000. The project was founded partly due to similar monitoring activities by the Swedish Broadcasting Commission and, in particular, to provide for background material for the debate on changing roles of public service broadcasting within the EU context.

Academic research has also produced both dissertations and continuous updates on Finnish media structures; the essence is reported in a textbook (Nordenstreng & Wiio, 2003). A major academic exercise on the topic has been the project 'Media Economy, Content and Diversity' funded by the Academy of Finland as part of a research programme on media culture in 1999–2002 (Picard, 2003). This study explored developments in Finland between 1950 and 2000 to determine changes in the nature and operations of Finnish media, the effects on the content available within Finnish media, and how emerging developments can be expected to affect Finnish media in the future.

Diversity in newspaper content
The Media Economy, Content and Diversity project involved both quantitative and qualitative analysis of content for nine newspapers, STT (the Finnish news agency), YLE (national public service broadcaster) main radio news, YLE television news, MTV3 (national commercial TV channel), and four public affairs magazines. A sample week's content was selected for the years 1955, 1970, 1990, and 2000. The method is grounded in traditional techniques of content analysis. In the quantitative analysis, 41 different genres of content were measured. A total of 30441 content items were coded.

Across the 50 years that were investigated, the total amount of content increased, not merely because of the proliferation of media but because the number of pages and articles in average issues of newspapers and magazines rose, and the number of broadcast hours in radio and television increased. The research showed that newspapers became more standardised in terms of formats and their agendas, that journalism became more professional, less partisan, and more willing to convey multiple viewpoints. The openly political 'propagandist' language seen earlier diminished when journalism turned more neutral as political party affiliations were discontinued in print media.

The content analysis also showed that differences in content between newspapers narrowed over time and that the topics covered and the amount of coverage became more uniform among newspapers across the second half of the century. Whereas there were large difference in what was covered and the amount of coverage in newspapers in the 1950s, there was high similarity in 2000. Other findings indicate that the percentage of content devoted to news declined and that the percentage devoted to non-news articles, especially with an entertainment orientation, increased. In terms of opinion material, the percentage of editorials, columns and letters to the editor increased.

Ownership and operation of media has both widened and concentrated at the same time. Changes in types of media and new opportunities for additional media units have brought new owners into the media and communication fields. At the same time, the largest media outlets in print, broadcasting, and new media have moved into the hands of a few large commercial firms that compete with the established public service broadcast media.

The trends are somewhat contradictory but the following aspects can still clearly be seen in the development of those monopoly papers that survived:

- fewer official records, more independent reporting;
- less overt political bias, more neutral platform;
- fewer topics, more comprehensive treatment of what is covered;
- fewer disparate items, more departmental organisation;
- less plain text, more pictures and graphics.

This trend is typically called professionalism and it is understood to mean greater journalistic autonomy from the authorities (local and national alike), with better service for the public. However, the trend has not automatically led to diversity of topics and pluralism of viewpoints. On the contrary, professionalism has brought homogeneity, both in terms of content and form – especially under conditions of media competition. Yet geography has led to regional diversity as each paper tends to focus on its local/regional affairs. Also, professional journalism has increased the number of actors represented in the news and other stories, balancing the earlier overwhelming dominance of official authorities by other actors in civil society, including so-called ordinary people. Likewise, earlier dominance of men in the news has been replaced by a somewhat better gender balance.

In short, content diversity has survived and even increased under the conditions of media concentration, but this positive trend has a negative countertrend. The qualitative analysis suggests that, while diversity prevails, it is far from complete and there is ample room for a better balance.

Consequently, the study showed that changes in media structure and content are both helpful and harmful to the goals of diversity in information and entertainment sources and content. There was a widening of content in the second half of the twentieth century in individual print media titles and broadcasts, but the media themselves became more uniform in term of content practices, becoming more professional and less partisan in presentation of news and information and increasing content that is less serious and more popular.

Paradoxically, these changes in media ownership and communications have created both more and less opportunity for political and social discourse and action. On one hand, changes in technology and deregulation resulted in increasing numbers of broadcast stations, cable and satellite distribution systems, and broadcast and cable/satellite networks in the past couple of decades. These media changes, along with telecommunications developments that have made possible wide diffusion of fax, e-mail, and related Internet services, have created more opportunities and means for communication. On the other hand, however, the changes have simultaneously resulted in communication to smaller audiences and fewer individuals than were reached by traditional mass media and have created conditions resulting in larger, more commercialised media firms.

A concise answer to what these changes mean to diversity is not available because contradictory tendencies are at work. On the one hand, loosening of political control and the increase in media availability seems to increase diversity. On the other hand, professionalism and ownership tends to produce uniform agendas and frames of reference. The researchers conclude that the observed changes cannot be explained merely as a result of structural changes in the media. A subtler qualitative analysis and case studies are needed to explore this delicate interplay further.

In terms of future policy, this study supports the idea that increasing the opportunities for multiple media sources and multiple providers of content is beneficial. Clearly, policy mechanisms that support those goals are desirable. The study has found that policy changes in the past 50 years have been useful in increasing both domestic and global diversionary and entertainment content, but that they have not necessarily increased content that supports the cultural, political and social needs of society.

Policy support for overall communication needs cannot come merely in the form of increasing the number of competitive media and employing antitrust laws, but will also require policies and professional practices that increase the ability of non-mainstream voices to be heard and promote alternative means of coverage of social and political issues.

Diversity in television supply

A major empirical study of television, including the aspect of diversity, was the doctoral dissertation of Hellman (1999) that researched the changing television markets and television programming in Finland in 1988–96. The study presented here (Aslama, Hellman & Sauri, 2004a, 2004b) was built on and developed from Hellman's dissertation as well as on annual studies commissioned by the Ministry of Communications.

The study in question examined the impact of changes in market structures and accompanying policies on the diversity of Finnish television programmes from 1993 to 2002. These ten years represent the period when Finland experienced a radical shift in thinking on broadcasting policy – which, however, did not replace the basic philosophy of structural regulation. The era marks a change in the relationship of public service television and commercial television 'from companions to competitors'; that is, it features the separation of YLE and MTV3, and the birth of second commercial channel Nelonen. The study investigated whether diversity of programme supply increased or decreased between 1993 and 2002, and whether these changes in diversity can be attributed to re-regulation and intensified competition since 1993. The study also assessed the implications of the findings for public service broadcasting.

The study took a multi-method approach. First, a descriptive, qualitative close reading of relevant media policy documents and decisions was conducted. Second, the diversity of television supply in terms of programme types was measured, focusing both on the breadth of programming as well as between channels. Programme breadth was measured with the Relative Entropy Index (H). The index can be used to examine the evenness of distribution of different programme types either on a single channel or in a television system as a whole. The index that indicates the programme type breadth in an individual channel is called *channel diversity*. On the other hand, *system diversity* stands for the overall programme output across all the channels of a television system. Differences between channels were measured with the Dissimilarity Index (D). This index indicates how much the content of one network, in terms of programme types represented in its schedule, deviates from the content of another (*channel dissimilarity*). By calculating the average dissimilarity per year, the index serves as a horizontal measure of difference across channels (*system dissimilarity*). Figure 3 depicts the development of channel and system diversity in the ten-year research period.

In the years between 1993 and 2002, the launch of the second commercial channel Nelonen in 1997 appears to mark a change in programme-type diversity. After all, both channel diversity and system diversity have decreased since 1997. This supports the theory that intensifying rivalry decreases rather than increases diversity. However, the dissimilarity indices show an increasing trend since the entry of Nelonen. This indicates that the new entrant encourages differences between channels rather than making channels more similar.

Combined, these results indicate that competition has multiple effects on diversity. At this stage, where four nationwide channels compete in the Finnish broadcasting market, increasing competition translates into decreasing system diversity. This contrasts with earlier periods, where competition was less intense and had not yet

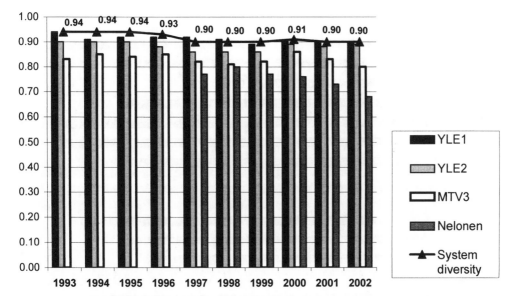

Figure 3 Channel and system diversity, 1993–2002.
Source: Aslama et al. (2004b)

resulted in a decline in system diversity (Hellman, 1999). On the other hand, the intensification of competition is also accompanied by an increase in system dissimilarity. This suggests that competition is strong enough to cause different channels to look for different positions in the television market, but not too strong – because otherwise programming would converge on cheap and middle of the road entertainment programmes. Nevertheless, the differentiation of channels results in an overall decline of diversity. Diversity therefore reacts more strongly and 'negatively' to increases in competition than dissimilarity.

Figure 4 portrays the situation in 2002, the first full year of digital broadcasting in Finland with three new thematic public service channels and two new commercial ones. The situation in 2002 again proves that the shift from a public service-led situation to that of a mixed system with two public service and two commercial nation-wide channels did not result in a drastic decline in the diversity of television programming. Strict, but pragmatic, market-entry regulation resulted in moderate competition, which appears to have favoured considerable programme-type diversity between channels. The entire digital supply of five new specialised channels offered almost as diverse programming as the four analogue full-service channels.

Finally, the diversity scores for the public service broadcaster YLE indicate a division of labour between the public channels that increase overall diversity. The two analogue full service channels together offer more diversity than each one separately. Also, YLE's digital channels – although more specialised than the analogue channels – together score higher on diversity than the commercial digital specialised channels or even the commercial full-service channels. The Finnish public service broadcaster therefore

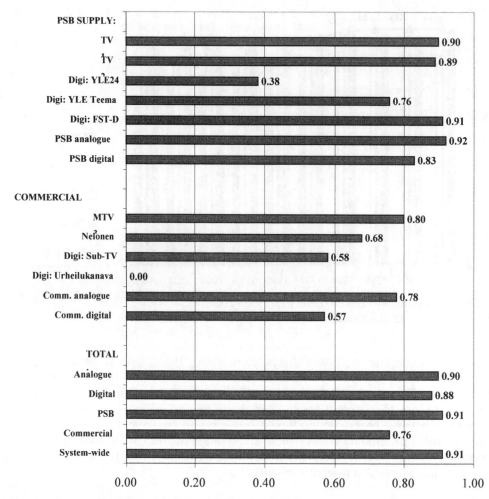

Figure 4 Diversity of Finnish television supply 2002.
Source: Aslama et al. (2004a)

managed to remain universal in its total programme output and to counter-balance the less diverse commercial output both via its analogue and its digital channels.

3. Germany
by Winfried Schulz

Germany, with its 82.5 million inhabitants, is the largest market for media and advertising in Europe; net annual advertising expenditure in the mass media comes to around €13billion. Of this, the largest proportion (€4.5 billion) is placed in daily newspapers, followed by television with €3.8 billion (Television, 2004).There is no official monitoring of media markets. Statistics are provided by media associations, by supervisory bodies in the sector and by academic research institutes. A selection of important statistics is provided by the journal *Media Perspektiven* (as an annual booklet *Media Perspektiven Basisdaten*, part of which is accessible online (cf. www.ard.de/intern/basisdaten).

Media landscape

For historical reasons, the German media market has a strong regional dimension with several key centres, including Hamburg, Munich, Cologne and Berlin. As a result, most of the daily newspapers distribute their daily print-run totalling 23 million copies within a limited local or regional market. Only a few daily newspapers have anything approaching an extensive national circulation. These include the mass-circulation tabloid *Bild-Zeitung* and the elite broadsheets, the *Frankfurter Allgemeine, Die Welt, Süddeutsche Zeitung*. Altogether, 355 newspaper publishers produce 1,537 different local editions; of these, however, only 138 differ in the general political section (2004). With one or two exceptions, the newspapers appear six times a week. There is, in contrast, a very small number of Sunday newspapers.

From a national perspective, the concentration ratio of the daily press is only moderate. The ten biggest newspaper publishers account for 56% of the total circulation. The Axel-Springer-Verlag has the largest market share by some considerable margin with around 23%, deriving predominantly from the tabloid *Bild-Zeitung* with its circulation of around 3.8 million. The market shares of the next largest newspaper publishers are between 2% and 6%. At the local level, however, the concentration ratio is often very high. In more than half of all local media markets, readers have only one newspaper with local content to choose from.

The market for radio broadcasting also has a strong regional character. There are only a few radio programmes with national coverage; their market shares are less than 1%. Nine public broadcasting organisations, which have their headquarters in various federal states (Länder), provide around 60 different radio channels. Their primary target group are the listeners in the respective federal states. A large proportion of these regional channels, however, can be received via cable or satellite throughout Germany. The market share of private radio stations is slightly less than 50% of the total radio broadcasting market. The market shares and the degree of competition vary considerably in the individual federal states and in the local markets (ALM, 2003). In common with public broadcasting, most of the more than 200 private radio channels only have a regional or local coverage.

The television market, on the other hand, is dominated by the national broadcasting companies. The regional or local providers, of which there are more than 150, only account for small market shares with channels broadcast for only a few hours at a time. Similarly, pay-TV with a full 3 million subscribers (as of September 2004) is still not very widespread. At the beginning of 2005, most TV-viewing households (93%) can receive more than 30 'free' German-speaking channels, as a rule via cable or satellite.

Public broadcasting had a monopoly until 1984, but since then private channels have achieved a market share of something over 50%. Developments in recent years have been characterised by an expansion of niche channels and of the small private stations catering for special-interests. The so-called Third Programmes (*Dritte Programme*) of the ARD (Association of Public Broadcasting Organisations in the FRG) have also expanded. This involves channels which – as public service stations – were supposed to be directed at regional interests, above all with information, education and culture, but which have since also started offering much entertainment; they can be received by cable and satellite in most of Germany's regional states.

While competition between channels is strong in Germany's television market, and has even increased further in recent years (see below), there has been a process of concentration in ownership. The two biggest providers control almost half of the viewer market. The RTL-Group, which belongs to the Bertelsmann Corporation, has a market share of 24.6%, and the ProSiebenSat.1 Media AG represents 22.2% of the market. In addition, US companies like AOL Time Warner, Viacom and Walt Disney own parts of German television broadcasters. The equity stakes in, and the market shares of, German television broadcasters are continuously monitored and published by the Commission for the Monitoring of Concentration in the Media (KEK) (ww.kek-online.de).

Regulatory and institutional arrangements
According to the constitution of the Federal Republic, it is the individual federal states – 16 in all – that are responsible for the regulation of broadcasting. They have all enacted their own broadcasting or media legislation which, on the one hand, defines the programming requirements and, on the other, provides the regulatory framework for the organisation of supervisory bodies which oversee compliance with the requirements. One of the most important requirements is the maintenance of diversity in the range of programmes. Attention is paid as much to the diversity of opinion as to the variety of genre represented.

The Länder Laws governing broadcasting and/or the media in general apply directly to the stations broadcasting regionally or locally in the respective federal states, but indirectly their validity also extends beyond the individual states, since regional television channels – the so-called Third Programmes – are accessible nationwide via cable and satellite and since the ARD's first channel – 'Das Erste' (The First) – is made up of parts produced jointly by the regional ARD organisations. In order to regulate the operations of the other main public provider ZDF (the Second German Television), the individual federal states agreed a State Treaty, the provisions of which are similar to those of the Länder broadcasting laws.

Apart from this, the Länder agreed to a 'State Broadcasting Treaty' with framework rules which are above all relevant to television broadcasts with national coverage. This includes the provision that 'the major political, ideological and social forces and groups' are given adequate broadcasting opportunities in the channels, and that the 'views of minorities' have to be taken into consideration.

These formulations correspond to the views and terminology of the Federal Constitutional Court which have permeated all German broadcasting jurisdictions since the first broadcasting judgement of 1961. They are orientated towards a conception of the process of political opinion formation which is often expressed in the metaphor of the 'forum' or of the 'opinion market'. According to this, the process of democratic opinion-formation produces the best results, if all 'forces and groups' that are involved, have their say in the media.

On the other hand, the concept of the 'diversity of genre' (*Spartenvielfalt*) denotes another dimension of the concept of diversity. The Broadcasting State Treaty refers to this by characterising so-called generalist channels (*Vollprogramme*) in terms of 'varied content' with significant proportions of information, education, advice and entertainment. This enumeration extends the obligation expressed in older legal statutes (e.g. in the Bavarian Broadcasting Law) and in the overall discourse of media law which included a 'Trio of Tasks' (*Aufgabentrias*) expected of public broadcasting, namely to provide information, education and entertainment.

The realisation of the requirement of diversity is monitored in different ways in the public and commercial broadcasting sectors. In each of the individual public broadcasting institutions there are supervisory boards (Broadcasting Councils or, in the case of ZDF, the Second German Television, the Television Council), which are made up of representatives of various societal groups and political organisations, e.g., the churches, trade unions, employers organisations, political parties. Their task consists in overseeing the overall diversity of programmes within the individual broadcasting channels. In this context, diversity is defined as 'internal pluralism' or 'balance'. The regulatory model implies that diversity is ensured by the fact that diverse societal interests are represented within the supervisory boards.

The regulatory model for the commercial sector corresponds in principle to a market model, i.e. it implies that broadcasting diversity is ensured when there is free competition between as many providers as possible. As a result, diversity in the commercial sector is monitored in terms of the market structure or the level of market concentration. The State Broadcasting Treaty thus stipulates under the concept of 'Ensuring Diversity of Opinion' that an individual company may not exceed a share of 30% of the total viewing market with its programmes. This threshold is lowered to 25%, if a company controls other 'media-relevant' markets. If the thresholds are exceeded, the company is granted no further broadcasting licences. The company can also be subject to various conditions, e.g. divesting certain equity holdings.

Various bodies are responsible for the monitoring of commercial providers. On the one hand there are the 15 Länder Media Authorities (in principle one for each federal state). Each one of these authorities can grant a licence for a local, regional or nationwide channel and is then responsible for supervising this channel or company. The Länder Media Authorities are institutions based in public law with internal supervisory boards that represent a diversity of interests (along the lines of the public broadcasting institutions). Secondly, there is a Commission for the Monitoring of Media Concentration (KEK), consisting of six experts appointed unanimously by all the heads of government of the federal states. The KEK monitors the market conditions in the television sector and publishes its results in annual reports and on its own website (www.kek-online.de). In the case of applications for licences and the endangering of competition it is KEK that makes final decisions on behalf of the respective Land Media Authority.

Apart from this, the Federal Cartel Office in Berlin can forbid the merger of media companies on the basis of the Law against Restraints on Competition, if with that merger an excessive degree of market power is reached – according to certain levels of turnover.

The regulation of the public and commercial broadcasting sector has been linked together by a judgement of the Federal Constitution Court in a unique manner. The Court ruled that the level of requirements imposed on commercial broadcasters – and thus also their diversity – depends on whether the public sector broadcasters provide a 'basic supply' of varied programmes. In this manner the commercial sector is dependent on the way in which public broadcasters function, creating on the one hand high demands on public sector channels, and on the other also helping to justify the existence and further development of public broadcasters in general.

The relevant market

It is generally accepted that, in the first instance, statements about the structure of a market make its limitation necessary – an enterprise that, in relation to the sphere of the media, only appears to be problem-free at first glance. It is customary to ask, when seeking a criterion for the demarcation of a relevant market, what products can be substituted in the short term from the consumer's point of view, in our case the television viewer. In the TV market an important yardstick for defining the limits of the market is that of being able technically to receive certain stations. The reception of channels in just a few regions or only by means of particular delivery systems (like cable or satellite) results quite naturally in a spatially or technically determined limitation of the market. On the other hand the thematic differentiation of the programmes provided by individual channels has a decisive influence on the limits of the television market. For example, one can assume that a music channel like MTV and a news broadcasting channel like CNN can hardly substitute each other from the perspective of the viewing public.

Considerations of this kind play a role in German media law, observable in the distinction between generalist channels and special-interest channels or in the term 'nationwide' ('*bundesweit*') in relation to television channels readily accessible or receivable throughout the country, as it appears in the regulations of the State Broadcasting Treaty (*Rundfunkstaatsvertrag*, RStV) governing concentration. The State Broadcasting Treaty defines a 'generalist channel' as 'a broadcasting channel with varied content, in which information, education, advice and entertainment make up a significant part of the overall programme'. A 'special-interest channel' (*Spartenprogramm*), in contrast, is 'a broadcasting channel with essentially similar content' (2 RStV). Whether a broadcaster provides a generalist channel or a special-interest channel is determined as a rule when the licence is granted. Also the question of technical reception can be clarified by reference to the licensing conditions. Thus, for example, in the lists of broadcasters published by the Länder Media Authorities, there are details of whether a channel is licensed for nationwide, regional or local coverage (cf. ALM, 1999). Strictly speaking, however, this only gives limited details of the possibilities for wider dissemination, not always on the actual coverage. Thus the receptability (the technical range) is only 100% in the case of ARD's First Channel and ZDF's Second Channel; other channels accessible 'nationwide' can often manage no more than 90%, in certain cases of just 50% or less of households in Germany.

Empirical studies

In Germany, many studies on (television) diversity have dealt implicitly or explicitly with the 'convergence hypothesis'. The underlying idea is that competition between commercial and public broadcasters may force both types of broadcasters to provide more similar (combinations of) programmes. The convergence hypothesis was originally introduced in a study by Schatz et al. (1989), who showed that the introduction of commercial channels in several German regions did not increase diversity. In the late 1980s and early 1990s, against the background of political challenges of public service broadcasting, the (negative) influence of commercial competition on public broadcasters was emphasised. The full picture, however, is more complex. In addition to public broadcasters accommodating their programming partly to commercial broadcasters, commercial television also became more similar to public television in the 1990s (e.g., Bruns & Marcinkowski, 1996; Pfetsch, 1996; Brosius & Zubayr, 1996; Maier, 2002: Rossmann, Brandl & Brosius, 2003). Other relevant studies include those of Weiss et al. (1991), Donsbach (1992) and Merten (1994). Since the mid 1990s, the convergence hypothesis is replaced by other research questions (Meier, 2003).

Arguably the most comprehensive and longitudinal analysis of television programme supply is provided by the annual studies conducted by Krüger. Commissioned by the public service broadcasters ARD and ZDF and published in the German magazine *Media Perspektiven*, Krüger's analyses provide an overview of (changes in) programming structures of the major public and commercial channels since 1985. Occasionally, he also includes smaller channels in his analysis. More recently, Weiss and Trebbe (2000) added another study, this time commissioned by the Länder broadcasting authorities.

This section reviews a recent study on the relationship between competition and diversity on the German television market between 1992 and 2001, conducted at the University of Erlangen-Nürnberg (Schulz & Ihle, 2005). This study follows approximately the same format as similar studies in Belgium, Finland and in particular the Netherlands that are also discussed in this chapter. It focuses on prime-time programmes of nationwide, free, generalist channels. It excludes the public regional channels (*'die Dritten'*), pay-TV channels, foreign channels, and digital-only channels. Thematic and niche channels are discussed, but could not be included in the quantitative measurement of levels of competition and diversity of programme supply – primarily because relevant data are missing. The lack of (comparable) data is one of the major obstacles for detailed investigations of the relationships between competition and diversity.

The development of the viewer market
In 1992 there were eight providers competing in the nationwide market for generalist channels. The number of broadcasters rose for a short while to 10 (with the arrival of Vox and RTL2 in 1993) and then, with the departure of 1Plus at the end of 1993, fell back to 9. Since then there has been no change in the period under examination. In terms of the number of providers, therefore, little has changed in the structure of the market. However, there have been changes in the viewer market share enjoyed by the generalist channel providers. This is reflected in changes in the competition intensity index, defined as the inverse of the Herfindahl-Hirschmann-Index (1–HHI). The fluctuations displayed in Figure 5 denote changes in market shares. These clearly reflect changes in the marketing strategies of the broadcasters and in the consumption patterns of the viewers as well as reciprocal effects between the two variables. The index relating to generalist channels

(upper graph line, left axis) rises relatively steeply at first. This may be partly explained by the market entry of Kabel 1, Vox and RTL2. From the middle of the 1990s the rise in the intensity of competition flattens off with mild fluctuations and then even falls again slightly after 2000. The index value hardly alters after the middle of the 1990s and appears to average out at around 0.84.

The aggregated market share of thematic and niche channels (defined as 100% minus the aggregated market share of nation-wide generalist channels) increased considerably in the same period (lower graph line, right axis). This increased the intensity of competition, also for generalist channels, even though the respective programmes are only partially substitutable. All the broadcasters are competing, if not for specific programme preferences, then at least for the scarce resource of television viewing; they thus increase the general pressure of competition in the market for viewers. Apart from this, the special-interest and niche broadcasters are likely also to influence the strategies of the generalist channels since, by dint of their greater affinity to target groups, they are potent competitors in the market for advertising.

Figure 5 Competition in the German Television Market 1992–2001.

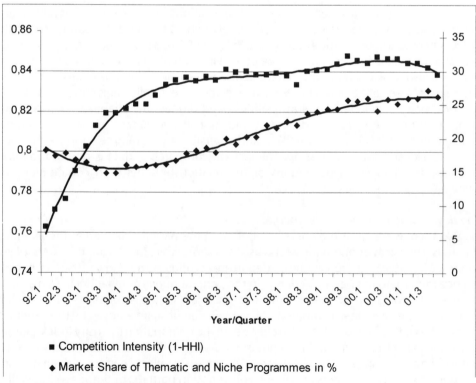

Source: Schulz & Ihle (2005): 278.

The development of diversity

As shown above, the German television market was characterised by a relatively intensive level of competition as early as the beginning of the 1990s as a result of a relatively high number of generalist channel providers. The intensity of the competition increased further, mainly at the beginning of the 1990s. If one takes a simple market model as one's point of departure, it can be expected that there will be an increase in programme diversity as a result of increasing competition. As van Cuilenburg and van der Wurff argue (see previous chapter) this only applies to a market with moderate levels of competition. For a market where the number of providers exceeds a certain threshold value, it was rather to be expected that there would be a process of ruinous competition with decreasing diversity and a concentration of the range of broadcasting on those programme categories most in demand among viewers ('excessive sameness').

The results of the German study shown in Figure 6 confirm neither of the two assumptions. The movements of the index, made clear by polynomic trend lines, certainly show an increase in the reflective diversity during the first part of the period under observation, which indicates an increasing adaptation of programme supply to the preferences of the viewers. This could be attributed to some of the new commercial broadcasters that had entered the market and added to the range of programmes. It is also possible that the established broadcasters altered their programme structures as a reaction to competition from the new entrants. As Krüger's programme analyses show, this really does apply, for example, to the big commercial broadcasters (Krüger, 2001, pp. 90ff.). From the middle of 1996 the reflective diversity decreases again, rising (temporarily) once more towards the end of the observation period. Overall, however, the changes in the diversity index are minor. The values would seem to hover around 0.9.

While the index of reflective diversity is rising, the index of open diversity initially falls, which is to be expected due to the theoretical relationship between the two indices. The programme supply in this period is concentrated more strongly on a few thematic categories. What is surprising, on the other hand, is that the index continues to fall even with a decline in reflective diversity (from the end of 1996), and then rises again towards the end of the observation period, more or less parallel to the rise in reflective diversity. According to the logic of the indices, the range of programmes is distributed more evenly during this period across the programme categories, while at the same time being more accommodating to viewer preferences.

Assessment

In principle, a variation in reflective diversity can be explained by changes in the supply structure, or in viewer preferences, or in both. However, the study assumes that the viewers' preferences are invariable, and measures reflective diversity with constant viewing-time averages for each category. If the viewing-time were supposed to have changed, however, this would lead to a false specification of the diversity index. A closer inspection of the data shows that the distribution of viewing-times has actually changed over time. This is confirmed by other studies (cf. Gerhards et al., 1996; Gerhards & Klingler, 2003). Since both programme supply and consumption varied in the observation period, the data do not support any conclusion that this can be interpreted as a convergence of supply in the direction of viewer preferences, or whether viewing habits have adapted

Figure 6 Diversity in the German Television Market 1992–2001

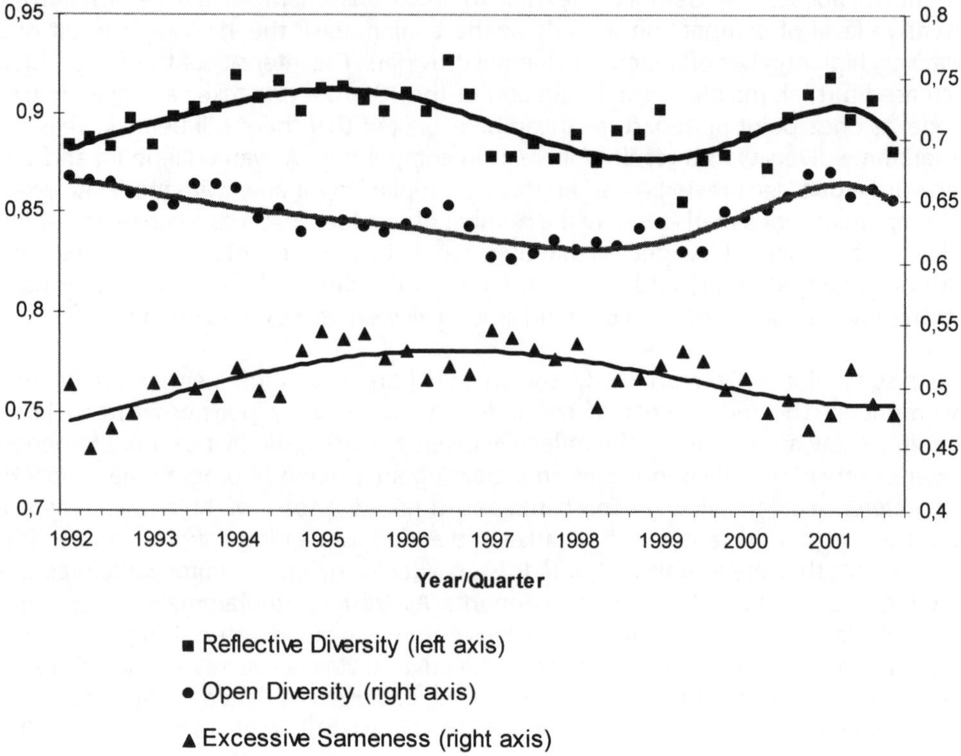

- Reflective Diversity (left axis)
- Open Diversity (right axis)
- Excessive Sameness (right axis)

Source: Schulz & Ihle (2005): 286.

to the supply of programmes. The way in which the index of reflective diversity has been operationalised probably exaggerates the variation of that diversity.

The study finally also indicates that, in line with the Hotelling-hypothesis, there has been a concentration of supply in those programme categories where viewer demand has been greatest ('excessive sameness'; see bottom graph line in Figure 6). However, a development of this kind seems to be confined to the beginning of the observation period and does not carry on after the middle of the 1990s. One can conclude from these results, on the one hand, that the German TV market tended to be characterised by moderate rather than by ruinous competition in the 1990s. A major difference between the German market and other markets investigated in this chapter is that the number of generalist channels in the German market was relatively stable during the 1990s, whereas the television markets in Flanders, Finland and the Netherlands witnessed a significant increase in channel numbers.

The German study, in contrast with the other studies, shows how a fixed number of incumbent channels compete for market share under moderately competitive conditions. It suggests that in the early 1990s, channels increasingly offered popular programmes (resulting in a decline in open diversity and an increase in excessive sameness) to conquer market share from competitors (resulting in a higher competition intensity index). The observation that reflective diversity increased as well in this period shows that there still was unmet demand for popular programmes that made these strategies fruitful. Around the mid-1990s, however, channels threatened to overshoot their target and provide too many popular programmes. This might have initiated a phase of ruinous competition, if channels would not have changed their programming schedules and established a new equilibrium in which market shares stabilised and diversity once more increased.

Also important for the stability of the German market, is the strong influence of regulating bodies (i.e., the broadcasting councils of PSB (*Rundfunkräte*) and the Land Media Authorities. This influence makes the German broadcasting system less market-driven than, for example, broadcasting in the Netherlands. Another important difference, of course, is the difference in market size. Combined, these differences explain why the German market can accommodate a larger number of channels than other markets in Europe without giving way to ruinous competition.

4. The Netherlands
by Jan van Cuilenburg & Richard van der Wurff
The Netherlands population is 16.1 million people (2001). Media concentration and media diversity are assessed annually by the Netherlands Media Authority. We here present some data from the Media Monitor as it is currently applied by the Media Authority (Commissariaat voor de Media, 2002, 2003; see also Ward, 2004, pp. 125–137).

Media landscape
In 6.9 million households (2001) in the Netherlands there is a circulation of dailies of 4.2 million copies. The market of daily newspapers consists of 35 editorially independent titles (2002); 7 national, 21 regional and 4 specialised newspapers. Editorial concentration is stable in the national market, but rapidly increasing in regional markets. From 2001 to 2002, however, the number of independent regional titles declined from 24 to 21.

Ownership concentration is very high in the national market, being dominated by two publishing companies (PCM: market share 2002 55%; De Telegraaf Holding: market share 2002 41%). The Herfindahl-Hirschman Index for the national market is HHI =. 46 (2002), indicating a very concentrated market structure (HHI in number equivalents = 2.2). Most regional markets in the Netherlands are nearly monopoly markets (average HHI in number equivalents = 1.38). The four largest cities all are one-paper cities (HHI in numbers equivalents = 1.0).

In the Netherlands radio market both ownership concentration and programming concentration are rather low. The high degree of radio channel plurality may be inferred from the following statistics (2002): 6 national public radio networks; 15 national commercial networks; 13 regional public networks; 47 regional commercial networks; and 287 local public radio stations. The overall public radio market share (national and regional) is 46%, compared to the total commercial market share of 54%. Competition between radio programme suppliers is very high. For the national radio market the

Media Authority calculated HHI = .16 (2002), corresponding to HHI in numbers equivalents = 6.1 radio programme suppliers.

Whereas the radio market in the Netherlands is structurally unconcentrated, with a high degree of programme plurality, the Dutch television market is highly concentrated – as is indicated by the Herfindahl-Hirschman Index being HHI = .26 (2002). Three main players, the Dutch public broadcaster and two commercial broadcasters (RTL and SBS) are dominant, with a total joint television market share of 85% (38%; 27%; 20%). All three of them operate three different channels. In spite of the high degree of ownership concentration, programming concentration is very low in the Netherlands, that is, there is significant channel plurality in the television market. The number of channels targeting the Dutch audience in Dutch and foreign languages has grown from four independent channels in 1990 to 24 in 1995. Since then there have been 30 stations in 2000 and 32 in 2002.

Regulatory and institutional arrangements

In broadcasting, the main institutional arrangement in the Netherlands to protect and maintain media diversity is public service broadcasting. Although there are currently many commercial stations operating in the Dutch broadcasting market, public service broadcasting still has a very prominent position on the national, regional and local level. On the national level, the public broadcaster has a concession for three television channels and five radio networks. The Media Act (1987: section 13C) defines the public broadcaster's tasks as follows:

1. The tasks of public broadcasting shall be:

   (a) to provide a varied and high-quality range of programme services for general broadcasting purposes at national, regional and local level in the fields of information, culture, education and entertainment and to transmit them, or cause them to be transmitted, on open networks; ...

2. Public broadcasting programme services shall provide a balanced picture of society and of people's current interests and views pertaining to society, culture, religion and belief, and:

   (a) shall be accessible to the entire population in the area for which the programmes are intended;
   (b) shall contribute to the development and dissemination of the socio-cultural diversity of the Netherlands;
   (c) shall be independent of commercial influences and, subject to the provisions laid down by or pursuant to the law, of government influence; and
   (d) shall be aimed at a broad audience and at population and age groups of varying size and composition.

As can be seen, the Dutch PSB remit is phrased in terms of programme *variety*, *quality* and *diversity*. To ensure programme diversity, the public broadcaster has to comply with a great number of specific rules prescribing, amongst other things, non-commercial and independent operations, and programme quota for informational and educational programmes (minimum of 35% on national television), arts (minimum of 12.5% on national television), and entertainment programmes (maximum of 25% on national television) (Media Act, Section 50.2 and 51.1).

In the press sector, emphasis is on the freedom of the press. It was not until 1974 that the government established the Press Fund as an instrument to create and maintain (economic) conditions that favour a free and diverse press. The Press Fund is a public fund, with an independent board of governors, that offers financial support from the Dutch government for the press media whose start-up or existence is threatened. The Fund was established in 1974 and since 1987 is regulated by the Media Act. Its main objective is to promote and guarantee a free, independent and diverse press in the Netherlands. This main objective is reflected in the Fund's remit and in the conditions that publishers must meet to become eligible for support. According to the Media Act,

> There shall be a Press Fund for the purpose of maintaining and promoting diversity of the press, in so far as this is in the interest of information provision and opinion-forming … (Section 123.1).

> Financial support may only be provided for press products which meet the following requirements: …

> (a) they must to a significant extent contain news, analyses, commentaries and background information covering the diverse aspects of present-day society, with a view to, inter alia, political opinion-forming;
> (b) they must be edited by an independent editing team on the basis of a statute expressing the editorial identity of the relevant press product … (Section 129).

Empirical studies on the Dutch television market

The Competition, Media Innovation and Diversity research programme (*CoMInDi*) of The Amsterdam School of Communications *ASCoR* at the University of Amsterdam investigates under which economic conditions media companies innovate their products and increase content diversity in media markets. The main hypothesis of the programme is that moderate competition stimulates innovation and diversity, while ruinous competition results in excessive sameness (Van Cuilenburg, 1999). The first studies in the programme focused on the relationship between the intensity of competition and the level of (open and reflective) diversity in the market (Van der Wurff & Van Cuilenburg, 2001). Subsequent studies looked in more detail at the strategies of individual media companies and their contribution to diversity (Van der Wurff, 2004a, b).

Empirically, projects in the programme focused on (1) the market for general-interest television channels in the Netherlands, (2) the markets in the Netherlands for agricultural, business services and transportation magazines in the 1990s, (3) the television market in the Netherlands, Germany and the UK, and (4) the newspaper market in the Netherlands, Germany and the UK.

The studies in the programme adopt a quantitative approach: the dependent variable is media diversity, described as the availability of different (medium-specific) types of information in a market. The level of diversity offered is assessed in terms of open and reflective diversity.

In the studies of print markets (trade magazines, newspapers), diversity is measured by content analysis of selected issues from selected outlets in the market. In these cases, the development of an appropriate content classification scheme is part of the project. In the television studies, on the other hand, diversity is assessed on the basis of classifications of programmes that are provided by Intomart and other ratings agencies. Independent variables (concentration, competition) are assessed on the basis of industry sources. Frequently, the researchers use the Herfindahl-Hirschman Index, or a related variable, to describe these market structural characteristics. In some studies, researchers also assess the level of diversity provided by individual channels (or magazines or newspapers) and the extent to which channels (or newspapers, or magazines) provide different content types. Other studies take policy variables as additional independent variables into account (Iossifov, 2001; Roth, 2004).

The relationships between competition and diversity on the Dutch television market are analysed in Van der Wurff & Van Cuilenburg, 2001; and Van der Wurff, 2004a, b. Since the late 1980s, the television market in the Netherlands developed in one decade from a public monopoly to one of the most competitive markets in Europe. Until the late 1980s, broadcasting in the Netherlands was the prerogative of public broadcasters. These public broadcasters were not state organisations, but not-for-profit, publicly funded private associations that were believed to represent the various social-religious 'groups' or 'pillars' in Dutch society. The objective of this public system of public broadcasting was to provide a combination of open and reflective diversity (cf. Van Cuilenburg & McQuail 1982, p. 144ff.). Each social and religious 'group' in Dutch society (or 'pillar') was entitled to its own broadcasting organisation, the amount of its broadcast time depending on the size of the group (consistent with the aim of reflective diversity), but never below a specific minimum, nor above a maximum number of broadcasting hours (consistent with the aim of open diversity). Since Dutch society consisted of relatively few, stable and docile 'pillars', this system worked relatively well, until the pillarised system itself started to crumble at the beginning of the 1970s.

Commercial broadcasters entered the Dutch market in 1989. Since then, their number has steadily increased. One additional RTL channel entered in 1993; three more commercial channels entered in 1995, and the ninth channel entered in 1999. After some changes in ownership, in which one broadcaster disappeared, these nine channels are now owned by three broadcasters. The public broadcaster owns three public channels. Three commercial channels are owned by the Holland Media Groep, a subsidiary of by Bertelsmann, and three others are owned by SBS SA. In addition, there are tens of new thematic channels.

In the 1990s, TV channels in the Dutch market provide more light informative programmes and series at prime time, at the expense of youth programmes and serious information. This contributes to a continuous decline of open diversity, signalling that different programme categories are less equally represented in supply. At the same time, these changes in programme supply resulted, until about 1995, in an increase in reflective diversity. This means that the described changes in supply resulted in a supply that better matched audience preferences. Since 1995, however, further changes result in a decline of both open and reflective diversity. Further shifts in supply therefore were no longer in conformity with audience demands.

Similar trends can be found for individual channels. Until 1995, channels became more similar, each developing into channels that provided those types of programmes that the audience preferred to see. This is witnessed in a decline of average open diversity per channel, and an increase in the average level of reflective diversity per channel. From 1996 onwards, however, trends changed. The average level of open diversity per channel started to decline more strongly, channels became less similar, and average levels of reflective diversity per channel also started to decline. Our research suggests that these changes in the levels of diversity provided both by the market and by individual channels occurred primarily because three new channels and two new broadcasters entered the market: VOO, at that time the third channel of the RTL group; SBS6, the first channel of the SBS group; TV10, an independent channel. Compared with the three public and two RTL channels that until 1995 operated in the market, the new channels offer a programming schedule with more series and movies and fewer informative programmes.

One factor that may lessen the effect of competition on diversity is the role of public channels. Public channels provide higher levels of open diversity than commercial channels. Also, two of the three public channels provide high levels of reflective diversity. These channels therefore succeed relatively well in their public task of providing diverse

Table 2: Key diversity indicators in the Dutch television market, 1988–1999

Years	Number of channels (channel plurality)	Reflective diversity	Open diversity
1988	3	0.80	0.73
1989	3	0.79	0.72
1990	4	0.82	0.72
1991	4	0.83	0.71
1992	4	0.87	0.74
1993	4	0.88	0.70
1994	5	0.88	0.69
1995	6	0.88	0.65
1996	8	0.85	0.60
1997	8	0.86	0.62
1998	8	0.84	0.60
1999	9	0.83	0.58

Note: Number of channels is average number of general-interest channels focusing on the Netherlands.
Source: Own calculations based on data from Intomart.

combinations of programmes that are attractive to viewers. If these public channels were to disappear from the market, it is probable that open and reflective diversity would decline. A second factor that may have reduced the negative effects of competition on diversity is concentration. When we look at the commercial segment of the market, we find that both broadcasters target their channels at different audience segments. They each have a main channel, and two more focused channels. The main channels in particular provide diverse programmes to a large audience. The other channels are in themselves less diverse, but because to some extent they provide different programmes from the main channels, they still contribute to diversity. In response, the public channels also started to cooperate more closely and to differentiate their channels. Nowadays, the first Dutch channel (NL1) is presented as a family channel, the second (NL2) as a sports and entertainment channel, and the third (NL3) as a cultural, progressive informative channel.

In spite of the decline in diversity, the audience continues to view a diverse combination of programmes. One major reason for this is that viewers at the end of the 1990s could choose from a larger supply of programmes than before. The supply of television programmes by general-interest channels increased from 23.4 hours per day in 1998 to 143.8 hours in 1999 (Van Meurs, 1999, Appendix 2). Many, but not all, programme types profited from this expansion. Of 110 programme types that are distinguished by Intomart (excluding continuity and commercials), 72 programme types are broadcast for more minutes in the period July 1998 - June 1999 than in the period July 1993 - June 1994. These include 7 programme types that were not broadcast at all in 1993/1994. 38 programme types, on the other hand, have fewer minutes of broadcasting time in 1998/1999 compared with 1993/1994.

This study shows that increases in the number of general-interest television channels in The Netherlands in the early 1990s resulted in a decline of open diversity; a decline, however, that was in accordance with audience preferences as the resulting supply better met audience demand. Only when three additional commercial television channels entered the market halfway through the 1990s did diversity levels drop significantly and the market started to provide less diversity than the audience wanted. Fortunately, the expansion in the absolute supply of television programmes still enables the audience to choose and find the types of programmes that it prefers.

Other studies and findings
The studies of the Dutch television market show that moderate competition contributes to diversity, while strong competition reduces diversity. Other studies of newspaper and trade magazine markets are also in line with this main argument.

The newspaper market in the Netherlands is a stagnating market, with a high ratio of subscription versus free sales, a gradual decline in readership and the time spent reading newspapers, and a declining share in total advertising revenues. Under those conditions the introduction of the free newspaper *Metro*, part of the international Metro chain, poses a serious threat to established newspapers, especially concerning their younger readers. Publishers look for various ways to improve their position: De Telegraaf Holding introduced its own free newspaper, *Spits!*; the Amsterdam newspaper *Het Parool*,

Table 3: Programme types on nine general-interest television channels in The Netherlands

That lost the most broadcasting time (19 hours or more per year)	That disappeared completely	That gained the most broadcasting time (213 hours or more per year)	That appeared new on TV
serious foreign movies	serious Dutch theatre	light foregin action	varied magazines
serious large game shows	serious Dutch drama for 13–19 year-olds	light foreign TV comedy	education for 0–19 year-olds
serious foreign TV series	serious foreign drama for 13–19 year-olds	serious informative magazines	education for 13–19 year-olds
Dutch talk shows	information for 0–19 year-olds	light foreign TV action	entertainment for 0–19 year-olds
nature programs	other sports reportages	light foreign TV drama	light Dutch drama for 13–19 year-olds
information for 13–19 year olds	serious Dutch drama for 0–19 year-olds	light foreign drama	other entertainment
light foreign drama for 0–19 year-olds	light Dutch drama for 0–19 year-olds	foreign talk shows	other foreign serious programs
art magazines		light foreign comedy	
serious Dutch TV series		other miscellaneous information	
		special services	
		small game shows	
		other light information	

Source: own calculations based on data from Intomart.

bought by the Belgian Persgroep, changed to the tabloid format; *De Telegraaf* and some regional newspapers introduced Sunday editions (which, until very recently, did not exist in the Netherlands); all newspapers also developed online editions.

As has been indicated in this section, the newspaper market in the Netherlands is highly concentrated. The national market is dominated by two publishers: PCM and De Telegraaf Holding. PCM became the primary publisher on the market for national newspapers when it bought NDU in 1994. In 2004, PCM was bought by the British-US investment company Apax. De Telegraaf Holding operates both on the national and regional markets. Wegener is the dominant publisher of regional newspapers. Research suggests that the lack of competition in newspaper markets in The Netherlands reduces diversity, but also that the entry of the free newspapers did not increase diversity.

The market for national newspaper includes, in the 1990s, five established generalist newspapers, two small religiously oriented newspapers, and one financial newspaper. The two free newspapers were launched in 1999. At the beginning of the 1990s, eight newspapers were published by three major and three small publishers. Since then, two major newspapers merged in 1994, and one foreign publisher (Metro) entered the market in 1999. Consequently, the Herfindahl-Hirschmann concentration index increased from approximately 0.31 in the early 1990s to 0.45 in 1995–1998. Open diversity at the same time increased, from 0.83 (1994) to 0.80 (1997 to .76 (2000) (Iossifov, 2005).

The regional markets for newspapers are mostly monopolies. In a few areas, two newspapers compete, and in one area (Limburg) in the South of the Netherlands, De Telegraaf Holding owns two regional newspapers that used to compete but now intensify their cooperation. Focusing on the ten most prominent news items, and comparing these three situations, diversity in terms of topics and article formats (e.g., news story, analysis, column) is highest in the competitive area (Leeuwarden) and lowest in the monopoly areas (Alkmaar, Den Haag and Breda). Diversity of topics and formats in Limburg (with partial competition) is similar to the diversity provided by the four largest newspapers on the national market (Van der Wurff & Lauf, 2004). In addition, a comparison across news media suggests that online editions of newspapers provide more diversity in terms of topics but less in terms of article formats than print newspapers. Regional newspapers provide more diversity on both dimensions than TV newscasts, but the national TV news is more diverse in topics than the major national newspapers – if we study the ten most important news items. Radio is the least diverse news medium, both in terms of topics and formats (Van der Wurff & Lauf, 2004).

Trade magazine markets differ from TV and newspaper markets because trade magazine markets are highly segmented and include a large number of very specialised titles. Competition within individual market segments, in particular specialised market segments, is weak. However, magazines also compete to some extent across market segments. Competition between general and specialty magazines makes competition on trade magazine markets vary between weak and moderate. A case study of agricultural magazines suggests that moderate competition on trade magazine markets is accompanied by relatively high levels of diversity. Results also show that the extent of competition between general and specialised magazines depends considerably on the demands of subscribers and advertisers. When subscribers are more willing to pay for information, markets are more concentrated and segmented, magazines are more differentiated and subscription prices are higher – and vice versa. Compared with these forces, the independent impact of competition on diversity is relatively weak (Van der Wurff, 2003 and 2005).

Three conclusions emerge from the *CoMInDi* research programme in The Netherlands on television, newspaper and trade magazine markets. The first important finding is that both too strong and too weak competition reduces diversity. On the TV market, the intensification of competition resulted in a decline in diversity, but weak competition in newspaper markets also reduces diversity. Only moderate levels of competition seem to lead to higher levels of (open) diversity. Secondly, the studies suggest that market levels of diversity depend much more on the diversity offered by individual outlets (channels, magazines) than by differences between outlets. In theory, a combination of focused but different outlets could provide as much diversity as a few internally diverse outlets, but in practice this is not the case. Considering, for the time being, that the consumption of diversity will also more strongly depend on the availability of internally diverse outlets (that confront audiences with diverse information) than on the availability of specialised outlets (that increase choice but also provide homogeneous information) the conclusion presents itself that the availability of internally diverse outlets should be an important indicator for market performance and policy. A third important finding is that the presence of different types of media organisations, in particular the combination of profit and not-for-profit organisations, contributes to diversity. In broadcasting, these are commercial and public broadcasters. In trade magazine publishing, these are commercial publishers and (not-for-profit) industry associations and research organisations that publish their own magazines. In news markets, these might be Internet news providers. The entry of publishers of free newspapers, on the other hand, did not contribute to diversity. This suggests that policies affecting the type of players (including market entry regulations and subsidies) might be as important as competition policy in promoting and maintaining diversity.

5. Other European cases

Hungary
by Ildiko Kovats
Diversity is an important goal of Hungarian media policy. The preamble of the Media Act 1996 lists 'diversity of opinion and culture' as one of the main objectives that the Act should accomplish. The notion of diversity has special meaning in the Hungarian context after fifty years of one (Communist) party rule. Diversity is connected with an understanding of society as a multiple articulated entity, contrasting with the idea of equality that long dominated policy and deprived people of the right to be different. Following the regime change, one of the main forms of difference emerging is connected to the rediscovery of national identity. Therefore it is not surprising that the two main forms of diversity discussed in media policy are the political and national dimensions of identity.

Diversity in the Media Act is interpreted as a *political diversity* (diversity of opinion), *cultural diversity* and *social diversity* (or access). Political diversity is defined as providing balanced information that reflects opinions and policies of both the ruling government and the opposition. This relatively narrow interpretation of *political diversity* implies that in media policy less attention is paid to voices of parties not in parliament and voices from civil society. *Cultural diversity* is related to defending and asserting the national heritage and traditions. It involves the availability of other than foreign (and in particular other than American) cultural/audiovisual products. *Cultural diversity* also means supporting and asserting minority (ethnic) cultural values and religious values – most of all those of the traditional Hungarian churches. In general, diversity in cultural terms is related to special forms of culture that seem to be endangered or threatened.

Social diversity, thirdly, refers to the right to have access to, and to be represented in, the media. The Media Act of 1996 places special obligations on public service broadcasters in this respect and rewards commercial broadcasters that serve minority or disadvantaged groups in society, including ethnic minorities, different regions, Hungarian minorities in neighbouring countries, religious communities, and people disadvantaged by age, mental situation or social conditions. Other groups are expected to be able to ensure themselves that their needs are covered and that they are represented in the media. Diversity in Hungarian media policy, therefore, reflects the social, political and cultural dimensions of society (reflective diversity), with the important modification that there is positive discrimination for the disadvantaged and that *access* of the powerful to the media is limited (open diversity).

The National Radio and Television Board is the main regulating authority in broadcasting. It monitors changes on the electronic media market and the content performance of broadcasting, in particular of the three public service programme providers: Hungarian Television, Hungarian Radio, and Duna Television (serving Hungarian minorities abroad). The Board has an obligation under the Media Act to report to the Parliament every year about the situation in the electronic media field. However, it must be mentioned that the Parliament did not put the Board's yearly report on its agenda between 1997 and 2002. Specifically, the Board monitors:

- the characteristics of radio and television programme providers and programme distributors, in terms of location, programme provision area, means of programme distribution, and ownership;
- the structure of the programmes on (public and commercial) national channels, by programme type, national origin, producer (in house, outside), target group and extent of replication (new or repeated programme);
- 'the equilibrium in the political and actual programmes'; that is, the representation of different political orientations, different activity spheres, social groups, different regions of Hungary and the world in the main information programmes; and the appearance of (representatives of) the main political parties in the news programmes in quantitative and qualitative terms;
- the consumption of programmes in quantitative and qualitative terms, including users' preferences and the effectiveness of different channels in covering the information needs of the audience.

Also, the Media Act established the Complaints Committee, a committee charged with assessing complaints that the criteria of providing balanced information have been violated:

If a broadcaster provides one-sided information on social issues concerning the population of the concerned area, especially if it only offers the opportunity to represent a single or one-sided view on the controversial issue, or if he seriously violates the fundamental principle of the provision of balanced information, then the representative of the undisclosed opinion or the injured party himself may raise an objection to the broadcaster.

Italy
by Gianpietro Mazzoleni

In the Italian Constitution there exists no reference to the concept of 'pluralism'. However, from one Article (Article 21) of the Constitution we may extract an embryonic definition of the concept – which finds a clearer specification in the ordinary legislation. Article 21 reads: 'All have the right to manifest his/her own thought with speech, writings and any other means of diffusion. The press cannot undergo any authorisation or censorship ….' In short, pluralism, i.e., the possibility that 'all manifest freely their own thought', is more than a policy goal. In Italy it is seen as a fundamental right.

In Italian legislation, there are three relevant references to the concept of 'pluralism', which is the equivalent of 'diversity' in the Italian language. The first law that dealt with media diversity was the so-called Mammì Law (1990). It actually photocopied the existing (unbalanced) situation. The law was intended to impede the concentration of media, banning cross-media ownership. Yet, it gave birth to a strong media duopoly (Mediaset and RAI) that has choked the whole system until today. In 1997 a new Law (the Maccanico Law) tried to solve this 'blockade', introducing more restrictive anti-trust norms. In practice, it envisaged a partial dismantling of RAI channels (to be put on the market place), and the dismantling of one of Berlusconi's network. But the law failed to attain both goals. The newest law, just passed by Parliament (2004), wanted by the Berlusconi government and named after the present minister Mr. Gasparri, declares:

> The founding principles of the broadcasting system are to guarantee freedom and pluralism of broadcasting media, to defend the freedom of expression of each individual, the objectivity, the completeness, the fairness of the information, the openness to diverse opinions and political-social-cultural-religious ideas, and the protection of ethnic diversities and of the cultural-artistic-environmental heritage (art. 3)

The norms about broadcasting – with the goal of defending the users – guarantee the users undiscriminated access to a wide variety of information and content provided by a plurality of local and national enterprises, in so favouring the fruition and the development – in a pluralistic and free-market environment – of those subjects that intend to operate in the communications system (art. 4).

The only dimension of media diversity specifically catered to is the 'political' one, but this is done in a rather limited way. Law (no. 28/2000) stipulates that all political forces should receive 'equal time' in the media during election campaigns. This has only loose relations with the concept of 'diversity'. The Authority for Communications has a direct role in enforcing this law, by monitoring all television broadcasts and counting the times dedicated during election time to each party and to each candidate. Usually it commissions this task to a private research institute and publishes the figures on its website. In case of violation of the law, the Authority issues fines and can order the halting of a programme. The only monitoring activity that has something to do with media diversity is the one related to the political party equal-time provision in television programmes, and then only during election periods. The Authority performs no other monitoring or assessment of diversity. A handful of private or academic institutions conduct some monitoring of mostly television content for their own purposes. In particular the Pavia's Observatory is the most prestigious and independent institution that has built a huge database on all television content since 1994 (see www.osservatorio.it). It is a business but the RAI and Mediaset have entrusted to the Observatory the monitoring of 'political pluralism' in certain periods.

United Kingdom
by Ralph Negrine
The structure of media regulation in the UK changed in 2003, when OFCOM took over the regulatory functions previously performed by the Radio Communications Agency, ITC, OFTEL, the Radio Regulatory Authority, and the Broadcasting Standards Commission. In effect, OFCOM has become very central in the organisation and regulation of structures and content in the media and telecommunications sector.

According to the Communications Act of 2003, the general duties of OFCOM are to further the interests of citizens and consumers, including securing (Section 3, article 2):

(a) the availability throughout the United Kingdom of a wide range of electronic communications services;
(b) the availability throughout the United Kingdom of a wide range of television and radio services which (taken as a whole) are both of high quality and calculated to appeal to a variety of tastes and interests;
(c) the maintenance of a sufficient plurality of providers of different television and radio services;
(d) the application, in the case of all television and radio services, of standards that provide adequate protection to members of the public from the inclusion of offensive and harmful material in such services;

In performing those duties, OFCOM must take into account (Section 3, article 4):

(a) the desirability of promoting the fulfilment of the purposes of public service television broadcasting in the United Kingdom;
(b) the desirability of promoting competition in relevant markets;
(c) the desirability of promoting and facilitating the development and use of effective forms of self-regulation;

The Communications Act acknowledges that concentration and media-cross-ownership can reduce media diversity. Thus the Act stipulates in Section 375 on 'Media public interest considerations' that in case of media mergers considerations specified as public interest considerations should be:

(2A) The need for:

(a) accurate presentation of news; and
(b) free expression of opinion; in newspapers ….

(2B) The need for, to the extent that it is reasonable and practicable, a sufficient plurality of views in newspapers in each market for newspapers ….

(2C) …

(a) the need, in relation to every different audience in the United Kingdom or in a particular area or locality of the United Kingdom, for there to be a sufficient plurality of persons with control of the media enterprises serving that audience;
(b) the need for the availability throughout the United Kingdom of a wide range of broadcasting which (taken as a whole) is both of high quality and calculated to appeal to a wide variety of tastes and interests;

Section 319 of the Communications Act on OFCOM's standards code imposes the following duty to OFCOM:

(2) The standards objectives are:

    (c) that news included in television and radio services is presented with due impartiality and that the impartiality requirements of section 320 are complied with;

    (d) that news included in television and radio services is reported with due accuracy;

    (e) that the proper degree of responsibility is exercised with respect to the content of programmes which are religious programmes;

Section 320 imposes impartiality requirements in 'matters of political or industrial controversy' and in 'matters relating to current public policy'. Although the Communications Act does not specify any specific procedure regarding how OFCOM should determine whether or not broadcasters comply with their relevant standards codes, OFCOM is required to carry out consultations and research as it sees fit in order to determine whether broadcasters comply with the terms of the Act.

It is important to note that OFCOM does not have complete oversight of the BBC. The BBC Governors retain powers and responsibilities over the governance of the BBC and such matters as editorial policy. In this respect, the governance of the BBC remains within the hands of the Governors. OFCOM nevertheless does have some regulatory powers over the BBC. For example, the BBC needs to consult or seek guidance from OFCOM over matters such as programming policy (see: www.ofcom.org.uk/about_ofcom/relbbc?a=87101). Besides, OFCOM is currently conducting a review of Public Service Broadcasting that will involve detailed analysis of all the UK public service broadcasters: BBC, ITV1, Channel 4, Five, S4C and all related television services taken together. OFCOM's review will be evidence-based and research-driven, and will take account of responses from viewers themselves. The outcome will feed into Government's review of the BBC's Charter.

6. Conclusions

Diversity is a major objective of media policy throughout Europe. Yet specific interpretations of diversity vary considerably across countries, and different instruments are applied to realise these more specific aims. On the one hand we find countries like Hungary and the Netherlands, where the supply and consumption of television programmes are continuously monitored. At the other end of the spectrum, we find countries like Italy where pluralism is only implicitly mentioned in legislation and political pluralism is monitored on an *ad hoc* basis.

Research in Europe on diversity and its 'friends' and 'enemies' (McQuail, 2000) is also varied. Results nevertheless consistently show that competition and concentration can both increase and reduce diversity, on television as well as on newspaper markets, depending on other market conditions, governmental policies and the role of public-interest players. Concentration on the Belgian press market, for example, in most cases results in a loss of diversity, yet in the case of *De Morgen* so far has rescued this newspaper from oblivion. The German and Finnish television markets show that moderate competition, in combination with a strong public service broadcaster, contribute to diversity of programme supply. The Flemish and Dutch cases, on the other hand, suggest that too strong competition causes a decline of diversity, perhaps even on public channels. The increase in media supply contributes at a more general level to the availability of diverse content. Yet, the analysis of print markets in Finland indicates that other than market forces, such as shared professional norms, once more reduce differences between available news products. This might also explain part of the observed similarities between the public and commercial newscasts in Flanders.

Finally, many studies indicate that competition may either increase differences between media products or make them more similar, but seldom contributes to a rise in the internal diversity of television channels or print services. Nevertheless, internally diverse outlets confront audiences more strongly than a wide range of focused outlets with diverse and thought-provoking information that audiences might not directly look for. The availability of internally diverse outlets as such, therefore, warrants more attention and perhaps policy intervention.

Comparative data

One serious problem for further research on (the causes of) diversity is the lack of comparable data across countries and sometimes even across time within countries. National studies of the diversity of television programme supply necessarily build on the programme classifications of national ratings agencies or national institutions of government. One problem with the available categories is that they sometimes conflate very distinct programme types under one heading. The German television study that was reviewed, for example, distinguished between news bulletins, news magazines, other information broadcasts, entertainment (including sports broadcasts), performances, films, series. The groupings are in part problematic because the category 'information broadcasts' covers both hard and soft information (infotainment).

At least as problematic for international comparisons is that different studies and different ratings agencies work with different (numbers of) categories. This is problematic because it affects the measurement of diversity (Kambara, 1992). These problems can, on the one hand, be ignored in an internal comparison of the results – i.e. in a longitudinal comparison, as in the studies reported here. However, the data used can only be interpreted in a qualified sense as absolute figures. Therefore comparisons between studies with different ranges of categories are only possible in terms of changes over time, but not in terms of the absolute values of the data.

Also other differences in definition need to be resolved before fruitful international comparisons can be made. The section on Germany already indicated some of the problems involved in defining the relevant television market. For the newspaper market, there still is some disagreement on the appropriate definition of (daily) newspapers. At one extreme, a news publication is considered a daily newspaper if it appears twice a week (Schütz, 2001, p. 602). In the Netherlands, on the other hand, newspapers are generally considered daily newspapers if they are published six times a week. In between, in Scandinavian countries newspapers are considered as dailies when they are published 3 or 4 times a week (De Bens & Ostbye, 1998). Also the World Association of Newspapers

(WAN) requires a periodicity of 4 times a week for a daily. Similar differences emerge when we consider the geographical orientation of newspapers and aim to distinguish between regional and national newspapers. And we have not even begun to understand the complexities involved in cross-media comparisons of media concentration and diversity.

To increase our understanding of the level of diversity available in various media markets across Europe, and to better investigate different factors that may alone or in combination contribute to a rise or decline in diversity, we urgently need more consensus on key indicators, and in particular the adoption of similar methodologies across countries and markets. The next chapter proposes some guidelines and starting points for such a common European approach.

Notes
1. Available at http://www.finlex.fi/pdf/saadkaan/E9990731.PDF.
2. Available at http://www.finlex.fi/pdf/saadkaan/E0030460.PDF.
3. Available at http://www.mintc.fi/www/sivut/dokumentit/viestinta/tavoite/Communications MarketAct_upto518_2004.PDF.
4. Available at http://www.mintc.fi/www/sivut/english/tele/massmedia/yle_legisl.htm.

References

ALM (1999) *Programmbericht zur Lage und Entwicklung des Fernsehens in Deutschland 1998/1999 der Arbeitsgemeinschaft der Landesmedienanstalten in der Bundesrepublik Deutschland (ALM)*. Berlin: Ullstein.

ALM (2003) *Privater Rundfunk in Deutschland 2003. Jahrbuch der Landesmedienanstalten, herausgegeben von der Arbeitsgemeinschaft der Landesmedienanstalten in der Bundesrepublik Deutschland (ALM)*. Berlin, VISTAS.

Aslama, M., H. Hellman, & T. Sauri (2004a) Digitalizing Diversity. Public Service Strategies and Television Programme Supply in Finland in 2002. *International Journal of Media Management 6*(3&4), pp. 152–161.

Aslama, M., H. Hellman, , & T. Sauri (2004b) Does market-entry regulation matter? Competition in television broadcasting and program diversity in Finland, 1993–2002. *Gazette, 66*(2), pp. 113–132.

Aslama M., & J. Wallenius (2003) Suomalainen tv-tarjonta 2002. [Finnish television supply 2002]. Helsinki: Ministry of Transport and Communications.

Brosius, H-B, & C. Zubayr (1996) *Vielfalt im deutschen Fernsehprogramm. Eine Analyse der Angebotsstruktur öffentlich-rechtlicher und privater Sender*. Ludwigshafen: Landeszentrale für Private Rundfunkveranstalter.

BRT (1979). *Jaarverslag* [Annual Report]. Brussels: BRT.

Bruns, Th., & F.Marcinkowski (1996) Konvergenz Revisited. Neue Befunde zu einer älteren Diskussion. *Rundfunk und Fernsehen* 44(4), pp. 461–478.

Commissariaat voor de Media (2002) *A view on media concentration: concentration and diversity of the Dutch media in 2001*, Hilversum: Commissariaat voor de Media [The Netherlands Media Authority]. Available: www.cvdm.nl/pages/mediaconc.asp

Commissariaat voor de Media (2003) *Concentratie en pluriformiteit van de Nederlandse media 2000* [Concentration and diversity of the Dutch media 2002]. Hilversum: Commissariaat voor de Media [The Netherlands Media Authority]. Available: http://217.148.171.193/documents/mmc2002.pdf.

De Bens, E. (1985). l'Influence de la cablodiffusion sur le comportement télévisuel des belges et sur les strategies de programmation. In IDATE (ed.), *Actes des 7es Journées Internationales de l'IDATE* (pp 318–329). Montpellier: IDATE.

De Bens, E. (1986) 'Cable penetration and competition among Belgian and foreign stations'. *European Journal of Communication* 1(4), pp. 478–492.

De Bens, E. (1997) 'Television: more diversity, more concergence?' pp. 27–37 in K.Brants, J. Hermes & L. Van Zoonen (eds), *Media in question.Popular cultures and public interest.* London: Sage.

De Bens, E. (2000) 'Media competition. Greater diversity or greater convergence? Evidence from two empirical studies', pp. 158–179 in J. Van Cuilenburg and R. Van der Wurff (eds.), *Media & open societies. Cultural, economic and policy foundations for media openness and diversity in East and West.* Amsterdam: Het Spinhuis.

De Bens, E. (2001) *De pers in België* [The press in Belgium]. Tielt: Lannoo.

De Bens, E. (2004) 'Media in Belgium', pp. 68–81 in M. Kelly, G. Mazzoleni and D Mc.Quail (eds), *The Euromedia Handbook.* London: Sage.

De Bens, E. & H. Ostbye (1998) 'The European newspaper market. Structural changes', pp. 7–23 in D. Mc Quail and K. Siune (eds.), *Media policy. Convergence, concentration and commerce.* London: Sage.

De Bens, E, & S. Paulussen (2004) *Nieuws op TV1 en VTM: anders of hetzelfde?* Ghent University. Available: http:/www.psw.ugent.be/comwet/documents/studiepublieke omroep_000.doc.

Donsbach, W. (1992) Programmvielfalt im dualen Rundfunksystem. *Baromedia* (8), pp. 10–23.

Geerst, Cl., & G. Thoveron (1979) *Télévision offerte au public, télévision regardée par le public ou les effets de cable.* Brussels: RTBF (Etudes de Radio et Télévision, nr 28).

Geerts, Cl., & G. Thoveron (1980) *Télévision offerte au public. Télévision regardée par le public.* Brussel: RTBF.

Gerhards, M., A. Grajczyk & W. Klingler (1996) 'Programmangebote und Spartennutzung im Fernsehen 1995. Daten aus der GfK-Programmcodierung'. *Media Perspektiven* (11), pp. 572–576.

Gerhards, M., & W. Klingler (2003) 'Programmangebote und Spartennutzung im Fernsehen 2002'. *Media Perspektiven* (11), pp. 500–509.

Hellman, H. (1999) *From companions to competitors: The changing broadcasting markets and television programming in Finland.* Tampere: University of Tampere.

Iossifov, I. (2001). 'The Dutch press policy: a model to follow or a model to change', pp. 164–192 in Y. N. Zassoursky & E. Vartanova (eds.), *Media for the open society. West-east and north-south interface.* Moscow: Faculty of Journalism / IKAR Publisher.

Iossifov, I. (2005) The Netherlands. Manuscript/draft chapter of Ph.D thesis, University of Amsterdam.

Kambara, N. (1992) 'Study of the diversity indices used for programming analysis'. *Studies of Broadcasting* (28), pp. 195–206.

Knockaert, I. (2004) *Synergie tussen Het Volk en Het Nieuwsblad* [Synergie between 'het Volk' and 'Het Nieuwsblad']. Unpublished MA thesis, Dept. of Communication Science, University of Ghent.

Krüger, U. M. (2001) *Programmprofile im dualen Fernsehsystem 1991–2000. Eine Studie der ARD/ZDF-Medienkommission.* Baden-Baden: Nomos.

Maier, M. (2002) *Zur Konvergenz des Fernsehens in Deutschland. Ergebnisse qualitativer und repräsentativer Zuschauerbefragungen.* Konstanz: UVK Verlagsgesellschaft.

McQuail, D. (1992) *Media Performance. Mass Communication and Public Interest.* London: Sage.

McQuail, D. (2000) 'Democracy, media and public policy; concluding note', pp. 257–262 in J. Van Cuilenburg & R. Van der Wurff (eds.), *Media and Open Societies.* Amsterdam: Het Spinhuis.

Meier, H.E. (2003) 'Beyond convergence. Understanding programming strategies of public broadcasting in competitive environments'. *European Journal of Communication* 18(3), pp. 337–365.

Merten, K. (1994). *Konvergenz der deutschen Fernsehprogramme. Eine Langzeituntersuchung 1980–1993.* Münster: Lit.

Nordenstreng, K., & O.A. Wiio (eds.) (2003) *Suomen mediamaisema* [Finland's media lanscape] Helsinki: WSOY.

Pfetsch, B. (1996). 'Konvergente Fernsehformate in der Politikberichterstattung? Eine vergleichende Analyse öffentlich-rechtlicher und privater Programme 1985/86 und 1993', *Rundfunk und Fernsehen* 44, pp. 479–498.

Picard, R.G. (2003) 'Media economics, content and diversity: Primary results from a Finnish study', pp. 107–120 in P. Hovi-Wasastjerna (ed.), *Media Culture Research Program.* Helsinki: Academy of Finland / Ilmari Publications, University of Arts and Design.

Rossmann, C., A. Brandl & Brosius, H-B (2003) 'Der Vielfalt eine zweite Chance? Eine Analyse der Angebotsstruktur öffentlich-rechtlicher und privater Fernsehsender in den Jahren 1995, 1998 und 2001'. *Publizistik* 48(4), pp. 427–453.

Roth, A. (2004) *The ecology of a dual television market: Competition and diversity in the Netherlands.* Paper presented at the 6th World Media Economics Conference, May 12–15, 2004, Montréal, Canada.

Schatz, H., N. Immer, & F.Marcinkowski (1989) 'sDer Vielfalt eine Chance? Empirische Befunde zu einem zentralen Argument für die 'Dualisierung' des Rundfunks in der Bundesrepublik Deutschland', *Rundfunk und Fernsehen* 37(1), pp. 5–24.

Schütz, W.J. (2001) 'Deutsche Tagespresse 2001'. *Media Perpektiven* (12), pp. 602–632

Schulz, W. & C. Ihle, (2005) 'Wettbewerb und Vielfalt im deutschen Fernsehmarkt. Eine Analyse der Entwicklungen von 1992 bis 2001', pp. 272–292 in C.-M. Ridder, W. Langenbucher, U. Saxer & C. Steininger (eds.) *Bausteine einer Theorie des öffentlich-rechtlichen Rundfunks. Festschrift für Marie Luise Kiefer.* Wiesbaden: VS Verlag für Sozialwissenschaften.

Souchon, M (1978) *La télévision et son public.* Paris: La documentation Française.

Souchon, M. (1980) *Petit écran, grand public.* Paris: INA.

Statistics Finland (2005) *Joukkoviestimet - Finnish Mass Media 2004.* Helsinki: Author.

Television 2004. International key facts (2004). Paris: IP and RTL Group.

Van Cuilenburg, J., & D. McQuail, (1982) *Media en pluriformiteit.* Den Haag: Staatsdrukkerij.

Van Cuilenburg, J. (1999) 'Between media monopoly and ruinous media competition', pp. 40–61 in Y. N. Zassoursky & E. Vartanova (eds.) *Media, communications and the open society.* Moscow: Faculty of Journalism / IKAR Publisher.

Van der Wurff, R. (2003) 'Structure, conduct and performance of the agricultural trade journal market in The Netherlands', *Journal of Media Economics, 16*(2), pp. 121–138.

Van der Wurff, R. (2004a) 'Supplying and viewing diversity: The role of competition and viewer choice in Dutch broadcasting', *European Journal of Communication, 19*(2), pp. 215–237.

Van der Wurff, R. (2004b) 'Program choices of multichannel broadcasters and diversity of program supply in the Netherlands', *Journal of Broadcasting & Electronic Media, 48*(1), pp. 134–150.

Van der Wurff, R. (2005) 'Business magazine market performance. Magazines for the agricultural, business services and transportation sectors in the Netherlands', *Journal of Media Economics, 18*(2), pp. 143–159.

Van der Wurff, R. & J.Van Cuilenburg (2001) 'Impact of moderate and ruinous competition on diversity. The Dutch television market', *Journal of Media Economics, 14*(4), pp. 213–229.

Van der Wurff, R. & E. Lauf, (2004) *Diversificatie en pluriformiteit van nieuws. Een onderzoek naar de bijdrage van print en online dagbladen aan de pluriformiteit van de nieuwsvoorziening in Nederland* (Differentiation and diversity of news). Amsterdam: ASCoR.

Van Meurs, A. (1999) *Switching during commercial breaks.* Unpublished PhD, University of Amsterdam, Amsterdam.

Ward, D. (2004) *A Mapping Study of Media Concentration and Ownership in Ten European Countries.* Hilversum: Commissariaat voor de Media [Netherlands Media Authority]. Available: http://www.mediamonitor.nl/html/documents/mappingstudy_ward_jun2004.pdf

Weiss, H-J., W. Demski, M. Fingerling & H. Volpers (1991) *Produktionsquoten privater Fernsehprogramme in der Bundesrepublik Deutschland. Eine Programmanalyse im Frühjahr 1990.* Düsseldorf: LfR.

Weiss, H-J., & J.Trebbe (2000) *Fernsehen in Deutschland 1998–1999. Programmstrukturen, Programminhalte, Programmentwicklungen. Forschungsbericht*

Toward Easy-to-Measure Media Diversity Indicators

Jan van Cuilenburg and Richard van der Wurff

A plea for easy-to-measure media diversity indicators

Lessons learned

The previous chapter described various empirical media diversity studies and illustrated the diversity in regulatory approaches in different EU Member States. From this overview, several lessons can be drawn. The first empirical lesson is that media diversity in the EU by and large reaches a high level, notably in the field of broadcasting where the introduction of commercial broadcasting has exponentially multiplied television and radio supply. On newspaper markets, on the other hand, diversity is more under threat.

The second lesson learned is that concentration of media ownership and competition can have both positive and negative effects. Concentration of channel ownership in competitive broadcasting markets contributes to diversification in products and thus to programme diversity, but concentration of newspaper ownership is frequently a first step towards the merger of titles and hence a loss in diversity. Likewise, competition between media owners has a beneficial effect on media diversity only to a certain point: if media competition deteriorates into fierce competition, media diversity decreases. This implies that the relationship between concentration/competition and diversity is curvilinear rather than linear. Both too strong and too weak competition reduces diversity.

The third lesson is that media diversity, especially in the field of journalistic products and services, may decline due to further professionalisation of media, resulting in growing adherence of media professionals to common professional standards, values, norms and best-practices. And, as a fourth lesson, EU Member States follow rather different approaches in measuring and assessing media diversity. It is still not possible to find a common European denominator as far as content diversity is concerned.

Media concentration data instead of diversity statistics?
Media diversity measurement and assessment in Europe is roughly speaking as diverse as media diversity itself. This being so, some may suggest that for media diversity assessment we had better rely on market structural statistics than on content diversity data. There is a lot of statistical information available on market structural factors (concentration and competition), even though in this area some problems with respect to market definition and measurement exist. Replacing diversity assessment for concentration analysis, unfortunately however, isn't very helpful, because the impact of market structural factors on media quality and diversity is not fully known and, more importantly, depends on country-, culture-, media- and market-specific conditions. This problem makes media-concentration and media-competition statistics far less useful for media-policymaking than many policymakers are aware of. The conventional policy approach to inferentially assess media diversity from market concentration and competition data doesn't make sense if the empirical relationship between diversity and concentration is either not known or not linear.

Inevitably, this problem of the unknown or non-linear relationship between concentration/competition and diversity leads to the conclusion that it does not suffice for media-policymaking to rely on market structural statistics alone. In searching policy instruments to maintain and enhance media diversity, policymakers somehow have to measure and assess media diversity independently from market structural factors. The country overview in Chapter 3, however, shows that there is no single content measurement system that can easily be applied to measure diversity in different countries for different media. And, to add a further complication, as research conducted in communication science on diversity always clearly demonstrates, the task of measuring the quality and diversity of media content requires laborious and expensive content analysis. For media-policymaking on a regular basis, full-fledged content analysis, taking a lot of time and money, is not a very practical option. Therefore we want to make a plea here to search for and to develop easy-to-measure diversity indicators, which can be easily used in policymaking.

Easy-to-measure media diversity indicators
A system of easy-to-measure diversity indicators should provide a simple way to assess whether media content available in the marketplace is sufficiently diverse and whether media system conditions favour (future) diversity. To be as efficient as possible, indicators of media content diversity should be based on existing data collections or on data that could be rapidly made adequate for use in policymaking.

Proxies for open diversity-as-sent
As discussed in Chapter 2, diversity is a multifaceted concept. Without claiming to be comprehensive, in measuring media diversity at least five different types of diversity can be identified. These types indicate the level of heterogeneity of media content at different

stages in the information chain, from original content producers to end-users. First, the type of diversity most frequently referred to in the studies described in Chapter 3 is:

- diversity-as-sent. Diversity-as-sent is heterogeneity of content supplied by media outlets in a media market.

The other four types of diversity that may be measured are:

- diversity-as-received: the heterogeneity of content that is actually consumed by audiences;
- diversity-as-demanded: the heterogeneity of content as it is demanded by audiences;
- diversity-as-proposed: the heterogeneity of content that is offered (proposed) to the media by various actors and individuals who seek to distribute their information; and
- diversity-as-choice: the total number of different options from which audiences can choose.

Likewise, diversity can be evaluated in different ways. We distinguish at least five approaches. First, we can estimate the heterogeneity of supply itself with the relative entropy formula (see Appendix A to Chapter 2) as a statistic for diversity-as-sent. Secondly, diversity-as-sent can be compared with diversity-as-demanded. This gives a measure of reflective diversity. Thirdly, diversity-as-sent can be compared with diversity-as-proposed. This gives a measure of access to the media for different social groups. Fourthly, diversity-as-sent can be compared with a theoretical optimum in which all options get equal attention. This gives a measure of open diversity. Finally, we can compare diversity-as-sent with diversity-as-received. This gives a measure of the use that audiences make of the available diversity.

Diversity-as-proposed and diversity-as-demanded are indicators that can only be estimated on the basis of relatively specific information. In a few countries this information will be collected on a regular basis. Information that can be used to assess diversity-as-sent and diversity-as-received, on the other hand, is more frequently available. For the television market, for example, there are at least two easy ways of measuring diversity without conducting a fully-fledged, costly content analysis. One is to use existing classifications of media content as used, for example, by television rating agencies, and to estimate the distribution of programmes (as supplied and as viewed) over different content categories. The other is to use available top-10/100 ratings lists and estimate how many different types of content are included in these top-lists. The former produces measures of open diversity-as-sent and open diversity-as-received; the latter gives a rather approximation of open diversity-as-received.

Another relatively easy-to-measure indicator could be the proportion of domestic versus foreign programming, differentiated by programme type. These kinds of data are periodically provided in, for example, the European Audiovisual Yearbook, and in publications of many national European rating agencies.

In cases where these data are not available, diversity could be measured by proxies that are indirectly linked to diversity, e.g., the audience reach of a programme type or media outlet. On the assumption that, on average, smaller minimum audiences suggest that more minority preferences are catered for, diversity can be considered to be the reciprocate of minimal audience reach. We may refer to this indicator as the audience size proxy. It deviates from other diversity measures in that is does not describe the relative distribution of content categories in supply, but rather indicates to what extent small minorities are being served in media content. To make this kind of indirect measurement more reliable, the average audience reach for a number of least viewed programme types could be ascertained.

Methodological limitations
The use of data that initially are collected for other purposes brings several methodological problems. These were already discussed at the end of chapter 3. One problem is that different data collection agencies use their own criteria to include some and exclude other media outlets in their analyses. Using available data, therefore, has consequences for how the *relevant market* is defined, and in practice implies that markets are defined differently for different countries. Secondly, different definitions and varying numbers of content categories are being used by different agencies. This again reduces the comparability of data across countries. On the other hand, as long as the same definitions and categories are used, estimates of diversity can be compared across time within countries.

Using available data to estimate diversity indicators for various media markets, therefore, does not allow us to determine once and for all whether media provide sufficient diversity in a particular year, or even to conclude that media in country A are more diverse than media in country B. Yet, using available data to monitor how media diversity is developing on different media markets in different countries does provide us with important – and hitherto still missing – basic information that subsequently can be used to investigate causes of time trends and even develop media policy thresholds for adequate levels of diversity. In interpreting these data, we must keep an open eye for the underlying differences and contradictions in approaches. Yet, we prefer to use these imperfect data, rather than waiting for a long time for the development of a perfect media diversity monitoring system.

Without pretending that it is the only approach possible, the next section describes some elements of the Netherlands Media Monitor as an example of how easy-to-measure media diversity indicators could look like. It focuses on the television market as a market where, relatively, much information is available throughout Europe. The section following the next section subsequently shows what indicators could be used for markets on which less information is available.

The Netherlands Media Monitor as an example of easy-to-measure media diversity
In Chapter 2 we introduced the Media Monitor Model for media concentration and diversity, developed by the Netherlands Media Authority, that may serve as an example of how easy media diversity indicators might look. For its monitor, the Media Authority uses standard statistical data collected by national media industry organisations. In the Dutch Monitor:

- media ownership concentration is measured in terms of market shares of media companies,
- editorial/programming concentration (or its inverse, title/channel plurality) is measured as the number of independent titles/broadcast channels,
- diversity is expressed in statistical indices for openness and reflection in media content, and
- the demand side is described in terms of audience preferences.

Television market: content diversity

The Netherlands Media Authority measures diversity of television programming on the basis of a content classification system, categorising all programme output in categories like news and information, education, drama, entertainment, sports and youth programmes. The percentages of programme time output in different categories are subsequently being compared to audience preferences, that is, the relative time people spend on viewing these programme categories. All these data are available from the Dutch Audience Research Foundation SKO. From these data easy-indicators for both reflective television diversity and open television diversity can be calculated (Commissariaat voor de Media, 2003, pp. 54–55). For the definitions of the various statistics used in this section, we refer to Chapter 2, Appendix B.

In 2002, nearly 40% of television output on the nine Dutch general interest channels was news, information and educational programmes, and also approximately 40% of programming time was spent on fiction (Dutch and foreign drama) (see Table 1). The diversity statistics indicate a reasonably diverse supply of television programmes; the entropy index $E =. 74$, where $E = 1$ signifies maximum diversity, and $E = 0$ means homogeneity in content. The programme supply by public broadcasters is a little bit more diverse ($E = .82$) than programme supply by commercial broadcasters ($E = .61$).

Table 1: The Netherlands Television Market 2002 (18–24 hrs): Programme Output and Audience Viewing Time.

	Programme Output		Audience viewing time	
	Public Channels %	Commercial Channels %	All Channels %	Programme category %
News, information and education	48	33	39	35
Fiction	18	53	39	41
Entertainment	14	8	10	11
Sports	10	5	7	10
Music	4	1	2	1
Children, youth	6	0	3	2
Total	100 (5534 hrs)	100 (10279 hrs)	100 (15813 hrs)	100 (682 hrs)

Source: Commissariaat voor de Media, 2003, pp. 54–55

Commercial broadcasters offer far more drama fiction and less news and information than their public competitor.

Audience viewing behaviour in The Netherlands correlates highly with the diversity of programme supply: reflective diversity RD = .94 (2002; RD = 1 being the maximum in case of full reflection of audience preferences by supply). Or, to put it the other way around, television programme supply in the Netherlands follows audience preferences. The reflective diversity index for the public broadcaster is RD = .77; for the commercial broadcasters we calculate RD = .88 (see Table 1 and Table 3).

From programme output data it is clear that the difference in reflective performance between public and commercial broadcasters is only small. Performance in terms of open diversity, however, results in a slightly different picture: the public broadcaster gives its audience more access to a variety of programme categories and genres than commercial broadcasters do (open diversity OD in 2002: .55 [all channels]; .67 [public channels]; .47 [commercial channels]). By far the main part of commercial programming consists, not surprisingly, of drama productions, notably inexpensive foreign soaps and series. It is in this respect that public service broadcasting in the Netherlands distinguishes itself from the commercial channels. This finding in the Dutch market is in accordance with a McKinsey study on public service broadcasters around the world. The McKinsey study (1999, p. 22) showed that *distinctiveness* of Dutch PSB measured as the percentage of programming time spent on factual, cultural and children's programmes is 57%, against PSB average distinctiveness of 52%.

The overall conclusion the Netherlands Media Authority has drawn from its analysis of the television market is that programme supply is very diverse and amply meeting media performance criteria of reflective and open diversity, notwithstanding the high degree of ownership concentration in the television market. Notably, the public service broadcaster with its distinctive programming and a very substantial market share of 38% contributes to the relatively healthy state of Dutch television market.

Television market: profusion and performance

The Dutch Media Monitor as it is currently used defines *media diversity* only in terms of the heterogeneity of media content, that is, the variety of content supplied to the readers, listeners and viewers. In Chapter 2 we argued, however, that *media diversity* should also include the sheer volume of media supply people can choose from. After all, content diversity on a high level of media supply in society should in general be preferred to the same diversity on a low level of media supply. This will become true particularly in the future when numerous digital channels will be available to the general public. Solely measuring content diversity of these channels, that for the most part are thematic channels supplying homogeneous content, gives an underassessment of media market performance. To take this notion into account we may use the concept of *media profusion*, introduced in Chapter 2. This concept correlates with the concept of diversity-as-choice we already referred to in this Chapter, and indicates the abundance or plenty of media supply in society. A media profusion index can easily be inferred from the same data already presented in Table 1.

Table 2: The Netherlands Television Market 2002 (18–24 hrs): Profusion (Choice) (own calculations based on: Commissariaat voor de Media, 2003: 54, 55)

Programme category	Audience viewing time			Profusion (supply exceeding viewing time)		
	Hours (per year)	%	Public Channels	Commercial Channels	All Channels
News, information and education	239	35	11.1	12.0	25.8
Fiction	280	41	3.6	21.4	22.1
Entertainment	75	11	10.3	11.6	21.1
Sports	68	10	8.1	6.5	16.2
Music	7	1	32.5	9.8	46.4
Children, youth	14	2	24.4	3.9	34.8
Total	682	100	8.1 (5534 hrs)	15.1 (10279 hrs)	23.2 (15813 hrs)

The analysis of television market data (2002) shows that in the Dutch market there is an abundance of television content provision: the nine general interest channels produce a programme output that exceeds television consumption with factor Profusion = 23.2 (for this concept see Chapter 2). The Dutch viewer, watching 682 hours of television viewing time a year (prime time, 18–24 hours), can choose from a programme supply (prime time) of 15,813 hours (see Table 2). So, for the Dutch audience there is no shortage of programme supply, especially if one also takes into account that in addition to the nine general interest channels there are also many niche channels (MTV, TMF, Discovery, Animal Planet, etc.) in Dutch language available to the Dutch public.

The abundance of television programme supply in the Netherlands is complemented by a high degree of content diversity, reflection and openness, as we saw before. Taken

Table 3: The Netherlands Television Market 2002 (18–24 hrs): Profusion (Choice), Diversity and Media Performance

	Public Channels	Commercial Channels	All Channels
Profusion (supply exceeding demand)	8.1	15.1	23.2
Diversity (relative entropy)	.82	.61	.74
reflective diversity	.77	.88	.94
open diversity	.67	.47	.55
Total Media Performance (= Profusion * Diversity)	6.63	9.26	17.27
Average Media Performance (average per channel)	2.21	1.54	1.92
Media Performance above / below average (on average = 1.00)	1.15	.80	1.00

together, the high profusion and high diversity in television programming result in a television market with very high media performance as we defined the concept in Chapter 2 (see Table 3). Media performance of the public broadcasting per channel is distinctly better than the performance per channel of the commercial broadcasters: per channel, PSB-channels outperform commercial channels by 44%.

The empirical data presented here indicate that, notwithstanding its oligopoly, the Dutch television market (see Chapter 3) is performing rather well on both diversity and profusion. This may be seen as corroboration and extension of the hypothesis introduced in Chapter 2, that under conditions of moderate competition media markets produce 'better' results than under conditions of full and fierce competition.

Examples of other easy-to-measure indicators
A similar approach as adopted in the Dutch Media Monitor can be applied to other media markets, although the approach obviously needs to be modified to the available data. We may illustrate this for the Dutch media market by using data regularly collected by industry organisations, primarily for advertising purposes, to estimate market structure and diversity indicators for the markets of newspapers, radio, magazines, and books.

We include three indicators for concentration:

- the number of providers;
- the Herfindahl index HHI for concentration of providers' market shares;
- and the number of outlets per provider. This statistic indicates how many publications/outlets are controlled by one publisher, which provides an alternative measurement of concentration.

For diversity, we also include up to four indicators, depending on the detail of information available.

The first indicator measures diversity-as-choice. It is defined as the total number of different outlets available to the public in a specific media market. Diversity-as-choice highly correlates with the concept of 'media profusion' introduced in Chapter 2.

The second indicator measures diversity as in-group choice. In general, competing media outlets fall into several groups of imperfect substitutes (e.g., generalist, news and sports TV channels; or popular, classic and jazz radio stations). In-group choice is defined as the average number of channels within these groups of imperfect substitutes.

The third indicator is open diversity-as-sent. At a minimum, open diversity-as-sent describes the distribution of outlets across the different groups of imperfect substitutes (referred to above). If the necessary data are available, it describes the distribution of more specific content categories in supply.

The fourth indicator is an audience size proxy, defined as the ratio between the audience size of the smallest outlet and average audience size per outlet.

We emphasise that the next sections are to be seen only as illustrations of the opportunities and obstacles for the development of easy-to-measure indicators.

Newspapers

Data on newspapers in the Netherlands are provided by media industry organisations, (Cebuco, newspapers, and HOI, newspapers and magazines). Circulation estimates reported by Cebuco and HOI differ slightly because of differences in definition – a common problem when using secondary data – but these differences do not compromise our analysis significantly. A more substantial problem emerges from the geographical division of the newspaper market. As elsewhere, the newspaper market in the Netherlands is an umbrella market where several national newspapers compete to some extent with regional newspapers that – in most cases – have a monopoly in the regional market. To calculate indicators for the overall market to the number of national newspapers that are available everywhere, we add the number of regional newspapers that on average are available in any region.

Table 4 provides indicators that can be estimated on the basis of available data, for the years 1990, 1995 and 2000. The first part of Table 4 shows indicators for concentration: the number of publishers (of regional, national, specialist, and free newspapers), the HHI for publishers' market shares, and the average number of titles per publisher.

Unlike television, there is no readily available data on content of newspapers. We therefore cannot calculate specific diversity indicators. Instead, we estimate diversity-as-choice, defined as the total number of titles available to the average reader. These include all national titles, and the average number of regional titles that an average person can receive in his region. This number differs substantially from the total number of (national and regional) independent titles, also mentioned in the table.

Table 4: Easy-to-measure indicators for newspaper concentration and diversity (The Netherlands)

Year	1990	1995	2000
Concentration			
Number of publishers	20	15	9
HHI publisher market			
Shares	0.09	0.16	0.22
Average number of titles per publisher	2.35	2.60	4.33
Diversity			
Diversity-as-choice	13.5	13.4	14.3
Number of independent titles	*47*	*39*	*39*
In-group choice	2.26	2.23	2.38
Open diversity-as-sent	0.83	0.82	0.84
Audience size proxy		0.10	0.08

Source: Calculations based on Bakker (2002, p. 12), Cebuco (2003), Commissariaat voor de Media (2002), Persmediamonitor (Bakker & De Ridder, 2003).

The available titles fall into one of four categories: national generalist, national specialist (e.g., financial, agricultural), national free, and regional generalist newspapers. If we consider these categories to represent imperfect substitutes, the distribution of titles across these categories becomes important. The average number of titles per category gives the indicator for in-group choice. The open diversity-as-sent indicator describes to what extent the available titles are equally spread across these four categories.

Finally, we estimated an audience size proxy, defined as the ratio between the circulation of the smallest newspaper and average circulation. This indicator informs us whether or not small audiences are being served with separate outlets, which indicates diversity.

The data show that concentration in the Netherlands newspaper market increased significantly, while diversity-as-choice and open diversity-as-sent remained the same. The audience size proxy declined slightly, which signals that there are fewer newspapers in 2000 than in 1995. These findings in concert suggest that diversity in the Dutch newspaper market did not decline, in spite of further ownership concentration and a reduction in titles.

Radio

Data on radio in the Netherlands is collected by Intomart GfK. As with TV and newspapers, this data is first of all collected for advertising purposes. The main results (ratings and market shares of about 20 stations) are available in the public domain.

Regional, public radio stations are relatively popular. Together, they attract a larger share of the market than any single national public or commercial channel. We include regional channels in our market definition. Furthermore, we focus the analysis on domestic channels.

Concentration is described with three indicators in Table 5. The first is the number of broadcasters – where all regional public broadcasters, all regional commercial broadcasters, and all broadcasters of 'other' (not identified) channels are counted as one broadcaster each. Calculations of HHI also consider the market shares of regional public broadcasters, regional commercial broadcasters, and 'other' stations as market shares of single broadcasters. The third indicator is the average number of channels per broadcaster.

To describe the diversity of supply, Table 5 gives indicators for diversity-as-choice (defined as the number of channels), in-group choice and open diversity-as-sent. The latter two indicators are calculated on the basis of a categorisation of radio stations in 8 different categories provided by the Netherlands Media Authority (Commissariaat voor de Media). Also provided is the audience size proxy, defined as the ratio of the market share of the smallest station and average market share. On the basis of these indicators, we may conclude that both competition and diversity in the Dutch radio market have increased considerably.

Table 5: Easy-to-measure indicators for radio station concentration and diversity (The Netherlands)

Year	1990	1995	2000
Concentration			
Number of broadcasters	3	10	9
HHI broadcaster market shares	0.63	0.24	0.16
Average number of channels per broadcaster	1.67	1.50	2.33
Diversity			
Diversity-as-choice	5	15	21
In-group choice	0.63	1.88	2.63
Open diversity-as-sent	0.38	0.70	0.71
Audience size proxy	0.12	0.05	0.05

Source: Estimates derived from and calculations based on Commissariaat voor de Media (2002).

Magazines

Information on magazines is available from two sources, the circulation auditing agency HOI and the Trade Book of Press and Publicity in the Netherlands. HOI provides circulation data per title, subdivided in 19 content categories, since 1998. The Trade Book lists a large number of print publications, and classifies them according to topic and also, more recently, to target audience. Unfortunately, the classification system was completely overhauled in 1998, making comparisons across time extremely complicated.

For this example, we focus on consumer magazines in eleven categories: cars and motors; computers and ICT; youth; men; opinion; tourism; sports; women; living; education and health; arts and culture. Bearing the above-mentioned limitation in mind, the number of publishers of consumer magazines is presented in the first row of Table 6. Market shares of publishers are calculated as the ratio of the total circulation of a publisher's magazines and the total circulation of all magazines. HHI on the basis of

Table 6: Easy-to-measure indicators for magazine concentration and diversity (The Netherlands)

Year	1995	2000
Concentration		
Number of publishers	248	405
HHI publisher market shares	0.04	0.08
Average number of titles per publisher	1.24	1.31
Diversity		
Diversity-as-choice	307	532
In-group choice	28	48
Open diversity-as-sent	0.75	0.67
Audience size proxy	0.003	0.002

Source: Calculations based on Handboek (1995, 2000)

these market shares is provided in the Table, as is the average number of titles per publisher.

The variety of supply is again assessed with four indicators: diversity-as-choice (or the number of different titles), in-group choice (the average number of titles per consumer magazine category), open diversity-as-sent (based on the distribution of titles across categories), and the audience size proxy. The concentration indicators show that there are many publishers and that concentration is very low. The diversity indicators show that the number of magazines increased considerably in the 1990s (both in total and on average per category), that the distribution of titles across these content categories (open diversity-as-sent) declined slightly in the same period, and that very small groups are served with their own magazines.

Books

Data on book sales is collected by Speurwerk, the market research agency of the Dutch Royal Book Publishers Association. Most of this data is not available in the public domain. To illustrate the possibilities, we use data on the numbers of literary fiction books published in the Netherlands in 1996, excluding comics. These are classified in 26 categories. The major categories included are: novels, poetry, essays, thrillers (includes detectives, science fiction, and westerns), romantic novels, myths and humorous stories, fiction in regional languages, and other fiction.

Speurwerk has, but does not provide, data on publishers' market shares, so concentration indices cannot be calculated. The level of variety provided by book publishers is summarised by three indicators: diversity-as-choice (the total number of books published), in-group choice (the average number of books per content category), and open diversity-as-sent, based on the relative number of books per category. Book circulation data is not available in the public domain. Hence, the audience size proxy cannot be estimated. Besides, because only data for one year is available, no interpretation of the estimated indicators can be provided.

Conclusion

Both media policy and scholarly research would benefit considerably if communication scientists and media-policymakers throughout the European Union came to an

Table 7: Easy-to-measure indicators for book diversity (The Netherlands)

Year	1996
Diversity	
Diversity-as-choice	3671
In-group choice	459
Open diversity-as-sent	0.63
Audience size proxy	n.a.

Source: Calculations based on Stichting Speurwerk (1998).

agreement to identify a few 'warning indicators' that inform policymakers when quality and diversity in media markets are under serious threat. Without pretending that it is the only possible approach, on the basis of data from the Netherlands we have outlined a possible way to develop 'easy-to-measure' indicators for media concentration and diversity and to show how these can be estimated from data already available.

Of course, using secondary data – data collected for other purposes – brings its own problems and risks. Implicit or explicit definitions of media markets and content categories may strongly influence estimates of competition and diversity. The discussion in the previous sections has illustrated these problems. Market definitions and diversity assessments are fundamentally normative exercises, and the multidimensionality of media content can never be completely captured in any diversity study. Under those conditions, media policymakers and scholars should opt for simple but consistent measurements of diversity that enable comparison across markets or time. We would like to propose an approach that makes the best use of available data, both to increase efficiency and to jumpstart a discussion of what is the best common denominator among existing practices of data collection. In many cases, data collection specifically targeted to address a specific research question is the preferred solution. Yet we believe that media policy and research on diversity would be considerably advanced if a similar set of indicators were to be used consistently. Besides, it should be emphasised that, at least in the Netherlands but as far as we know also in other countries, various industry organisations are collecting relevant data in a continuous and consistent way that makes such a search for easy-to-measure indicators a fruitful exercise.

Data and indicators
The type of data we need per media sector is data on the number of providers, the number of outlets (titles, channels) and on media consumption (circulation, visitors, viewing time). We also need a breakdown of media outlets per content category (genre, country of origin). If we have this data, concentration of ownership can easily be measured with the number of providers, the average number of outlets per provider and the HHI (on the basis of providers' market shares).

As our empirical analysis shows, the number of outlets could be measured in all cases discussed above once we have defined the relevant market. Some measurements will be biased (for example, the Trade Book for Press and Publicity does not include all magazines), but if we can use the same source for different years, we may expect the bias to be constant. Hence, we can make comparisons across time. One issue that must be carefully considered is the difference between the formal number of outlets and actual availability (for example, not all regional newspapers are actually available to all users, nor are satellite channels).

The assessment of diversity is more complicated, but not impossible. Sometimes we could use more or less satisfactory classifications of content in content/genre categories (television, movies, magazines). Sometimes we are forced to use other dimensions of diversity. And sometimes, we have no content classification at all (newspapers, radio). In the latter case, we can only assess diversity if we classify outlets ourselves or assume that each outlet represents its own unique category. Equally serious problems arise when the content classification system is changed over time. As we have shown in this Chapter, however, for the television market it is quite easy to measure diversity of content if we use standard content classification systems from the television ratings industry. From this data, in combination with standard television ratings, concepts like 'media profusion' (correlating with the theoretical concept of diversity-as-choice) and even the complicated, yet for media policy most interesting concept of 'media performance', can be inferred in a very efficient way. And our empirical analysis in this Chapter illustrates that the open-diversity formula works well and is intuitively valid. It measures exactly what it aims for, namely the extent to which supply differs from an equal distribution. It requires, however, relatively sophisticated data.

Recommendations

The overall conclusion that emerges from the empirical data presented in this Chapter and Chapter 3 is that concentration or competition does not straightforwardly improve or reduce diversity. In general, media markets produce 'better' results under conditions of moderate rather than full and fierce competition. However, it is not obvious which economic data can be used to decisively draw the threshold between moderate and ruinous competition. One major reason is that economic considerations and forces are but one set of factors that influence the behaviour of media professionals, the competitive conduct of media companies, and the performance of media markets. To develop adequate and market-compatible media policies, policymakers cannot only rely on economic indicators: they also need valid and reliable time series of quality and diversity indicators.

Diversity is a multifaceted phenomenon. The development of indicators that assess diversity in all its important dimensions would require a massive research effort that would not be efficient or likely to produce policy-relevant information in a short period of time. Instead, we propose to use available data to assess diversity on a few, indicative dimensions. This requires that the data collected by industry organisations is made available for this type of research without unnecessary restrictions and on cost-based tariffs. These indicators are best validated with a number of in-depth studies that assess to what extent trends in the chosen indicators also reflect changes in other, unobserved, dimensions of diversity, and that additionally determine (country, market and indicator-specific) thresholds below which diversity is seriously threatened. Subsequently, these indicators can be tracked on a regular basis, and additional research can be developed to improve these indicators.

For the time being, we propose two sets of indicators, as illustrated in the previous sections: three indicators for concentration: the number of providers, HHI for providers' market shares, and the number of outlets per provider; and four indicators for diversity: diversity-as-choice, in-group choice, open diversity-as-sent, and an audience size proxy.

In the medium term, we recommend that industry organisations and policy makers together aim for the development of common content classification systems throughout Europe. The advantage for the assessment of indicators is obvious. But also media organisations themselves, which are increasingly confronted with one European market and European advertisers, will profit if sales and advertising revenues can be described throughout Europe in one common currency – which implies the use of shared content classification systems to describe media markets and media market players in similar terms.

At the national level, we see the development of common approaches in audience measurement that cross media boundaries. We also see more efforts to audit circulation and reach estimates. In the television market, we see attempts to combine TV ratings from many different countries in a comprehensive European presentation. Policymakers should stimulate such developments, ensuring both that content classifications systems become similar and that objective criteria are used, both for the measurement of audiences as well as the classification of media outlets and media contents. That would benefit the media and advertising sector as well as facilitating the measurement of better easy-to-measure indicators.

References

Bakker, P. (2002) *Twee decennia regionale en lokale printmedia in Nederland* [Two decades of regional and local print media in the Netherlands]. Amsterdam: The Amsterdam School of Communications Research ASCoR.

Bakker, P., & J. De Ridder (2003) *Nederlandse PersMediaMonitor. Dagbladen. Concentratie* [Dutch PressMediaMonitor. Newspapers. Concentration]. Available: http://www.persmediamonitor.nl/cgi-bin/display.cgi?path=1_7 [April 2003].

Cebuco (2003) *De ontwikkeling van de binnenlandse oplage per dagbladtitel* [Development of domestic circulation per newspaper title]. Amsterdam: Cebuco. Available: http://www.cebuco.nl/cms/data/images/jacqueline/Oplageontwikkeling%20tabel%202.xls [April 2003].

Commissariaat voor de Media (2002. *Mediaconcentratie in beeld. Concentratie en pluriformiteit van de Nederlandse media 2001* [Mediaconcentration in the picture. Concentration and diversity of the Dutch media 2001]. Hilversum: Commissariaat voor de Media [The Netherlands Media Authority]. Available at: www.cvdm.nl.

Commissariaat voor de Media (2003) *Mediaconcentratie in beeld. Concentratie en pluriformiteit van de Nederlandse media 2002* [Concentration and diversity of the Dutch media 2002]. Hilversum: Commissariaat voor de Media. Available at: www.cvdm.nl.

Handboek van de Nederlandse pers en publiciteit [Trade book of Dutch press and publicity]. Electronic edition (October 1995). Schiedam: Nijgh Periodieken.

Handboek van de Nederlandse pers en publiciteit [Trade book of Dutch press and publicity]. Electronic edition (October 2000). Schiedam: Nijgh Periodieken.

McKinsey & Company (1999) *Public Service Broadcasters Around the World: A McKinsey Report for the BBC.*

Stichting Speurwerk (1998) *De aantallen in 1996 uitgebrachte boeken per genre (NUGI-rubriek) en de gemiddelde prijs bij verschijning* [Numbers of books published in 1996 per genre (NUGI category) and average price when published]. Amsterdam: Stichting Speurwerk. Available: http://www.speurwerk.nl/bc/96nugi.html [April 2003].

5

Public Service Broadcasting: A Pawn on an Ideological Chessboard

Karol Jakubowicz

Introduction

Ideology, not technology (as is sometimes claimed), will determine the fate of public service broadcasting. A discussion about PSB is in reality a discussion about the values and principles governing society and social life – in short, about the kind of society we want to live in. In other words, it is, in reality, a purely ideological and axiological discussion, in that different approaches spring from clearly distinct social principles and value systems.

On this basis, three main approaches to PSB can be distinguished.

According to the first, neo-liberal approach, the proper mechanism for the satisfaction of individual and social needs is the market where required goods or services can be purchased. The law of supply and demand, together with the profit motive, will ensure provision of these goods and services. State or public sector involvement in meeting these needs is unnecessary and unwelcome. Therefore, PSB should be dismantled.

According to the second approach, the market should indeed predominate, but since it does not meet every need, there is room for the public sector to supplement what the market has to offer. Nonetheless, public institutions should under no circumstances compete with private enterprise, nor engage in any kind of activity that private entrepreneurs might wish to pursue. So, what is needed is 'pure PSB' as a niche broadcaster, offering only broadcast content and services which private broadcasters find commercially unrewarding. This could be called liberalism with a human face.

In both these instances, any other arguments used to argue the case for the abolition or marginalisation of PSB are, in fact, pretence, a cover-up for the ideological stance which motivates the participant in the debate.

And finally, the third approach proceeds from the view that whatever the market may offer, the community still has a duty to provide broadcasting services free from the effect of the profit motive, offering the individual a 'basic supply' of what he/she needs as a member of a particular society and culture, and of a particular polity and democratic system. Proponents of this approach cherish more values than just those related to the market and more motivations than just the profit motive. From this point of view, the market-failure argument in favour of PSB is insufficient, precisely because that argument should turn on the vision of society we want to live in and the kind of service PSB provides to that society.[1]

The future of PSB will depend on the resolution of the growing conflict between these three approaches. Let us immediately say, however, that this is not the first time in the 80 years of public service broadcasting that it is in the thick of a major controversy. It has always faced challenges that were at once conceptual and contextual. For one thing, difficulties with defining PSB have led to the concept being understood in a multitude of different ways (Syvertsen, 1999, pp. 5–6; see also Jakubowicz, 2001). For another, changing contexts of PSB operation have always affected the shape, nature and objectives of that media institution and positioned it in society and on the media scene in a variety of ways. As a result, there was hardly a time in the eight decades of PSB's existence when it was not 'in transition'.

At a policy level, difficulties with defining PSB and the changing historical context for its operation have produced several critical junctures for this media organisation, requiring a reappraisal of its identity, goals and functions (see e.g. Head, 1988, Blumler, 1992; Syvertsen, 1992; Achille & Miège, 1994, McKinsey & Company, 1999). Today, we are at yet another critical juncture for public service broadcasting. For example, Recommendation 1641 on public service broadcasting, adopted by the Parliamentary Assembly of the Council of Europe in January 2004, minces no words in stating that PSB 'is under threat. It is challenged by political and economic interests, by increasing competition from commercial media, by media concentrations and by financial difficulties. It is also faced with the challenge of adapting to globalisation and the new technologies'.

This is not to deny that there are countries where a degree of consensus concerning PSB has been achieved, and it is not seriously challenged. Nevertheless, even in those countries the consensus may be breaking down and change may be in the offing. While some protest that 'Public service broadcasting is not dead yet' (Steemers, 2003), others ask whether there is still a reason for its continued existence

Richard Collins (2002, p. 1) asks precisely the question 'Why continue with Public Service Broadcasting?' and seeks to explain the reasons why it is being posed:

Why is reassessment of Public Service Broadcasting (PSB) now so pervasive? There are two reasons, both associated with failure. First, the notion that market failure in broadcasting is over and that technological change makes PSB unnecessary. Second, the belief that PSB is failing – whether this notional failure is manifested in falling ratings, elite criticism or the sense that PSB has 'dumbed down' its programming.

In this chapter we propose briefly to analyse the process of change which has led to the present situation. In this context, we will examine different schools of thought on how PSB should redefine its tasks and obligations to remain relevant. We will then look at media policy *vis-à-vis* public service broadcasting at the national and European levels to ascertain the extent to which it favours (or not) any particular form of PSB readjustment to new realities, and what prospects this creates for its long-term survival and development, especially in terms of its distinctiveness and financing.

Public Service Broadcasting in a Changing Europe
In order fully to comprehend the present situation, it will be useful to go back briefly to the origins of public service broadcasting and trace, in very general terms, the process of change which has unfolded since then.

We may identify three main motives behind the creation of public service broadcasting, or the transformation of state into public service broadcasting:

- Paternalistic – as in the UK, where PSB was originally born in 1926 in the form of the BBC, an independent[2] public corporation with a public-service remit, understood in part as playing a clearly normative role in the country's cultural, moral and political life, and as promoting 'the development of the majority in ways thought desirable by the minority' (Williams, 1968, p. 117);
- Democratising – as in some other Western European countries (e.g. France or Italy), where erstwhile state broadcasting organisations began to be transformed into public service broadcasters in the 1960s and 1970s, a time when State (government) control of the then monopoly broadcasters was no longer tenable and a way was sought to associate them more closely with the civil society and turn them into autonomous PSB organisations;
- Systemic – as in West Germany after World War II, Spain, Portugal and Greece in the 1970s, and in Central and Eastern Europe after 1989, when change of the broadcasting system was part and parcel of broader political change, typically transition to democracy after an authoritarian or totalitarian system.

We will leave aside the state of PSB in post-Communist countries (see Jakubowicz, 2003), as well as the many differences between PSB systems in different countries (and especially the fact that in Southern Europe – Greece, Portugal, Spain, Italy – real emancipation of public service broadcasters from direct, 'hands-on' political control has been prevented by 'political clientelism', 'state paternalism' and 'partitocrazia'; see Statham, 1996; Hibberd, 2001; Hallin & Papathanassopoulos, 2002; Papatheodorou & Machin, 2003). Concentrating on the origins of public service broadcasting in Western Europe, one can point to some fundamental features shared by all these systems, stemming from the historical circumstances in which they were born. PSB is always very much a product of a particular historical period, closely attuned in its fundamental principles and goals of operation to the social, cultural and technological realities of the time. Hence, some participants in the debate argue today that the challenge is to preserve PSB – described by Silvo (2003, p. 3) as one of 'the most invaluable socio-political inventions of the Western democracies in the 20th century' – in a form suited to the conditions of the 21st century.

First of all, PSB originally emerged at a time of 'an economy of scarcity' in broadcasting. As a monopoly broadcaster,[3] it was naturally forced to develop a generalist orientation for its programme services and assume a universal service obligation. It was able to operate undisturbed by any competition and have a captive audience deprived of any choice.

Secondly, public service broadcasting was everywhere what Van den Bulck (2001, p. 54) has called 'a typical modernist project of the cultural elite'. PSB in general appears to be the very epitome of the Modern Project, with its roots in the Age of Enlightenment, which saw the intellectual maturation of the humanist belief in reason as the supreme guiding principle in the affairs of humankind. The belief was that the 'truth' revealed thereby could be applied in the political and social spheres to 'correct' problems and 'improve' the political and social condition of humankind, and thus create a new and better society. At the root of this thinking is the belief in the perfectibility of humankind (Szacki, 2002). These could be described as the philosophical underpinnings of the concept of public service broadcasting and its Reithian ethos.

Thirdly, public service broadcasting emerged during what McQuail (2000) has called the 'public service' phase of media policy development in Western European countries that reached its apex in the 1970s. It was dedicated to the achievement of cultural and social goals (mainly in broadcasting) and also to the provision of 'communication welfare'[4] by ensuring the social responsibility of the print media and limiting the power of monopoly owners of the media. The ultimate goal was protection of the public interest and enhancement of democracy. PSB was thus a product of what might be called collectivistic, social-democratic social arrangements (the Welfare State), assigning an important role to the State in providing for the satisfaction of the needs of the individual. An important element of this was the culture of 'non-commercialism': 'the political and cultural forces ranged against private exploitation of broadcasting were strong and the main available model of commercialism, that prevailing in the USA, was not viewed with much favour by most social and political elites' (McQuail, 1986, p. 153).

And finally, despite its 'fundamentally democratic thrust' (in that it made available to all virtually the whole spectrum of public life and extended the universe of discourse), and the original purpose for its introduction to introduce social equality in access to information and all other content, it was a system based on unequal and asymmetrical relations between broadcasters and the audience. In this system of representative communicative democracy, power accrued 'to the representatives, not those whom they represent' (Scannell, 1989, pp. 163–164).

As shown above, the audience also stood in an unequal and asymmetrical relation to the state and the cultural elite involved in the social institution of public service broadcasting. Both the state and the cultural elite had varying degrees of control of the nature and contents of programming reaching that audience. Far-reaching social divisions and stratification, also in educational and cultural terms, led to popular acceptance of that situation at the time.

Very few of the original circumstances of PSB development remain today. There has, of course, been profound media and socio-cultural change since then. Kopper (2000, 2002) lists 'spheres of change' in European media: technological change and convergence; progressive fusion of public and private spheres and of information and entertainment; commodification; changing structures and functions of the media; economics and financing; visuality, interactivity, etc. Raboy (1998) lists three sets of parallel developments directly affecting PSB: explosion of channel capacity, disintegration of the state broadcasting model with the collapse of the Socialist bloc, and the upsurge in market broadcasting in the countries with former public service monopolies. He adds that the unfolding structural change in broadcasting involves an ideological dimension (circumstances are not favourable to suggesting measures that depend on increased involvement of the State), and a socio-cultural one (changing needs and expectations of the audiences and the individuals who compose them).

Some of the cultural and ideological reasons for changing approaches to PSB are brought into sharp relief by Bardoel and Brants (2003). They note that the Dutch policy discourse on role and functions of public service broadcasting has shown 'a further increase and refinement of the social responsibility concept in light of social (individualisation) and economic (competition) changes affecting public broadcasting. There is clearly more attention to the audience-as-consumers, and programmes should thus not only have quality but also attractiveness'. They detect four general tendencies and shifts:

- From political to cultural motives, i.e. from predominantly political motives (related to basic values as communication freedom and democracy) towards mainly cultural motives (related to preserving national culture and identity) and greater concern for choice, authenticity, creativity and quality of programming;
- From collectivism to individualism, with policy primarily individualist and citizen-centred, while in previous periods it was more collectivist and state-oriented. Issues of importance are citizen and consumer protection, greater concern for access of citizens to the entire broadcasting system, and the maintenance of pluralist and independent programming for an increasingly diversifying society;
- From ambiguous to positive assessment of economic and market forces. With liberalisation of the media sector, the market mechanism is by now considered to induce a more efficient use of resources and an expansion of choice;
- From purely national to also minority cultures, with more attention to minority groups and different cultures. It was also felt that the public system had to be more attractive to the young who seemed to be more interested in commercial than in public channels.

Bardoel and Brants comment that the old, modernist paradigm – with freedom and equality as the core values – is being replaced by a more postmodernist approach. There is more room for individual cultures, styles, and tastes and less for paternalistic policies. This is highlighted by many authors, including for example Syvertsen (1999) who noted an evolution of the definition of PSB from (i) 'public service' in the sense of a public utility; to (ii) broadcasting in the service of the public sphere; and finally to (iii) broadcasting in the service of the listener/viewer, that is to say broadcasting whose prime purpose is to satisfy the interests and preferences of individual consumers rather than the needs of the collective, the citizenry. Attallah (2000) notes a similar evolution of the concept of PSB in Canada. After Umberto Eco, Ociepka (2003) describes the two original concepts of public service television identified by Syvertsen as 'paleo-television', now buried deep in history, and the third one as 'neo-television'.

In all, technological change, market evolution and socio-cultural change have far-reaching consequences for the context and rationale of PSB operation. We will subsume these changes under two headings: convergence and marketisation. They may not do full justice to the complexity of these processes, but do highlight perhaps their most important dimensions.

Convergence

According to the European Commission's *Green Book on Convergence* (1997), the process described by this term leads to the ability of different network platforms to carry essentially similar kinds of services. Mueller (1999) sees convergence as a take-over of all forms of media by one technology: digital computers. The computing power of information technology invests the digital media with the ability to process content potentially without any restrictions. Telecommunication networks provide diverse and distant people with connectibility and access to content anywhere. Digitisation additionally makes possible signal compression, reprocessibility of content as data, text, audio and video and its transference across distribution networks. This changes or eliminates constraints heretofore limiting communication, such as bandwidth, interactivity and network architecture.

We may thus identify the following main features of convergent digital communication:

- Interactivity: interchangeable sender/receive roles;
- Pull technology (on-demand communication and access to content, i.e. 'take what you want, when you want it') gradually replaces push technology ('take what you are given, when it is available');
- Asynchronous communication: content can be stored and await the user's decision to access it, ultimately doing away with traditional linear-time delivery of content in electronic media (unless it is wanted or needed);
- Individualisation/personalisation (customisation): both the sender and the user are able to guide communication flows in such a way that the sender can address individual users with content selected according to different criteria, or users can select content from what is on offer;
- Portability of terminals and mobility: the ability to receive content while on the move, as well as the ability to receive specific, time-sensitive and often location-sensitive information;

- Disintermediation (elimination of intermediaries, e.g. media organisations, as anyone can offer information and other content to be directly accessed by users and receivers) and 'neo-intermediation' (emergence of new intermediaries, especially on the Internet, capable of offering new services or packaging content in new ways);
- Development of new payment and micro-payment systems (moving from credit cards to 'click and pay', required to sell non-tangible goods over the Internet);
- 'Anyone, Anything, Anytime, Anywhere' – the ultimate goal of access to anyone from any place and at any time, and to all existing content stored in electronic memory.

Eli M. Noam (1995) describes television as developing in three stages: (1) Privileged TV (a handful of channels, behaving in an oligopolistic way); (2) Multichannel TV, characterised by greater commercialism, greater diversity, and greater specialisation in channels; (3) Cyber-Television – distributed, decentralised cyber-television. Galperin and Bar (2002) list the following 'three generations' of broadcasting: 1st generation – Fordist television (one way broadcasting of a few channels); 2nd generation – Multichannel television (one way broadcasting of multiple video channels); 3rd generation – Interactive TV (two-way delivery of multiple video channels and other services).

Challenges to public service broadcasting arising out of this process of change are outlined in Table 1.

The situation described in the last column of Table 1 would put an end to traditional public service broadcasting in the form of linear 'flow' channels, assembled by a broadcaster and broadcast as point-to-multipoint communication. At the present stage, however, it is too early to predict whether, and, if at all, how soon, broadcasting as such will disappear,[5] so we will leave this matter out of account here.

The impact of convergence on the media goes beyond technology and extends to social and political issues: 'Reinventing regulatory frameworks in an era of convergence is all about redefining national competitive advantage within a global information economy, the digital economy [will determine] how countries can restructure to participate in the new sources of wealth creation and of economic growth.' (Cutler, 1998) In this sense, convergence constitutes yet another stage of redefining the media into a sector of the economy, and media policy from a 'cultural' into an 'industrial' one.

Marketisation
Transition to post-industrial society and what is now seen as the need to develop a knowledge-based economy and Information Society have created an 'industrial imperative' for media policy (Kleinsteuber, 1986). That and the general ideological evolution of society have led to a shift in perception and definition of the media in the area of public policy. With the old social-democratic social arrangements now a thing of the past, and with the media seen as crucially important for technological and economic development (Ostergaard, 1998), policy in this area has been redefined sharply, with primacy given to the market as the driving force of media development. This is reflected, for example, in the European Commission's (1999) Communication *Principles and Guidelines for the Community's Audiovisual Policy In The Digital Age* which states that 'the basic rationale' for regulation to meet general interest objectives 'should be the

Table 1: Challenges to PSB as Electronic Communication Evolves

	1st Generation Broadcasters[a]	2nd Generation Broadcasters[b]	3rd Generation Broadcasters[c]	Non-linear, on-demand communication, 'pull technology'
Funding	Public Advertising	Advertising Subscription	Subscription Advertising	VOD, Pay-per-view, micro-payments, commission on transactions, etc.
Output	General	General (but more entertainment) Premium Pay-TV	Thematic	No, or few 'flow channels', most content (except for live news and live coverage of events) available on demand
Licence Conditions	Strong	Moderate	Weak	Unknown at this stage
Programme Expenditure	Mainly originated	Mainly originated, but a lot of acquired	Mainly acquired	Unknown at this stage
Challenge to PSB	None, PSB monopoly or domination	Loss of monopoly on audience. Need to compete for audiences and (in most cases) advertising revenue	Loss of monopoly on most 'PSB genres'	Channels, schedules disappear; PSB broadcasters may have gradually to evolve into public service content providers (PSCP)
Effect of challenge	None	PSB identity, funding and legi-timisation crisis, need to redefine remit and the way it is pursued	Need to reinvent institutional and financial guarantees of 'basic supply,'if still required	

[a] Mainly public; [b] Mainly commercial; [c] Mainly new digital thematic channels.
Adapted from The Impact of Digital Television on the Supply of Programmes (Anderson 1998).

failure of the market, real or potential, to reach these objectives (except in certain cases, such as the protection of minors or copyright, where market forces are not adapted to the achievement of such objectives).'

This is indicative of what McQuail (2000) calls a 'new paradigm' of media policy emerging in Western European countries since the 1980s, oriented more to economic goals than to social and political welfare and concentrating primarily on such issues as continuation of commercial competition and technological innovation, openness and transparency of ownership and control, maximum access for all and choice for consumers. This phase is marked by deregulation and removal of as many constraints to the operation of the media market as possible. Policy-makers and regulators accept the *de facto* commoditisation and commercialisation of mass media in the hope that this will set the stage for the media's expected contribution to economic and technological growth (Ostergaard, 1998). Accordingly, current developments in television and audiovisual services in Europe are spurred on almost exclusively by commercial motives and private investment. Moreover, the principle of non-commercialism has been effectively transformed into one particular minority value. The old anti-commercial paradigm has almost disappeared (McQuail, 1998). The very notion of the public interest in mass communication is in question (Brants, Hermes & van Zoonen, 1998). If Europe is to move forward in its economic and technological development, it is argued, the process must be driven by private entrepreneurs. Commercialism is the engine of change and privatisation is seen by some as best serving the public interest.

Thus, the terms of the debate about the future of European communications and the balance of power between the main actors involved have, over the last decade or so, shifted decisively under the impact of two parallel movements:

- the ascendancy of marketisation policies within both the European Union and its major member countries,
- and accelerating convergence of the computing, telecommunications and audio-visual industries.

Murdock and Golding (1999, p. 3) define marketisation as 'all those policy interventions designed to increase the freedom of action of private corporations and to institute corporate goals and organisational procedures as the yardsticks against which the performance of all forms of cultural enterprise are judged'. It comprises privatisation, liberalisation and corporatisation (i.e. encouraging or compelling organisations still within the public sector to pursue market opportunities and institute corporate forms of organisation) (see also Murdock, 2001). Richard Collins (2002) confirms this trend by pointing out that 'PSB is also the victim of pervasive disenchantment with public provision of goods and services itself' and adding that 'the striking efficiency gains that liberalization has realized in a host of sectors from telecommunications to air transport, from retailing to energy means that more and more credence is given to Adam Smith's model of the public interest being best achieved through the pursuit of a host of individual private interests.'[6] The European Commission (1999) whose approach to media policy could be seen as having foreshadowed the 'new paradigm' (see Jakubowicz, 2004)[7], has accordingly formulated the following view:

> The future of the dual system of broadcasting in Europe, comprising public and private broadcasters, depends on the role of public service broadcasters being reconciled with the principles of fair competition and the operation of a free market, in accordance with the Treaty, as interpreted by Protocol n° 32 on the system of public broadcasting in the Member States.

Though this referred primarily to the need to adjust PSB to EU competition law, the implications of such a sentence are quite chilling.

Taken together, social, economic, cultural and technological change, combined with ideological evolution, have contributed to eliminating or reversing practically all the sets of circumstances which originally helped shape public service broadcasting. Table 2 provides a non exhaustive overview of these changes.

In these changing circumstances, the continued existence of publicly-controlled broadcasters dedicated to providing 'communication welfare' is being challenged more and more – not only by commercial competitors and some politicians, but also, to some extent, by the audience. The result is a crisis of legitimation for PSB broadcasters. For the first time in their history, public service broadcasters no longer seem able to set, or seriously influence, the agenda or terms of the debate concerning its vital interests. More than that, it largely seems unable take part in this debate in a forceful, active, persuasive way.

Not so the commercial broadcasters. As attested by the number of complaints against PSB they have lodged with the European Commission (see Ward, 2002, 2003), they are on the attack and could be said to pursue goals in the following four generally defined areas:

Table 2: Evolving socio-cultural and technological context of PSB operation

Circumstances of PSB emergence	Current social and audiovisual landscape
'Economy of scarcity' in radio - generalist programming and a universal service obligation, 'take what you are given' mode of communication	Multichannel, increasingly specialised broadcasting, personalised online communications, audience control of communication
Top-down 'push' communication	Arrival of 'pull', on-demand communication; everyone a potential communicator
No competition	Growing competition
A modernist project	Post-modernism
Collectivistic, social democratic Welfare State, culture of non-commercialism	Neo-liberalism, individualism, marketisation and commercialism
Public service, financed from 'solidarity funding' (licence fees)	Dwindling legitimacy of the public sector and its involvement in satisfaction of individual needs
Unequal, asymmetrical relations between audience, broadcasters, cultural elite and the state, legitimated by social divisions and stratification	Levelling of living and educational standards and democratisation lead to rejection of such asymmetrical relations
PSB part of a media system largely confined to the nation-state	PSB operating on a globalised media market

- 'Semantic' – public service *broadcasting* should remain just that, best in the traditional mould of generalist 'one-size-fits-all' channels;
- Programming: PSB should be restricted to programme genres which commercial broadcasters find commercially unrewarding:
- Financial: no advertising money for PSB, which should be funded from public funds;
- Technological: ICTs and the Information Society will not develop without investments by the private sector; those investments should be protected so PSB should not branch out into the new technologies, or only marginally so;

The commercial sector (see VPRT et al, 2003) also intimates that PSB is no longer really necessary, in that public and commercial broadcasters offer increasingly similar content and fulfil increasingly similar social and market functions. The strategy of the commercial sector is to condemn PSB to marginalisation and ultimate extinction by, as noted above: (1) pressuring governments and international organisations to adopt highly restrictive definitions of the PSB remit, confining it to a role of a niche broadcaster, with a view to then using these definitions to prevent any change; (2) blocking PSB's entry to, and use of, new technologies; (3) using domestic and EU competition law to deprive PSB of advertising revenue (see also Association of Commercial Television et al., 2004) and – ultimately – of the licence fee, to be replaced by subscription (Broadcasting Policy Group, 2004). It is acknowledged that the market may not deliver all 'socially valuable programming', but – despite the failure of the New Zealand project based on the same principles (Lealand, 2002; Norris, 2004) – it is proposed that it is possible to have PSB without PSB institutions, as 'PSB content' can be commissioned, out of public funds, from all broadcasters, as well as Internet and 3G telephone content providers (Broadcasting Policy Group, 2004). In some countries, this strategy is gaining influential political allies. One such example is Poland, where the Civic Platform, a centre-right political party, has sponsored the development of policy proposals which in effect amount to the abolition of PSB (see Bierzynski, 2004).

Rationale for PSB: Continuity and Change

The rationale for the existence of PSB has so far grown and evolved over the years in three distinct stages. In the first stage, the original role of the monopoly PSB broadcaster was to provide 'communication welfare' and a 'basic supply' – in short, to provide all genres of programming for all groups of the audience, in order to satisfy every need.

In the second stage, after the emergence of the first generation of commercial broadcasters (typically offering generalist channels), this rationale was supplemented by the obligation to provide a quality alternative to commercial broadcasting (as a 'merit good' that audiences would, given a choice, probably not demand or sustain), and to redress market failure by providing content commercial broadcasters did not offer because it was commercially unrewarding. That is how it retained its 'distinctiveness.'

In the third stage, the situation changed again with the emergence of multi-channel broadcasting and of a second generation of commercial broadcasters with a different business model, allowing them to offer thematic channels. At least on big markets, commercial channels now provide many elements of 'basic supply' content which may also meet minority needs, though it is also true that in the UK, for example, arts, education, multi-cultural programmes, investigative current affairs programming, natural history programmes and the like continue to be under-supplied by commercial broadcasters, and that, apart from sport, there is little first-run programming on multi-channel television which was made specifically for a UK audience (*ITC Consultation ...*, 2000). Of course, this content is often available for additional payment or on thematic satellite channels, reaching minuscule audiences, but it can be argued that the audience can (though with extra effort and expense) obtain most 'PSB content' from commercial channels.

This is a major change which shows that one of the ways of defining PSB – in terms of the programme genres it broadcasts – is no longer valid. It also requires a redefinition of such terms as 'market failure' and 'distinctiveness', which have traditionally also referred primarily to programme formats and content.

Some attempts to redefine 'market failure' and the way PSB corrects it, have been rather lame: they portrayed PSB content as being the same, but better[8] than in the case of commercial broadcasters, or PSB itself as performing the same functions as the private sector, but in a different way.[9]

In fact, correcting 'market failure' means somewhat different things on different markets. On smaller markets, it may retain much of its traditional meaning of the provision of genres and programme types that are not available elsewhere. On big, media-rich markets, it increasingly means the provision of such content as free-to-air universally accessible radio and television, while elsewhere it may be available for additional payment. In a long-term perspective, it is important to remember that the commercial sector may not, due to growing competition, persist in providing 'PSB content' for very long. It has thus been made clear that neither Channel 3 nor Channel 5 in the UK would probably be able to 'deliver PSB in the longer term, well beyond digital switchover' (*ITC Consultation ...*, 2000, pp. 8–9; OFCOM, 2004). Therefore, correcting market failure also means that, while commercial broadcasters may change their programming concepts, PSB broadcasters have the obligation to serve as 'the provider of last resort' by guaranteeing that 'basic supply' programming will always be easily and universally available. On all markets it means, in addition, that this programming will be domestically produced and operate within the cultural, historical and other frames of reference within which the audience actually lives. Moreover, as noted by Bob Collins (2003), the difference is not just the presence of this content, but the entire schedule: 'the public service character and obligations are of the essence and must inform the very fabric and texture of the broadcaster. ... It also follows that the public character is reflected in the overall schedule and is not something which inheres in individual programmes which are then distributed across a schedule, somewhat like sultanas in a fruitcake.'

And thirdly, the rationale for PSB today also encompasses the fact that it acquires growing importance as an element of 'structural regulation' oriented to shaping the broadcasting and electronic media system as a whole. Already in the second stage it was recognised that though PSB no longer defines the market by itself, it can play a vital role in influencing it: 'If the PSB is healthy, with distinctive programmes and meaningful share, it can be a strong shaper of the broadcasting ecology' (McKinsey & Company, 1999, p. 16; 2004). It can keep audience demand for high-quality programming alive in the market and thus produce a 'demonstration effect' by encouraging commercial broadcasters to imitate PSB distinctiveness and emulate programme genres and formats successfully pioneered by public service broadcasters.

This role of PSB is growing in importance, as policy-makers and regulators find 'behavioural regulation' less effective and rely more and more on structural regulation in pursuing their four principal objectives (1) ensuring access to networks and services (2) setting standards (3) promoting quality, and (4) ensuring a healthy, technologically up-to-date industry:

> In most countries, the primary regulatory mechanism [of structural regulation] is the funding of one or more public service broadcasters (PSBs), which are mandated to deliver key aspects of quality and diversity to the national audience and to selected audience segments. Most countries around the world continue to support public service broadcasting, primarily through the licensing of specific public service channels (McKinsey, 2002, p 4).

Today, as we face the arrival of the Information Society, we are in a fourth stage of redefining the rationale for PSB. By now, the issue has gone far beyond the matter of programming content on generalist channels. It concerns a whole range of questions, pertaining to:

- The PSB remit;
- Programme and content formats;
- Technologies used for delivery of programming and content;
- PSB and the market;
- PSB funding and competition law.

The overarching question is to what extent and in which of its aspects PSB needs, and will be allowed, to change – both to remain true to itself and to keep abreast of developments in society and on the media scene and to remain attuned to the needs of the audience. The strategy employed by opponents of PSB amounts to an attempt to prevent its evolution and modernisation by holding it to remits and definitions formulated in an altogether different historical era. This is justified on competition grounds with the argument that 'a dual system of broadcasting at national level can only function if there is a clear delimitation of tasks and financing methods' (VPRT et al. 2003). Any departure from the old definition or any extension of services or use of new means of delivery is condemned as 'mission creep.' It must be noted, at the same time, that this entire campaign amounts to a self-fulfilling prophecy: if PSB can be prevented from modernising, it certainly will very soon become a relic of the past, fit only to be consigned to the rubbish heap of history. And that appears to be the intention.

The questions listed above cannot easily be separated, but for the sake of clarity we will try, in general terms, to examine the debate about them one by one.

Remit

Three main schools of thought may be distinguished here:

- 'Pure Public Service'
- 'New Tasks for a New Age,'
- 'All-embracing Public Service.'

These, of course, are ideal types and elements of each may sometimes be found in the other approaches. These schools of thought manifest some affinity with the ideological stances described at the outset.

The first school of thought can be further subdivided into two approaches: that of supporters of 'true' public service broadcasting (Pure PSB-1[10]), and that of commercial broadcasters and media in general whose only real concern seems to be removal or marginalisation of PSB as a market competitor ('Pure PSB-2'). The net effect of the implementation of both approaches would be the positioning of PSB as a complement to commercial broadcasting, dedicated to redressing whatever is left of market failure as it used to be understood.

The 'New Tasks for a New Age' approach seeks to identify new tasks or redefine old tasks in keeping with the requirements of new circumstances. In general, it bespeaks an awareness of the need for more social actors and processes than just market forces. Public service broadcasters themselves (see *Media with a purpose*, 2002) signal an awareness of the need to go beyond their traditional obligations, for example by

- Spreading awareness of the additional (both supra- and sub-national) dimensions of political citizenship, as well as individual and societal co-responsibility for developments at these other levels;
- Provision of more in-depth information on the situation prevailing on the international scene and in individual foreign, and especially other European, countries, helping develop the international/global public sphere and serving as a watchdog of international bodies and organisations;
- Engaging, where appropriate, in 'peace broadcasting' and promotion of post-conflict reconciliation;
- Reflecting the increasingly multi-ethnic and multicultural societies, without unduly accentuating differences or 'ghettoising' different social and ethnic groups by locking them into 'walled gardens' of programme services, dedicated solely to them.

'New tasks' refer also to new ways of performing the traditional role of PSB in promoting societal cohesion, now interpreted also as promoting digital inclusion. Thus, PSB should be active in all areas of new multimedia where the audiences will be in the future. Public broadcasters must do so by:

- developing strong and recognisable programme and institutional brands, serving as a beacon for people among the multitude of new content providers;
- being available on all digital platforms, and thus attracting people to gain access to them;

- supporting traditional broadcasting content with Internet and interactive resources;
- providing multimedia interactive services, independent and complimentary web services;
- serving as a trusted third party, a reliable and trustworthy guide to content in the online world;
- actively promoting digital media literacy and awareness of the tools of the information society, in particular the use of Internet;
- providing content in local and minority languages in order to encourage minorities to use the tools of the information society;
- promoting open standards in API, CA/CI, etc. (*Media with a purpose*, 2002).

Another concept advanced by PSB broadcasters in this context is that of 'portality', with the totality of the PSB organisation's offer across different programme and service formats and different delivery methods (including the on-line media) serving as a 'portal' to a wide-ranging universe of content (Silvo, 2003).

For her part, Barbara Thomass (2003, pp. 34–35) seeks to redefine some of the old objectives with a view to their performance in the Knowledge Society and points to the need to reconfigure PSB delivery methods to make this possible:

> The old triad of information, education and entertainment will have to be modified and enlarged [and] reconceived as knowledge. ... The principle behind this education ... could be well transferred to the notion of knowledge as participation. The capability to use information for social action and activities in the economic, as in the political sphere, is of central importance for the Knowledge Society.

If the all-encompassing notion of education is altered to the need for a flexible concept of knowledge, this means that individualised forms of supplies must be possible ... it no longer makes sense to reduce broadcasting to mass communication. Video on demand, enhanced programming services, individualised news bulletins, etc. are forms of content delivery which should be involved in the knowledge communication strategy of PSB. (Thomass 2003)

Thomass also believes that the Knowledge Society will set in train a revitalisation of the public sphere into a deliberative model, emphasising inclusion, transparency and access. If the public sphere is to be understood as a space where citizens speak out and express their interests towards the political system, and thereby try to influence and control it, the media must serve as informant, controller and also as a platform for participation and debate. The job of PSB will therefore be to ensure participation of all parts of the public sphere, of all groups of civil society, in the public discourse.

This point is also made by Kearns (2003) who said that the old Reithian description of the remit should be extended:

> Our citizens now need to be educated, informed, entertained and *empowered* [my emphasis] ... the possibilities of online interactive communication offer a potential way out of the crisis in democratic communication ... online [public service] media

offer the opportunity of a new democratic public sphere ... the BBC needs to view itself not just as a communications channel but also as a provider of social space. It needs to provide participation spaces so that it serves the function of empowering citizens. Now, when the processes of our democracy do not appear to be working well, the purpose should be to help the informed and educated voices of the people be more effectively and regularly heard ... there is a need for a Public Service Communications to work toward universal access to the services provided. Not just in terms of access to technology (although this is vitally important) but also access to the tools needed to access the promise of the online world ... there is a need for A Civic Commons in Cyberspace. A trusted platform for citizens to deliberate, to come together and to be heard.

The 'All-Embracing Public Service' approach calls for extending the concept of public service broadcasting among other things in terms of content (both full-fledged public service and non-public service activities). This seems to be supported by public service broadcasters themselves (see e.g. *Media with a purpose*, 2002), the Council of Europe and the European Union.

Recommendation Rec (2003) 9 on Measures to Promote the Democratic and Social Contribution of Digital Broadcasting, adopted by the Committee of Ministers (2003) of the Council of Europe, says in an appendix that PSB 'should preserve its special social remit, including a basic general service that offers news, educational, cultural and entertainment programmes aimed at different categories of the public.'

As for the European Union, complaints against what was regarded as State aid to PSB (Harrison & Woods, 2001; Ward, 2002, 2003) have forced the organisation to develop a view of PSB based – in view of the Community's determination to treat all media, including public service ones, as actual or potential business operations – on the application to public service broadcasting of Treaty provisions concerning protection of competition. That involved a prolonged debate within the EU, including a stage when the EU seemed to be backing the 'Pure PSB' approach, based on defining PSB in terms of selected programme genres (see DG IV, 1998). Finally, the European Commission – under pressure from member states and other institutions of the EU – (see Tongue 1996; European Parliament, 1996; European Commission 1998; Council, 1999; European Commission, 2001; Harrison & Woods, 2001; Coppieters, 2002) – came down in favour of the 'All-Embracing PSB' approach. As reflected in a variety of documents, the EU view can be summed up as follows:

■ PSB is directly related to the democratic, social and cultural needs of society and media pluralism;
■ PSB has a comprehensive mission: wide range of programming in order to address society as a whole, including a suitable balance of entertainment, culture, spectacles and education and a natural overlap with commercial broadcasting in popular programming: sport, comedy, drama, news and current affairs (i.e. PSB is no longer defined as a broadcaster dedicated to providing selected programme genres);
■ PSB can legitimately seek to reach wide audiences;

- PSB is important in promoting new audiovisual and information services and the new technologies;
- PSB can legitimately be engaged in both public service and non-public service (commercial) activities;
- PSB can legitimately compete on the market, as long as public funding does not distort competition.

Programme and Content Formats

This concerns primarily the question whether PSB broadcasters can go beyond generalist terrestrial channels and offer thematic channels, as well as other formats (e.g. Video on Demand) and on-line content.

Complaints by the commercial sector to the European Commission against Germany and the UK, concerning PSB thematic channels (Kinderkanal and Phoenix in Germany and BBC News 24) argued, among other things, that thematic channels, by definition catering to just a part of the audience, went beyond the definition of services of general interest (Ward, 2002, 2003). The same argument is used with regard to Internet activities of PSB broadcasters. Objections are raised against such activities on the grounds that they violate the fundamental PSB principle of universality of content and audience.

This view is rejected by supporters of PSB. For example, according to the Council of Europe Recommendation cited above, 'the means to fulfil the public service remit may include the provision of new specialised channels, for example in the field of information, education and culture, and of new interactive services, for example EPGs and programme-related on-line services.'

Technologies used for delivery of programming and content

As we have already seen, the use of new information and communication technologies by PSB organisations is challenged by the commercial sector and other opponents of PSB. Meanwhile, public service broadcasters themselves call for extending the concept of PSB also in a technological sense (presence on all significant platforms, since PSB 'has to follow its audiences wherever they tend to look for content' – Thomass, 2003, p. 34, see also Wessberg, 2000), and in terms of its relationship to its audience (e.g. provision of a 'personalised public service' via on-line delivery).

The prevailing trend of international opinion supports these changes. The Recommendation of CoE Committee of Ministers (1996) states that 'public service broadcasters should play a central role in the transition process to digital terrestrial broadcasting.' That is also the EU view, as we saw above. Thomass (2003) argues that the aim of social integration can no longer be supported only by the means of broadcast media, with their ability to reach millions, but also must include all the new possibilities of online transmission. The Internet, digital distribution, interactive services and wireless services – all of these are means wherein a public service orientated content must be available for users.

Accordingly, Thomass formulates the following principles:

- PSB must be available on all technical platforms of distribution.
- Platforms and Electronic Programme Guides (EPG's) must give priority to PSB.
- Integration is realised no longer via the appeal to the largest possible audience for one programme, but rather of one branded 'type' of contents and services.
- Integration also means leading those who are not integrated in the knowledge society to the new structures offering knowledge.
- PSB must provide help for orientation within the market of content and services.

The strategy of opponents of PSB appears to be one of setting a semantic trap: public service broadcasting should remain public service *broadcasting*: the very name suggests that it should not move to the next stage of development when, as noted above, digitisation is set to change the traditional mode of mass communication beyond recognition. The answer to that is provided, among others, by Kearns (2003): 'Social and technological change means facing the challenge of renewal - from public service *broadcasting* to public service [online] *communications* ... the BBC and the entire Public Service Communications community needs to move away from the broadcast paradigm of content delivered to a mass public and toward the usage and participation paradigm of the network age' (my emphases)

PSB and the Market
This issue again unites supporters of both versions of 'Pure PSB.' Some prefer PSB organisations to be untarnished by any contact with the market and commerce and to receive sufficient financing to be able to concentrate on programme production without the need for additional advertising or other commercial revenues. The commercial sector opposes PSB involvement in entrepreneurial activities, especially in new, non-traditional areas, for fear of market foreclosure and competition. This is why VPRT et al. (2003) protest against what they see as the expansion of public broadcasters in other segments of the market: the online sector and into e-commerce; the TV production business; or cross-border digital satellite television.

On the other hand, most governments accept advertising as a source of revenue for PSB organisations. In some cases (as in Spain and Portugal or Belgium), public service organisations are mainly dependent on advertising, with no licence fee revenue.

In at least one case, a PSB organisation is actively encouraged to become a global media market player. This concerns the BBC, which, though it carries no advertising, derives almost 25% of its budget from commercial revenue via its commercial arm BBC Worldwide. Its Royal Charter expressly allows the BBC to engage in entrepreneurial activity.[11]

In any case, it is clear that it is no longer possible to isolate PSB from the market. Digital technology changes the value chain in the audiovisual sector and decides for the PSB broadcaster when to continue concentrating on programme production and channel assembly, or whether also to become involved in other elements of the value chain, exploiting other possibilities of entrenching its position. Also, in the digital world, more and more delivery networks and digital gateways will be controlled by commercial entities. PSB organisations will have to enter into cooperation and alliances with such entities or they may find they are cut off from important segments of the audience.

As long as core programme activities of PSB organisations are properly non-commercial and devoted to implementing the remit, additional commercial and economic activities undertaken by PSB organisations are – assuming fair trading rules are observed – less likely to introduce the commercial logic into programming decisions than advertising or sponsorship.

PSB Funding and EU Competition Law

This is another battlefield, arising on the one hand out of the exploitation by the commercial sector of EU Treaty provisions (art. 87) concerning State aid, and on the other out of the unwillingness of EU bodies to adjust its legal framework in this area to the special case of public service broadcasting – due, in part, to the ruling of the European Court of Justice in the 1974 *Sacchi* case, recognising PSB as a service.

As noted above, numerous complaints lodged by the commercial sector with the European Commission sought to use State aid rules to: (1) resolve the question of dual funding of PSB, hopefully by eliminating advertising from PSB programming; (2) promote a 'Pure PSB' regulatory model, recognising that public funding may only be used to finance 'non-commercial programming'; (3) eliminate PSB as a competitor in any field of interest to commercial broadcaster (see e.g. Association of Commercial Television et al., 2004).

The Amsterdam Protocol of 1997 and the European Commission's (2001) subsequent *Communication on the application of State aid rules to public service broadcasting* were designed to resolve the question of the compatibility of PSB with 'the principles of fair competition and the operation of a free market'. At the same time, the *Communication* in para 33. accepts a 'wide' definition of PSB, 'entrusting a given broadcaster with the task of providing balanced and varied programming in accordance with the remit, while preserving a certain level of audience, may be considered, in view of the interpretative provisions of the Protocol, legitimate under Article 86(2). Such a definition would be consistent with the objective of fulfilling the democratic, social and cultural needs of a particular society and guaranteeing pluralism, including cultural and linguistic diversity'. This is an important turnaround in EU policy. Since the adoption of this *Communication*, the European Commission has had a policy instrument to apply to this issue, enabling it to rule on some long-standing complaints by commercial broadcasters against what they perceived as distortion of competition by State aid – practically in all cases in favour of PSB. Recent rulings by the European Court of Justice have also contributed to elucidating the EU rules in terms of how competition law relates to the existence of public service broadcasting.[12]

Conclusion

It is clear that PSB organisations cannot resolve these issues – and the PSB identity crisis inherent in them – all by themselves. National and international media policy must provide an answer on how PSB may readjust to changing circumstances, and what sort of service is expected of PSB in the new circumstances, as well as how it should be performed – especially in terms of the interpretation of the remit, financing and access to new technologies.

As will be clear from the following chapters, a great deal is happening in the area of national and international policy on such issues as definition of the PSB remit, financing and PSB *vis-à-vis* the new technologies. The question is whether all this activity will indeed deliver a new concept of PSB suited to the conditions of the 21st century.

The following contributions by Marcel Betzel (Appendix to Chapter 5), Stylianos Papathanassopoulos (Chapter 6) and Minna Aslama and Trine Syvertsen (Chapter 7) tell their own story in this regard. We will also seek to address this question in Chapter 8 'Looking to the Future' at the end of this part of the book.

Notes

1. This point is eloquently made by the BBC (2004, *passim*) in its most recent manifesto *Building public value: Renewing the BBC for a digital world*: 'An economist might conclude from this that the BBC has an important role in preventing various kinds of market failure in the new digital world. Yes – but our vision is far bolder than that suggests. … Broadcasting is a civic art. It is intrinsically public in ambition and effect. We may experience it individually, but it is never a purely private transaction. To turn on a TV or radio is to enter a communal space and to be constantly aware of and influenced by that fact. This shared experience may itself represent a significant public value – the communal glue which some call *social capital*. But that is only one of many potential wider benefits. A programme may make me more likely to vote, or to look at my neighbour in a new, more positive light. … The BBC exists to create *public value*. … Public value is a measure of the BBC's contribution to the quality of life in the UK.' The BBC says in the document that it creates five main types of public value: democratic value, cultural and creative value, educational value, social and community value, global value.

2. Interestingly, it was the politicians who established the principle that public service broadcasting should be autonomous and keep an arm's length distance from the politicians. In 1933, the House of Commons confirmed that in a resolution which said: 'it would be contrary to the public interest to subject the Corporation to any control by government or by Parliament other than the control already provided for in the Charter and the Licence; that controversial matter is rightly not excluded from broadcast programmes but that governors should ensure the effective expression of all important opinion relating thereto' (quoted in Burns, 1977, p. 12).

3. Radio was born everywhere as small, private stations in competition with one another. It was then nationalized and centralized, for expressly political reasons. Whatever the extent of a PSB organization's independence, it was designed to prevent the power of broadcasting from falling into unwanted hands. So, in the UK, the Beveridge Broadcasting Committee's 1949 *Report* puts it in the following way: 'Right use of the great power of broadcasting must be safeguarded … We believe that it will be easier in practice to apply safeguards to one corporation than to several' (quoted in Heller, 1978, p. 19; see also Smith, 1979).

4. The German Constitutional Court subsequently coined the term 'basic supply' (*Grundversorgung*) to describe the provision of information and content to which everyone is entitled and which must be offered by PSB (see e.g. Holtz-Bacha, 2003).

5. Existing forecasts in this field do not venture beyond the outlining of possible 'scenarios', without committing themselves to any one of them. See *Outlook of the*

development of technologies and markets for the European Audio-visual sector up to 2010, Arthur Andersen, June 2002, http://europa.eu.int/comm/ avpolicy/ stat/tvoutlook/tvoutlook_finalreport_long.pdf (Commissioned by the European Commission); *Television and Beyond. The Next Ten Years*. London: Independent Television Commission, 2002; *Future Reflections. Four scenarios for television in 2012*. A Condensed Report of a scenario analysis study for the Future Reflections Conference. Bournemouth: Bournemouth Media School, November 2002 (with research support from the Independent Television Commission and the British Screen Advisory Council).

6. John Whittingdale, the UK Conservative Party culture spokesman, made this ideological approach very clear when he said that his party would switch off a swath of the BBC's digital services, including its website and the youth channel BBC3, if it won the next general election. He said he was 'not persuaded' of the case for a public service website and that he was 'not convinced the BBC needs to do all the things it is doing at the present', including providing 'more and more channels'. And he added: 'As a free-market Conservative, I will only support a nationalised industry if I'm persuaded that that is the only way to do it and if it were not nationalised it would not happen.' (Happold, 2003).

7. Opinion is divided on this subject. According to Michalis (1999, pp. 164–165) the EU has traditionally found it difficult to develop a regulatory regime concerning content and culture. Rollet (2002) contends that the EU pursues an 'integrated communication policy', covering both telecommunications and media institutions, which the EU has treated in a very similar way. Kaitatzi-Whitlock (1996, p. 455) says that the EU's 'media policy' is in fact an 'industrial policy', arguing on the example of abortive debates on EU-wide regulation of media concentration that it is impossible to fit 'the political and cultural issue of [media] pluralism on to the economistic Procrustean bed of the Single European Market' (see also Hirsch, Petersen, 1998; Harrison & Woods, 2001; Näränen, 2003; Llorens-Maluquer, 2002; Göktepeli, Christensen, 2002; Iosifidis, 2002). On the other hand, Ward (2003, p. 230) opposes the view that 'overtly economistic, industrial and ultimately destructive European Union policies are complicit in the demise of the public sector of broadcasting' and argues that 'the Commission has a far more sophisticated and sympathetic approach to the question of public service broadcasting in the EU'.

8. This line of reasoning has been offered by Michael Souchon: 'In producing the same type of broadcasts as others, it [PSB], it will have to try to produce them better, with stricter standards and more precision, and with more marked concern for professional ethics. Public television must broadcast the genres that the public at large expects of television (information, fiction, entertainment), but the quality must be higher than that of commercial television channels' (cited after Atkinson, 1997, p. 47).

9. See the UK Independent Review Panel's attempt to provide a rationale for PSB: 'the second principle is that some form of market failure must lie at the heart of any concept of public service broadcasting. Beyond simply using the catch-phrase that public service broadcasting must 'inform, educate and entertain', we must add 'inform, educate and entertain *in a way* which the private sector, left unregulated, would not do" (*The Future Funding of the BBC* ... 1999, p. 10; emphasis added).

10. 'Pure PSB-1' is represented by, among others, Lord Puttnam (2003): 'In the new world of the Information Society [each broadcaster] must focus on its strengths, in the case

of the Public Service broadcasters, some very specific and fairly well-honed strengths.' In his view, PSB should make a special effort to differentiate itself from the rest of television and to this end should be committed especially to local and regional programming ('local arts, local sports, indeed local events of every conceivable kind') and education: 'opportunities that never can and never will be provided, in quite the same way, by the 'market."

11. The 1996 Royal Charter allows the BBC (see Article 3 (u)) to 'enter into joint ventures or partnerships with other companies and to establish companies whose objects include any of the objects of the Corporation or whose business is capable of being carried on in such a way as to facilitate or advance any of the objects of the Corporation, and to purchase or otherwise acquire stocks, shares or securities of, and to subsidise and assist, any such company.' Article 16(1) authorizes the Corporation to 'receive all other moneys which may be obtained by or given to the Corporation or derived from any source not hereinbefore mentioned (though the BBC is to use such funds 'exclusively in furtherance of the purposes of this Our Charter') and may treat such funds and moneys either as capital or as income at its discretion.'

12. The European Court of Justice ruling (EJC, 2003) of 24 July 2003 in the *Altmark* case seems to tilt the debate on whether public funding for PSB represents 'compensation' or 'State aid' in favour of the former. According to this and other EJC rulings, financial support which merely represents compensation for public service obligations imposed by the member states does not have the characteristics of State aid. In other words, public funding cannot be regarded as State aid under Article 87 of the EC Treaty where such funding compensates for the services provided by the recipient undertakings in order to discharge public service obligations. Only public funds granted to a PSB broadcaster above and beyond the cost of discharging the remit can recognized as State aid. Thus, where the national system for funding PSB ensures the reasonableness of the compensation provided for the discharge of public service obligations within a pre-defined public service remit, there is no over-compensation, and consequently no State aid.

References

Achille, Yves & Bernard Miège (1994) 'The Limits of the Adaptation Strategies of European Public Service Television', *Media, Culture & Society*, 16(1) pp. 31–46.

Andersen Arthur (1998) *The Impact of Digital Television on the Supply of Programmes*. A Report for the European Broadcasting Union.

Association of Commercial Television in Europe et al., (2004) *Safeguarding the Future of the European Audiovisual Market*. A White Paper on the Financing and Regulation of Publicly Funded Broadcasters. Brussels

Atkinson, Dave (1997) 'Public Service Television in the Age of Competition', in Dave Atkinson, Marc Raboy (eds.) Public Service Broadcasting: the Challenges of the Twenty-first Century. Reports and Papers on Mass Communication, No. 111. Paris: UNESCO.

Attallah, Paul (2000) 'Public Broadcasting in Canada', *Gazette*, 62(3–4), pp. 177–205.

Bardoel, Jo & Kees Brants (2003) 'From Ritual to Reality. Public Broadcasters and Social Responsibility in the Netherlands', pp. 167–186 in Taisto Hujanen & Greg Lowe (eds.) *Broadcasting and Convergence: New Articulations of the Public Service Remit.* Gothenburg: NORDICOM.

BBC (2004) *Building public value: Renewing the BBC for a digital world.* London. http://www.bbc.co.uk/thefuture/pdfs/bbc_bpv.pdf.

Blumler, Jay G. (1992) (ed.) *Television and the Public Interest. Vulnerable Values in West European Broadcasting.* London: Sage Publications.

Bierzyƒski, Jakub (2004) 'Inwestycja w misj´', *Rzeczpospolita,* September 17.

Born, Georgina & Tony Prosser (2001) 'Culture and Consumerism: Citizenship. Public Service Broadcasting and the BBC's Fair Trading Obligations'. *The Modern Law Review,* 64(5), pp. 657–687.

Brants, Kees, Joke Hermes, Liesbet van Zoonen. (1998) (eds.) *The Media in Question. Popular Cultures and Public Interests.* London: Sage.

Broadcasting Policy Group (2004) *Beyond The Charter. The BBC after 2006.* London: Premium Publishing.

Burns, T. (1977) *The BBC. Public Institution and Private World.* London and Basingstoke, Macmillan.

Collins Bob (2003) *'A New Future for Public Broadcasting',* conference speech, Wellington, New Zealand.

http://www.newfuture.govt.nz/docs/SpeechByBobCollinsAtWellington.doc

Collins, Richard (2002) *The Contemporary Broadcasting Market and the role of the Public Service Broadcaster -A View from the UK.* Paper delivered at a conference 'Public Service Broadcasting – Changing Scenes', organised by the Union of Radio and Television Journalists in Finland, Helsinki. http://www.proyleiso.org/frameset.htm.

Committee of Ministers (1996) *Recommendation No. R (96) 10 on the Guarantee of the Independence of Public Service Broadcasting.* Strasbourg: Council of Europe.

Committee of Ministers (2003) *Recommendation Rec (2003) 9 on Measures to Promote the Democratic and Social Contribution of Digital Broadcasting.* Strasbourg: Council of Europe.

Coppieters, Sandra (2002) *The Financing of Public Service Broadcasting.* Paper presented during the 94th Ordinary Session of the EBU Legal Committee, Tunis.

Council (1999) 'Resolution of the Council and of the Representatives of the Governments of the Member States, meeting within the Council of 25 January 1999 concerning public service broadcasting'. *Official Journal of the European Communitie,.* C 030, 05/02, 1.

Cutler, Terry (1998) *Re-inventing Regulation in the Era of Convergence.* World Telecommunications Day Forum, Kuala Lumpur, May 19, http://www.cutlerco/com.au/content/speeches/WTD/WTD.html.

DG IV (1998) *Application of Articles 90, paragraph 2, 92 and 93 of the EC Treaty in the broadcasting sector.* Discussion paper. Brussels.

Dorfman, Ben (2002) 'Postmodernism, Knowledge and J-F Lyotard'. *IMPACT,* an electronic journal on formalisation in text, media and language. http://www.impact.hum.auc.dk

EJC (2003) Judgment Of The Court 24 July 2003 in Case C-280/00 (Reference for a preliminary ruling from the Bundesverwaltungsgericht): Altmark Trans GmbH, Regierungspräsidium Magdeburg v Nahverkehrsgesellschaft Altmark GmbH. *Official Journal of the European Union,* C 226/1, 20.9.2003

European Broadcasting Union (2002) *Media with a purpose. Public Service Broadcasting in the digital era,* The Report of the Digital Strategy Group. Geneva.

European Commission (1998) *The Digital Age. European Audiovisual Policy.* Report from the High-Level Group on Audiovisual Policy. Brussels-Luxembourg.

European Commission (1999) *Principles and Guidelines for the Community's Audiovisual Policy in the Digital Age.* COM(1999) 657 final. Brussels.

European Commission (2000 a) *Communication from the Commission - Services of general interest in Europe* (COM/2000/0580 final). Brussels: The European Union.

European Commission (2000 b) 'Commission Directive 2000/52/EC of 26 July 2000 amending Directive 80/723/EEC on the transparency of financial relations between Member States and public undertakings', *Official Journal of the European Communities,* 29.7.2000.

European Commission (2001) 'Communication from the Commission on the application of State aid rules to public service broadcasting', *Official Journal of the European Communities,* 15.11, p. 5–11.

European Parliament (1996) 'Resolution on the role of public service television in a multi-media society', *Official Journal of the European Communities,* No C 320, October 28.

Galperin, Hernan & François Bar (2002) 'The Regulation of Interactive Television in the United States and the European Union', *Federal Comunications Law Journal,* Vol 55, pp. 61–84.

Göktepeli, Miyase, Christian Christensen (2002) *The Transformation of EU Media Policy: Toward a Market-Based Framework.* Paper presented at the RIPE@2002 Conference, Helsinki-Tampere.

Hallin, Daniel C., S. Papathanassopoulos (2002) 'Political clientelism and the media: Southern Europe and Latin America in comparative perspective', *Media, Culture and Society,* 24(2), pp. 175–198.

Happold Tom (2003) "Tories would close BBC website." *Media Guardian,* August 26. http://media.guardian.co.uk/newmedia/story/0,7496,1029616,00.html

Harrison, Jackie & Lorna M. Woods (2001) 'Defining European Public Service Broadcasting'. *European Journal of Communication,* 16(4), pp. 477–504.

Head, S.W. (1988) *The Future of European-Style Public Service Broadcasting: An Unorthodox View.* Paper presented at the BEA Annual Convention, Las Vegas, MS.

Heller, C. (1978) *Broadcasting and Accountability.* British Film Institute

Hibberd, Matthew (2001) 'The reform of public service broadcasting in Italy', *Media, Culture and Society,* 23(2), pp. 233–252.

Hirsch, Mario, Vibeke Petersen (1998) 'European Policy Initatives', pp. 207–217 in Denis McQuail, Karen Siune (eds) *Media Policy. Convergence, Concentration and Commerce.* Euromedia Research Group. London: Sage Publishers.

Holtz-Bacha, Christina (2003) 'Of Markets and Supply. Public broadcasting in Germany', pp. 109–122 in Taisto Hujanen, Greg Lowe (eds.) Broadcasting and Convergence: New Articulations of the Public Service Remit. Gothenburg: NORDICOM.

Iosifidis, Petros (2002) "Digital Convergence: Challenges for European Regulation". *Javnost/The Public.* Vol. 9:3, pp. 27–48.

ITC Consultation on Public Service Broadcasting (2000), http:\\www.itc.uk.org.

Jakubowicz, Karol (2001) *We Know It When We See it? Public Service Broadcasting: Definitions, Descriptions and Policy Dilemmas,* MS.

Jakubowicz, Karol (2003) 'Ideas In Our Heads: Introduction of PSB as Part of Media System Change In Central And Eastern Europe', *European Journal of Communication,* 19 (1), pp. 53–75.

Jakubowicz, Karol (2004) 'A Square Peg in a Round Hole: The EU's policy on Public Service Broadcasting', *Journal of Media Practice,* 4(3), pp. 155–175.

Kaitatzi-Whitlock, Sophia (1996) 'Pluralism and Media Concentration in Europe. Media Policy as Industrial Policy', *European Journal of Communication*, 11: 4, pp. 453–483.

Kearns, Ian (2003) *A Mission to Empower: PSC. From Public Service Broadcasting to Public Service Communications.* Speech presented on behalf of the Institute for Public Policy Research, Westminster e-Forum, www.ippr.org/research/files/team25/project61/WMFSpeech.doc

Kleinsteuber, Hans, J. (1986) 'The Industrial Imperative', pp. . 179–198 in Denis McQuail & Karen Siune (eds.) *New Media Politics. Comparative Perspectives in Western Europe.* London: Sage Publications,

Kopper, Gerd G. (2000) *Changing Media. Spheres of Change and Steps of Research.* Paper presented to a meeting of Working Group No 3, European Science Foundation Programme 'Changing Media - Changing Europe', Seville, June 22–23.

Kopper, Gerd G. (2002) *Media, Change and Cultures in Europe. Meta-problems of Social Science Research in the Area of Media Change within Europe.* Paper presented to a meeting of Working Group 3, European Science Foundation Programme 'Changing Media - Changing Europe', Copenhagen, April 20–21.

Lealand, Geoff (2002) *Reviving Public Service Television in New Zealand: A Road Too Far?* Paper presented at the RIPE@2002 Conference 17–19 January 2002, Finland.

Llorens-Maluquer, Caries (2002) *The European Union Policy, Pluralism and Public Service Broadcasting.* Paper presented at the RIPE@2002 Conference, Helsinki-Tampere.

Lord Puttnam (2003) *The Role of Public Service Broadcasting in the Changing Television Landscape.* Delivered at the "Public Service Broadcasting – Changing Scenes" conference, organised by the Union of Radio and Television Journalists in Finland, Helsinki, http://www.proyleiso.org/frameset.htm.

McKinsey & Company (1999) *Public Service Broadcasting Around the World.* London.

McKinsey (2002) *Comparative Review of Content Regulation.* A Report for the Independent Television Commission. www:\\itc.org.uk.

McKinsey & Company (2004) *Review of Public Service Broadcasting around the world.* London.

McQuail, Denis (1986) 'Commercialisation', pp. 152–178 in Denis McQuail & Karen Siune (eds.) *New Media Politics. Comparative Perspectives in Western Europe.* London: Sage Publications.

McQuail, Denis (1998) 'Commercialisation and beyond', pp. 107–127 in Denis McQuail & Karen Siune (eds.) *Media Policy. Convergence, Concentration and Commerce,* Euromedia Research Group. London: Sage Publishers.

McQuail, Denis (2000) *Mass Communication Theory.* London: Sage Publications.

Michalis, Maria (1999) 'European Union Broadcasting and Telecoms: Towards a Convergent Regulatory Regime?' *European Journal of Communication,* 14(2), pp. 147–171.

Mueller, Milton (1999) 'Digital Convergence and Its Consequences', *The Public/Javnost,* Vol. VI, 3, pp. 11–28.

Murdock, Graham (2001) 'Digital Divides. Communications policy and its contradictions', *New Economy,* 8 (2), pp. 110–115.

Murdock, Graham & Peter Golding (1999) 'Common Markets: Corporate Ambitions and Communication Trends in the UK and Europe', *Journal of Media Economics,* 12(2), pp. 117–132.

Näränen, Pertti (2003) 'European Regulation of Digital Television. The Opportunity Lost and Found?' p. 57–68 in Taisto Hujanen & Greg Lowe (eds) *Broadcasting and Convergence: New Articulations of the Public Service Remit.* Gothenburg: NORDICOM.

Noam, Eli M. (1995) *Towards the Third Revolution of Television.* Presented at the Symposium on Productive Regulation in the TV Market 'Beyond All National Borders? Political, Economic, and Regulatory Perspectives of Media Development in the USA'. Bertelsmann Foundation, Gütersloh, Germany, December 1, http://www.columbia.edu/dlc/wp/citi/citinoam18.html.

Norris, Paul (2004) *Reshaping Public Broadcasting: the New Zealand Experience 1988–2003.* London: IPPR.

Ociepka, Beata (2003) *Dla kogo telewizja? Model publiczny w postkomunistycznej Europie Ârodkowej.* WrocTTaw: Wydawnictwo Uniwersytetu WrocTTawskiego.

OFCOM (2004) *Review of public service television broadcasting. Phase 2 – Meeting the digital challenge.* London, 24 November.

Ostergaard, Bernt Stubbe (1998) 'Convergence: Legislative Dilemmas', pp. 95–96 in D. McQuail & K. Siune (eds.) *Media Policy. Convergence, Concentration and Commerce.* London: Sage Publications.

Papatheodorou, Fotini & David Machin (2003) 'The Umbilical Cord That Was Never Cut. The Post-Dictatorial Intimacy between the Political Elite and the Mass Media in Greece and Spain', *European Journal of the Media*, 18(1), pp. 31–54.

Raboy, Marc (1998) 'Public Broadcasting and the Global Framework of Media Democratization', *Gazette*, 60(2), pp. 167–180.

Rollet, E. (2001). 'Connecting to the Information Age. A Challenge fur the European Union', *Gazette*, 63(5), pp. 371–386.

Scannell, P. (1989) 'Public service broadcasting and modern public life', *Media, Culture and Society*, 2, pp. 134–166.

Silvo, Ismo (2003) *Securing Access to Diverse Services and Content on Digital TV Platforms: Experiences of a Public Service Broadcaster, YLE of Finland.* Paper delivered at a conference on 'Digital Television in Europe: What Prospects for the Public?' Council of Europe, Rome, November 3.

Smith, Anthony (1970) (ed) *Television and Political Life. Studies in six European countries.* London and Basingstoke: The Macmillan Press Ltd.

Statham, Paul (1996) 'Television News and the Public Sphere in Italy. Conflicts at the Media/Politics Interface', *European Journal of the Media*, 11(4), pp. 511–556.

Steemers, Jeanette (2003) 'Public Service Broadcasting Is Not Dead Yet. Strategies in the 21st Century', pp. 123–135 in Taisto Hujanen & Greg Lowe (ds.) *Broadcasting and Convergence: New Articulations of the Public Service Remit.* Gothenburg: NORDICOM.

Syvertsen, Trine (1992) *Public Television in Transition. A Comparative and Historical Analysis of the BBC and the NRK.* Oslo/Trondheim: NAVF.

Syvertsen, Trine (1999) 'The Many Uses of the "Public Service" Concept', *NORDICOM Review*, Vol. 20, No. 1, pp. 5–12.

Szacki, Jerzy (2002) *Historia myÊli socjologicznej.* Warszawa: Wydawnictwo Naukowe PWN.

The Future Funding of the BBC. Report of the Independent Review Panel (1999) London: Department for Culture, Media and Sport.

Thomass, Barbara (2003) 'Knowledge Society and Public Sphere. Two Concepts for the Remit', pp. 29–39 in Taisto Hujanen & Greg Lowe (eds) *Broadcasting and Convergence: New Articulations of the Public Service Remit.* Gothenburg: NORDICOM.

Tongue, Carole (1996) The *future of public service television in a multi-channel digital age.* Available at http://www.poptel.org.uk/carole-tongue/pubs/psb_b.html

Van der Bulck, Wilde (2001) 'Public service television and national identity as a project of modernity: the example of Flemish television', *Media, Culture and Society*, 23(1), pp. 53–69.

VPRT et al. (2003) *Broadcasting and Competition Rules in the Future EU Constitution- a View from the Private Media Sector*, http://www.vprt.de/dateien/sn_020503_verbaende_zu_eu_konvent.pdf

Ward, David (2002) *The European Union, Democratic Deficit and the Public Sphere. An Evaluation of EU Media Policy*. Amsterdam: IOS Press, Ohmsha.

Ward, David (2003) 'State aid or band aid? An evaluation of the European Commission's approach to public service broadcasting', *Media, Culture & Society*, 25(2), pp. 233–250.

Wessberg, A. (2000) *Public Service Broadcasting, Information Society and Small Markets*. Paper presented at a conference on 'Public Service Broadcasting. The Digital and Online Challenge', London, 28–29 February.

Williams, Raymond (1968) *Communications*. London: Penguin.

Appendix to Chapter 5

Public Service Broadcasting in Europe: distinctiveness, remit and programme content obligations

Marcel Betzel

Introduction

Public service broadcasting is expected to offer programming that differs from that from commercial broadcasters and to serve both a large audience and specific groups in society. There are several ways to fulfil the objective of diversity and distinctiveness and in this manner to justify legitimacy of national PSB. The aim here is to provide an overview of the different approaches that can be found in Europe today. It will mainly focus on regulation: (legal) remits and programme content obligations. It also looks at the extent to which PSB activities in the field of the new media are regulated. The aim is to point out the main trends and establish which approach is most preferable to reach distinctiveness and legitimacy of PSB.

Most of the data was collected in May 2003 for a survey conducted among members of the European Platform of Regulatory Authorities (EPRA) concerning the remit and programme content obligations of PSB broadcasters (Betzel, 2003). Information provided below is based on replies to the questionnaire.

Remits of PSB

A wide variety of PSB remits can be found throughout Europe (the EPRA study found that Romania and Albania are the only countries with no remit or similar arrangements). They might differ little in general programme tasks of PSB, but they do so to a high degree in specific ones. They have been laid down in a broadcasting act, a similar legal instrument or a contract between the State and the broadcaster. Most countries prefer to define the remit in legislation or its equivalent, though in a large minority of countries remits take the form of contractual arrangements: this is at least the case for Denmark (both law and contracts), Norway (for TV2 and Radio P4), Sweden, UK (only BBC), Luxembourg, France (*cahier des charges*), Portugal (both law and contract of concession) and Italy.

It is hard to say whether legal or contractual arrangements are preferable; a legally-binding remit is likely to have more status and impact. On the other hand contracts or similar arrangements are definitely more flexible, can more easily be adapted to new developments, and leave more room for details.

In most countries the remit is described in general terms and – as far as programming is concerned – further elaborated in programme content obligations. In some countries, however, even the (legal) remit is extremely detailed regarding the programming of PSB, while in other countries both remit and programme content obligations consist of very general requirements.

In a majority of cases, the remits, regardless of how they are established, are based on the following assumptions that PSB programming will:

- contribute to a democratic and/or pluralistic society;
- contribute to national culture and language;
- provide high quality programming;
- meet high journalistic or moral standards and values (like impartiality, respect of privacy and human dignity);
- provide a universal service.

All public service broadcasters in Europe must meet content requirements in remit and/or programme obligations. In most cases, they are obliged to provide a wide range of programming, including information, culture, education and entertainment. Diversity is a main requirement, based on the idea that PSB should cater to a range of different interests and produce a programme schedule for the whole national population.

The frameworks for establishing these requirements differ considerably in detail. They vary from extremely general formulations, as in the Netherlands where PSB must meet minimum thresholds for information, culture and education, to highly detailed ones. The following main systems can be observed in Europe:

- Qualitative programme content requirements: a requirement to broadcast certain programme types (e.g. news) or programmes belonging to a certain genre (information), without specifying percentages or amounts;
- Quantitative programme content requirements: a requirement to broadcast a minimum percentage or amount of certain programme types (news) or programmes belonging to a certain genre (information);
- Other requirements focus more on the audience. This includes the obligation to reach certain (shares of) audiences, serve specific target groups, broadcast certain programmes at peak time or satisfy certain needs of the public.

Qualitative content obligations

All countries have qualitative content programme requirements, amounting in most cases to the obligation to broadcast programmes belonging to the categories of information, culture, education and entertainment. Some countries stick to general terms; other countries have described which categories or even which types of programmes should be broadcast in a very detailed way.

Entertainment is mentioned in many countries as a required programme category, either in general terms in the remit, or in the programme content requirements. This is the case for Denmark, United Kingdom, Ireland, the Netherlands, Belgium (Flanders), Germany, Austria, Spain, Portugal, Turkey and Latvia. The Netherlands are unique as they are the only country where a maximum limit for entertainment has been laid down in law, which is stated as not more than 25% per TV channel. The remit in the Dutch Media Act refers to general programme categories, requiring broadcasters: 'to provide a varied and high-quality range of programme services for general broadcasting purposes at national, regional and local level in the fields of information, culture, education and entertainment and to transmit them, or cause them to be transmitted, on open networks.'

When it comes to more detailed arrangements, some remits and content obligations specifically refer to the quality and innovative nature of programmes. The remit in Flanders states that 'All VRT programmes must be characterised by quality, not only in their content and form, but also in their use of language. In all its programmes, the VRT will strive for maximum quality, professionalism, creativity and originality. New talent and innovative forms of expression should be given a chance.'

The need for innovative and experimental programming is also highlighted in PSB remits in Sweden, Ireland, Italy, UK and Portugal. In the UK this is explicitly stated for Channel 4. In Portugal the remit requires public service broadcaster RTP: 'To transmit an innovative and diversified plan of programmes which stimulates the formation and the cultural valorisation having in mind particularly the young public'. Central and Eastern European countries display a tendency to describe topics to be covered by PSB in a very precise manner – probably due to the fact that PSB is a novelty in these countries. In Lithuania, for example, the remit prescribes the role of the public service broadcaster LRT as follows:'LRT must collect and publish information concerning Lithuania and the world, acquaint the public with the variety of European and world culture and principles of modern civilization, reinforce the independence and democracy of the Republic of Lithuania, create, nurture and protect the values of national culture, foster tolerance and humanism, culture of co-operation, thought and language, and strengthen public morality and civic awareness and develop the country's ecological culture.' Furthermore the remit states that 'priority in LRT programmes shall be accorded to national culture as well as informational, world culture, journalistic, analytical, educational and art broadcasts. Mass culture has to be reflected in review, informative and analytical type programmes.'

In Latvia the remit of national PSB is formed on the basis of comprehensive studies of the wishes and expectations of viewers and listeners. One of the stipulations is that the programming must reflect as extensively as possible the current opinions of society, as well as political philosophical and cultural trends.

Slovakia is another country where the remit is very precise in mentioning the subjects of the programmes to be broadcast by the public service broadcaster, such as:

■ programmes aimed at educating and training, science and research;
■ programmes which provide legal and other information, supports a healthy life-style, the protection of nature, the protection of the environment, the protection of life, health and property, and road safety.

This tendency can also be found in countries with more established PSB. For example, Austria and Italy have been very precise in describing which topics or issues should be covered by PSB programming. In Austria the programme mandate states that the Austrian Broadcasting Corporation must provides services like:

- comprehensive information on all important political, social, economic, cultural and sports related issues;
- promotion of understanding for all questions of democratic society;
- promotion of Austrian identity from the perspective of European history and integration;
- promotion of understanding for European integration.

In Italy, the remit lays down extensive quantitative programme content requirements, and in addition obliges PSB broadcasters to broadcast programme categories such as the so-called social programmes, in which social communication shall be promoted on topics such as environment, health care, consumer rights, employment, multiculture, immigration and disabled persons.

Qualitative programme content requirements can also be defined in more detail by describing certain aspects of society to which programme services should pay attention. In Sweden the detailed remit states the obligation to cover and examine cultural events and developments. The Irish public service broadcaster RTE is explicitly required to cover proceedings in the national as well as European Parliament.

Quantitative content obligations

Such programme content requirements can be found in Denmark, Norway, the Netherlands, Luxembourg, France, Italy, Portugal, Malta, Turkey, Lithuania, Hungary and Bulgaria. It is remarkable that percentages or amounts usually apply to transmission time; few countries have an obligation to spend a certain amount or percentage of the budget for certain programming, though such requirements can be found in the case of independent production in France, Italy and some other countries, where broadcasters are given a choice between a transmission time, or investment quota (Austria, Czech Republic, Denmark, Finland, Ireland, Malta, Slovakia, Sweden). Also different approaches can be observed throughout Europe, varying from percentages for general categories of programmes – as in the Netherlands – to absolute numbers of specific programmes, which is the case in Portugal.

In the Netherlands, PSB must meet percentages for general categories defined in law: at least 25% of the broadcasting time shall be used for cultural programmes and at least 35% must be used for programmes of an informative or educational nature. At least 12.5% of the total television broadcasting time used by all the broadcasting associations together shall consist of, or relate to, the arts.

France, too, has developed a system of quotas. This begins with the more general requirements to broadcast programmes aimed at culture, education or science on France 2 (40%), France 3 (45%) and France 5. But above that, PSB must meet more detailed provisions laid down in the *cahier des missions et des charges*, for example, to broadcast 15 plays (lyric, drama or choreography), musicals (2 hours a month), concerts performed by national, regional or European orchestras (16 hours a year). Each PSB channel has a different set of detailed requirements of this nature to fulfil.

Portugal is another country where PSB broadcasters must respect detailed quantitative requirements, expressed in absolute numbers:

■ musicals and ballets: minimum 26 hours per year;
■ Portuguese works by qualified authors of fiction: minimum 26 hours per year;
■ original documentaries: 26 hours per year;
■ original fiction, with the aim to encourage new talent.

In Bulgaria the public service broadcaster is subject to very detailed and extensive quantitative programme content requirements, expressed in its licence. Some of the stipulations are:

■ news: no less than 5.1% from the current day;
■ actualities: no less than 16.6% of the weekly programmes;
■ education: no less than 3.7% of the weekly programmes;
■ culture, science, religion: no less than 4.7% of the weekly programmes;
■ children's and youth programmes: no less than 7.6% of the weekly programmes;
■ programmes in support of integration of socially disadvantaged and risks groups: no less than 1.8% per month.

Specific quotas for such programmes can be found in Denmark: public service broadcasters are obliged to broadcast at least the same amount of news in the evening as in the previous year, including subtitling for the deaf (as in 2002); children's programmes and Danish fiction should average a certain amount of time over a four-year period. Furthermore there is the obligation to broadcast at least one main news bulletin in primetime and to increase the broadcast hours of Danish music.

In Norway, only the public radio channel P4 has a quantitative requirement: the obligation in the licence that 35% of the music must be Norwegian. In the UK, there are only real quantitative programme content requirements for ITV, Channel 4 and 5. As far as BBC and S4C are concerned, it is left to the BBC Board of Governors and the Welsh Authority to interpret their remits in detail.

Audience-related programme content obligations

The last special category of programme content requirements is focused mainly on audience reach. Often the question is not whether PSB broadcasts enough programmes of a public nature, but whether they are, or can be, seen by an appropriate part of the national population. For example in the Netherlands, PSB has been criticised for broadcasting more 'commercial' programmes during peak time, while programmes devoted to arts, science, information and documentaries are shown relatively late in the evening. A way of tackling this problem is to oblige PSB to broadcast certain programmes during time slots that traditionally enjoy high ratings.

France has some quantitative programme content requirements with sometimes detailed stipulations for the time of transmission, such as the obligation to broadcast 12 genres of different programmes between 8.30 and 10.30 p. m. or to broadcast 35 plays in the course of a year, to be broadcast before 11.00 p. m.

In Italy the remit requires RAI to carry in the annual programming in the time band between 6 a.m. and 12 p.m. at least 65% of the following programmes: news, information on politics, economics, science, society, programmes on institutional matters, programmes on social and public utility events, programmes devoted to minors, programmes devoted to cultural matters; programmes with interest for scientific and environmental subjects; sports, auteur films, films and fiction of European or national origin. For the channel RAI 3 this percentage is even set at 80%.

Belgium (Flanders) offers an interesting example of programme requirements defined in terms of audience reach. The five-year management contract with the Flemish government for the period 2002–2006 contains stipulations such as:

■ a weekly reach of 70% of Flemish population;
■ a weekly reach of 70% of the viewers between 4–12 years old;
■ a daily reach of 1.5 million people by news and current affairs programmes;
■ a weekly reach of 15% of Flemish population by culture;
■ a weekly reach of 10% of Flemish population by education;

Often the remit mentions specific audiences at which PSB should aim its programmes. In most cases the following target groups can be indicated:

■ children and youth
■ ethnic minorities
■ disabled people

The extensive remit for SVT in Sweden highlights the need to reach the younger audience: 'SVT shall devote greater effort and resources to programmes for children and young people and programmes in which young people take part. Programming for young viewers shall feature news and current events as well as cultural and artistic expressions, taking into account the special linguistic needs of children in cultural and ethnic minority communities.'

The obligation for PSB to pay attention to the culture and language of (ethnic) minorities in its programming is laid down in the remits in Norway, Finland, Spain (including Catalonia), Portugal, Italy, Latvia, Hungary, Slovakia and Albania. In Finland the remit requires the public service broadcaster Yleisradio Oy in its broadcasting to treat Finnish and Swedish speaking citizens on equal terms and to produce services in the Sámi and Romany languages and in sign language as well as, where applicable, for other language groups in the country. In Bulgaria the PSB licence explicitly states that news in the Turkish language should be offered.

The remit in Hungary mentions programmes for handicapped people and minors: 'Public service broadcasters and public broadcasters shall pay special attention to the following: …providing important information to groups that are severely disadvantaged due to age, mental and psychological state or social circumstances, in particular broadcasting programmes on children's rights, on child protection and on conveying information regarding available services in prime time programming.'

Regulation of digital activities of PSB

In all countries, public service broadcasters have engaged in different Internet activities. In a growing number of countries they are launching digital (terrestrial) broadcasting. From this point of view, it is remarkable that European broadcasting legislation is almost silent on the need to safeguard the public nature of PSB activities in the digital environment. Denmark, Spain and Austria are the only countries where the current remit deals explicitly with role of PSB in the sphere of the Internet. In some countries, the Internet can be regarded as part of the PSB remit because reference is made to new technological developments in which PSB should take part. This is the case for the Netherlands, Flanders and Portugal.

In the Netherlands, Internet activities of public service broadcasters come under the main task of PSB. This means that Internet activities have to comply with the remit and should be in accordance with one of the main characteristics of PSB, i.e. non-commercial. This should result in limited advertising and sponsorship, and a clear and recognisable distinction between editorial content of a public service broadcaster on the Internet and commercial information of third parties. In the UK there are no restrictions on Internet activities; until now, all websites have displayed a strong educational character. If there were websites with mainly commercial purposes, the code on cross-promotion would forbid promotion of such a website on the broadcasters' main programme services.

In Flanders and Germany, advertising and sponsoring are not allowed on PSB websites. In Germany, controversy surrounds the Internet services of PSB broadcasters. ARD and ZDF may legally offer Internet services primarily with programme-related content. The respective laws for the other public service broadcasters contain regulations that in part correspond to the regulations for ARD and ZDF. Such is the case as regards Bayerischer Rundfunk, for example. The NDR-treaty stipulates that NDR may offer new services using new forms of technology. The content of this permission is controversial. What is not controversial, however, is that the broadcaster may provide programme-related information and references online.

ARD and ZDF's Internet offerings go beyond these limits. They offer free-of-charge services such as live chats, E-commerce, SMS services as well as a news service financed by a commercial partner (T-Online). The broadcasters view all this as referring to the future convergence of television and Internet and as part of their basic broadcasting services. Those outside public service broadcasting, however, view this development as distorting competition with commercial providers.

In Austria, online services have to be 'associated with broadcasting programmes' and have to 'serve the purpose of fulfilling the programme mandate'. The Federal Act on the Austrian Broadcasting Corporation lays down further rules for the content of these services; in particular they also have to comply with key aspects of the programme mandate. The proportion of advertising in the provision of such services has to be determined by decision of the Foundation Council.

The same pattern of light – or no – regulation occurs in the case of digital channels. Besides the UK, Spain is the only country where digital programmes/activities are explicitly mentioned in the PSB remit. In some countries, digital channels can be regarded as being covered by the PSB remit because it makes reference to new technological developments in which PSB should take part, where necessary or desired. This is the case for Finland, the Netherlands, Flanders and Portugal. In Flanders, the management contract for 2002–2006 gives the VRT an important role in helping to bridge the digital gap and offering new media applications to the audience. In the field of digital TV the VRT has set up an experimental project where 100 households are provided with a set-top box for interactive TV.

In the UK, the 5 BBC thematic television channels offered via all digital platforms are defined as part of the remit and have to provide services that are not provided by the free market. The remit of each channel has to be approved by the Secretary of State, following public consultation.

In Germany public service broadcasters are authorised to transmit their (analogue) programme services digitally and are also authorised to create additional programme services using digital technology. Except for general competition rules, the digital programme services of German PSB are not subject to the same broadcasting regulations and restrictions as the analogue programme services. Also in Austria, the digital satellite theme channel (TW1) operated by a daughter company (half-owned by ORF) is not subject to a specific public service remit and obligations.

Conclusion

The aim of this appendix was to outline how PSB in Europe is regulated to foster the public nature and distinctiveness of programmes. There are a lot of different systems employed throughout Europe and the huge differences between countries with regard to the cultural background, the historical tradition and size of national PSB demand a sensitive approach when it comes to drawing general conclusions.

When we take into account the way in which the remits and programme content obligations are described, it becomes clear that in most countries the legislator opts for an all-embracing PSB approach. In a vast majority of countries PSB has the legal obligation to serve a large general audience as well as specific target groups. This is implemented by both quality and audience-related programme content obligations. Programme obligations connected to Pure PSB-task occur in the broadcasting legislation of many countries but only to a certain extent; in almost every country the remit emphasises that PSB is entitled to broadcast programmes that are also offered by commercial broadcasting.

As far as the remit is concerned, the 'less is more' policy might be adopted, so that it can be restricted to the key elements that demonstrate the public and distinctive nature of PSB. The following elements can be observed all over Europe, however only rarely does the remit in any one country embrace all these aspects:

■ universality of content, understood as both universality of basic supply on generalist programmes as well as programmes specialised or tailored for specific audiences;

- universality of access, a clear presence on all significant relevant media and platforms, including the online and on-demand environment;
- basic journalistic standards, editorial freedom and independence from both political ties and commercial parties;
- high quality of programmes and services to constitute a benchmark of quality and professionalism.

In a large majority of countries, the role of PSB with regard to digital channels is not yet defined in broadcasting legislation. The same goes for the online strategy of PSB; in most countries there is a clear absence of legal provisions concerning Internet activities. There is a risk, taking into consideration recent discussions in countries like Germany and the UK, that this can easily affect the legitimacy and ability to expand on new platforms. Therefore it is recommended that the remit contains clear provisions on the role of PSB in the area of the new digital media. These provisions could include certain (content) obligations to ensure fair competition and avoid sensitive discussions about the role of PSB; this is also the backdrop to the growing number of complaints by private broadcasters lodged within the European Commission.

There is also the trend, in the Eastern European countries in particular, towards very detailed provisions, not only in programme content obligations, but even in remits. It can be questioned whether this is a desirable approach since it might restrict the necessary freedom and flexibility of PSB to adapt to new programme strategies. On the other hand there is in Europe a growing tendency to go beyond the traditional forms of public service broadcasting regulation and define PSB obligations more precisely, often by contracts backed up by accountability reports to parliament, government and/or a regulatory agency, as is the case in Flanders. This approach might be preferable, since these documents can be adapted more easily and quickly to the new circumstances, demands and challenges that PSB face in a rapidly changing media environment.

References

Betzel, M.P.H. (2003) Programme performance of PSB and its mission in the digital age, 17th meeting of the European Platform of Regulatory Authorities

6

FINANCING PUBLIC SERVICE BROADCASTERS IN THE NEW ERA

Stylianos Papathanassopoulos

Public broadcasters face a severe threat concerning their future, i.e., their source of income in the new television landscape. This chapter tries to describe these challenges by providing an account of the current situation showing the trends in the ways of funding public broadcasters and discussing the challenges they face in the new environment.

Ways of funding: emerging trends

Public broadcasters in Europe, with a few exceptions,[1] used to have two main sources of revenue: the licence fee[2] and advertising. A few pubic broadcasters, such as in the case of Spain and Portugal, are mainly funded by advertising and to a lesser extent by public subsidies. A recent trend is the replacement of the licence fee by public funding, as in the Netherlands and the Flemish Community of Belgium (Table 2). By and large, a general trend is that those European public broadcasters that carry advertising have experienced a decrease in their share of advertising revenue. This has been compounded by the fact that even for the most successful public channels the arrival of competition has reduced rates.

According to the European Audiovisual Observatory (2002), the total income attributable to public broadcasters in the European Union totalled 26.3 billion euros in 2000, against 22.8 billion euros in 1997, representing an annual growth rate of 4.9%. This was considerably less than that of private television over the same period (17.7%). Moreover, there has been, throughout Europe, a growth in commercial income (from 28.4% of all income in 1995 to 32.3% in 2000) to the detriment of public income (which fell from 69.1% in 1995 to 65.4% in 2000). Furthermore, the losses registered by a total

Table 1: The Funding of Public Broadcasters in Selected European Countries *

Way of funding	Public broadcasters
LICENCE FEE	BBC (UNITED KINGOM) DR (DENMARK) YLE (FINLAND) STV (SWEDEN) NRK (NORWAY)
PUBLIC FUNDS	VTR (BELGIUM-Flandres) NOS (NETHERLANDS)
LICENCE FEE & ADVERTISING	ARD + ZDF (GERMANY) *Advertising is allowed only 20:00 and for 20 minutes per day* RTE (IRELAND) ORF (AUSTRIA) FRANCE TELEVISION (FRANCE) RAI (ITALY) RTBF (BELGIUM) ERT (GREECE) *Licence fee is charged on the electricity bills*
PUBLIC SUBSIDIES & ADVERTISING	RTP (PORTUGAL) RTVE (SPAIN) MTV (HUNGARY)

* Broadcasters funded from advertising also derive revenue from sponsorship; in some cases that are funded solely by the licence fee, such as NRK, there is also some sponsoring. All PSB broadcasters in addition obtain funds from sales of programmes, services, etc., and, in some cases (like the BBC), from involvement in commercial activities and channels.

of 55 companies studied are continuing to grow: 193 million euros in 1998, 220.7 million euros in 1999 and 578.5 million euros in 2000. The profit margin, which was still positive in 1997 and 1998, became negative in 1999 and 2000 (EAO, 2002).

Grants or contracts with the public authorities are sometimes given for specific services, particularly for international services. On the other hand, there have been pressures from private interests, described below, that accuse public broadcasters of unfair competition due to their dual way of funding. In one way or another, it seems the traditional way of funding public broadcasters through the traditional licence fee may have entered a new phase concerning its future, and probably the future of the public service broadcasting system itself, at least as we know it.

Of course, for the time being the licence fee still plays a pivotal role in the financing of public broadcasting in Western Europe. Therefore, if its level stays unchanged or falls but costs of talent and broadcasting rights inexorably rise as competition intensifies (Molsky, 1999) public broadcasters have either to cut some of their organisational expenses or even decrease their production costs (with obvious consequences for their quality).

Table 2: Public Broadcasting in Europe: Audience Shares and Funding

Country	TV audience market share – all public services (2002) (%)	Funding		
		Public	Advertising	Other
Austria	54.1	49.3	49.9	0.9
Flemish Belgium	36.0	60.1	33.4	6.5
French Belgium	19.7	70.6	27.6	1.8
Denmark	70.1	89.1	10.9	
Finland	45.4	74.5	25.4	
France	39.6	52	45.5	
Germany	46.5	78	17.1	3.1
Greece	12.5	38.1	43.1	17.8
Hungary	16.7	55.4	45.6	
Ireland	43.0	34	66	
Italy	41.1	50	43	
Netherlands	37.6	66.5	22.5	11.1
Poland	46.8	25	46	29
Portugal	29.6	43	55	1.5
Spain	33.0	11.5	77.6	10.9
Sweden	42.9	92.6	7.3	0.1
United Kingdom	39.0	77.8	15.8	6.4

Sources: Television 2001–European Key Facts. IP RTL Group (2003), European Audiovisual Observatory-*Statistical Yearbook 2000, Television, Video and New Media in Europe (2000)*; De Bens, 2003, p. 218.

In terms of TV market share, public broadcasters, with a few exceptions, have managed to retain a considerable share of their national audiences, even though they do not attract the same ratings as in the past. In Austria, Germany, Ireland, Finland, France, the Netherlands, Norway, Sweden, Italy, and the United Kingdom a combination of public broadcasters has managed to retain approximately 40% and more of the national television audience. On the contrary, public broadcasters who used to work under strict state control, such as in Spain, Portugal and Greece, as well as in the Eastern Europe, have seen a significant decrease in their television audience with the entry of private television.

Trends in European countries

All public broadcasting systems are to some degree subject to political influence (Etzioni-Halevy, 1987), and disputes over the independence of public broadcasting are general to the history of European media. Most countries in Western Europe, however, have succeeded in developing institutions that separate public broadcasting from the direct control of the political majority. The countries of Southern Europe, however, have not moved as far in this direction, and of those of Eastern Europe much further (Hallin & Papathanassopoulos, 2000). This situation is reflected not only in the legitimacy of public broadcasters in the public conscience and public support but also in their performance *after* the entry of private television.

It is therefore no coincidence that public broadcasters perform better in Northern Europe than in Southern and Eastern Europe. In Northern European countries, public broadcasters not only perform well (e.g., Denmark, Sweden, UK, Finland, etc), but also traditionally enjoy the greatest amounts of public funding (De Bens, 2003) and sound public support. In contrast, in Southern Europe, public broadcasters failed not only to get widespread support, but also were never granted financial stability and full independence from political influence. In Eastern Europe, public broadcasters never had the chance to get public legitimacy during the transitional period and had to compete from the start with their private counterparts. But in either case, the fate of public broadcasters in Europe will be related to the fate of the public broadcasters in the larger European countries.

Germany, the UK, France and Italy dominate in terms of public broadcasting revenues. Combined revenues of these public broadcasters account for 72% of the total of public broadcasters' revenue in Western Europe. These countries also represent slightly more than the half of the entire European audience and at the same time play a central political role within the European Union (Molsky 1999; Papathanassopoulos 2002). In other words, as in most cases, the direction their public broadcasters follow will be significant to the future of the entire public broadcasting sector in Europe – as in the past, the smaller countries should follow – but, the future of large public broadcasters may not be too secure.

The BBC will face Royal Charter renewal in 2006, preceded by a full-fledged review of its remit, performance and funding. The UK Labour government is sending ambiguous signals about its intentions,[3] but suggests that in the run-up to Charter renewal the BBC has to demonstrate that it does not only continue to reach the vast majority of the audience, but that it also fulfils its public service remit of delivering high quality, innovative programmes (White Paper, 2000).

In France, new regulations in 2000 have decreased the amount of advertising time allowed on public channels. France 2 and France 3 used to carry up to 12 minutes of commercial breaks per hour. With the new law, the government needs to heavily increase the licence fee, but many wonder how easy it will be to do this on the eve of the digital and PPV television era.

In Germany the amount of the fee is fixed by the state governments and has to be ratified by the state parliaments. Since all Germans pay the same amount, all 16 states have to come to an agreement. This is done in an Interstate Treaty on Broadcast Financing, effective for approximately three years. Recently, the VPRT, the association representing Germany's private broadcasters and telecommunications sector, lodged a complaint with the European Commission in 2003, alleging competition law infringements due to state support for public service broadcasters. It seeks to change the regulatory framework for broadcasting in Germany in favour of private broadcasting media operators. Its aims are to reduce the licence fee, tighten taxation arrangements and block the Internet activities of the public-service broadcasters (Holtz-Bacha, 2002).

In Italy, RAI is about to undergo a major reform, which will partly privatise its holding company. In fact its licence fee remained stable for the fourth consecutive year. Most importantly, stagnating income comes at a time when RAI is required to invest more, especially in content rights in the digitising and converging television market.

From the licence fee to the direct public fund

Countries that have abolished or replaced the licence fee merit some attention. However, as noted, one has to define the abolition of the licence fee. There are countries that abolished the licence fee and replaced it with public grants, and countries that replaced it with direct public funding.

In the first case, in Portugal the licence fee for television was abolished in 1991–92. Since then, RTP has received annual state grants. From 1992 to 1995, the state grants represented about 15% to 18% of RTP's annual revenues. In Spain, RTVE is financed mainly from commercial sources. State grants represent about 12.9 % of RTVE's revenues.

In the second case, the Dutch government abolished the licence fee from 2000 and replaced it with a levy on income tax. Similarly, in Belgium the Flemish government replaced the licence fee for the Vlaamse Radio en Televisie (VRT) in 2000 with public funding, while the French retained it. The Flemish government wanted to show that it considered it its duty to provide for a well-functioning public broadcasting system.[4] Political opponents argued that the government wanted to boost its popularity by replacing the licence fee with public funding, considering it as more socially fair tax for the public and more effective for the public broadcaster (De Bens, 2003). In Hungary, in June 2002, the new right wing government abolished the licence fee and replaced it by state subvention.

However, the cases of Portugal and Spain are worth noting. The question of how to finance the public broadcaster RTP is becoming an increasingly difficult issue for the Portuguese government. The *Public Television Service Concession Agreement* (31 December 1996) introduced an annual state subsidy in order to support the public service. The estimation methodology for that subsidy is based on the real cost of the public service, controlled by the Finance Ministry and the Opinion Council of the RTP (an independent body). With the progressive loss of the TV market share and the increase of costs in production and acquisition of TV products, the revenues of advertising for RTP had decreased and the state subsidy was not able to support the budget of the public broadcaster. Since 1994 RTP has lost more than 22% of market share, mainly due to increased competition from the private channels. The downward curve seems unstoppable and it makes the case for public subsidies for the public broadcaster more difficult to justify. On the other hand, RTP cannot easily return to the abolished licence fee (Traquina, 1995 & 1998), even if the 2003 law on the Financing of the Public Service Radio and Television Broadcasting says that public television can receive any surplus from the licence fee still collected to finance public radio.

Spain's RTVE, which receives no licence fee money, faces serious financial problems. Despite leading the audience ratings, RTVE is burdened with debts. Financed by a combination of advertising (77.6%) and state subsidy (11.5%), the broadcaster's accumulated debt reached a staggering 6 billion euros in 2003. The government plans to restructure RTVE through a cost-cutting plan, but it seems unlikely that it will introduce a licence fee to finance the public broadcaster. On the contrary, limits on advertising time have been proposed for the public channels and there is consideration of the privatisation of certain of RTVE services. Moreover, the private channels claim that they lose advertising due to RTVE's commercial policy to lower its prices in order to capture more advertising (see below).

On the other hand, the above examples, although derived from different cases, indicate that when the licence fee is either abolished or replaced or has limitations imposed on it, it is extremely difficult to reinstate. The case of the Netherlands is indicative: since the replacement of the licence fee by a levy on the income tax, the budget of NOS is fixed by law at the 1998 level, with yearly indexing. But the new government intends to cut the budget by 5% (Brants, 2004).

In other words, direct public or government funding may, in one way or another, seriously affect public broadcasters' independence, or in the best case, the public perception of their independence. Moreover, it seems much more difficult to increase the licence fee in comparison to the past – at least it is more difficult compared to electricity or telephone bills. On the other hand, the licence fee also has (or used to have) a social dimension. By contributing to their national public broadcaster, citizens felt that it was more accountable to them than to the politicians.

The future of dual funding: the role of the European Union

According to some views, in the future television will rely more on subscription fees and less on advertising (Norcontel, 1998), but it is almost certain that, unless the law changes, advertising will continue playing a significant role in the funding of public television. On the other hand, there is general agreement that one of the factors that will decide the future of public broadcasting in Europe is the level of financial support (Brants & Siune, 1992, p. 114). That, in turn, will depend on whether the system of dual funding of public broadcasters (licence fee and advertising) can survive. The issue has been the object of heated debate for a considerable time now, as commercial broadcasters continue to press their point that advertising should be the sole domain of private broadcasters.

The matter goes back to 1988 when leading private broadcasters such as the French TF1 and Italian Fininvest were asking for a breathing space to enable them to establish themselves in the increasingly fierce competition between private and public broadcasters. In effect, they were arguing that PSB broadcasters should not be allowed to carry advertising. With the European Union now encompassing 25 countries, its policies in this matter are likely to be decisive in determining this question. The European Commission and the European Court of Justice have received a considerable number of formal complaints on this issue since 1992.

Private broadcasters have accused their public rivals of enjoying an unfair competitive advantage because they are financed both from public funds and advertising revenues. In their view, public broadcasters have received 82.2 billion euros of State aid between

Table 3: Complaints made to the European Commission against Publicly Funded Broadcasters (1992–2003)

Year	Market	Basis of complaint
1992	Spain	Different form of illegal state aid including the authorisation of debt
1993	Spain	Different form of illegal state aid including the authorisation of debt
1993	France	Capital increases and other ad hoc subsidies
1993	Portugal	Grants that distorted competition
1996	Portugal	New state aid, capital increase and guarantees
1997	Portugal	Incompatible state aid
1996	Italy	Combination of licence fee and tax exemptions, capital increases & other measures
1997	Germany	Launch of two thematic channels
1997	UK	Use of licence fee money to finance a restricted cable offering
1999	UK	Unlawful state aid for internet activities
1999	Ireland	Dual-funding mechanism
2000	Denmark	Excess funding, reduction of advertising prices
2002	Netherlands	Unclear public service remit, the absence of adequate and independent supervision and the lack of transparency and structural overcompensation.
2003	Germany	Breaches in competition law by benefiting from hidden state aid, financing online ventures with revenue from the licence fee, distortion of premium sports rights and inadequate implementation of the Financial Transparency Directive.

Source: White Paper, 2004: 6.

1996 and 2001 and a 'massive 15 billion euros in 2001, making it the third largest recipient of state aid since 1998, more than the state aid in agriculture' (White Paper, 2004).

Other complaints concerned public funding for activities of PSB broadcasters (thematic channels, Internet activities, etc.), which, according to commercial broadcasters, went beyond the scope of the PSB remit and allowed PSB to compete unfairly in areas that should be the sole domain of private enterprise.

The EU was originally ill-equipped to deal with these complaints. On the one hand, it refused to consider PSB as an exception to rules on State aid enshrined in article 87 of the Treaty. On the other it needed, also under pressure from Member States, to recognise the special case of PSB. Its first effort to create a legal framework for dealing with this issue was the adoption of the well-known 'Amsterdam Protocol' in 1997, which is annexed to the EU Treaty of Amsterdam. The Protocol states that:

the funding of public service broadcasting insofar as such funding is granted to broadcasting organisations for the fulfilment of the public service remit …does not affect trading conditions and competition in the Community to an extent which would be contrary to the common interest, while the realisation of the remit of that public service shall be taken into account.

Under this framework, public aid would be prohibited when subsidies, coupled with advertising revenues, exceed the costs of meeting public service obligations. However, the Amsterdam Protocol only formulates some general principles and, in addition, does so in an ambiguous way. Further development of the EU's policy on this matter was needed. A first effort was a *Discussion Paper* prepared by the Competition Directorate.[5] It sought to propose a very narrow definition of the PSB remit, reduced to information, educational and cultural programming as well as programmes with a regional scope or directed at social and ethnic minorities. Films and series could not automatically be included in the remit (only if PSB broadcasters had special obligations in this respect), and there was no mention of entertainment and sports. It was also stated that the Commission would assess the compatibility of the aid with the EC Treaty (i.e. proportionality of funding to the cost of public service obligations) only in case the Commission established that the measures could not be considered as existing aid (i.e. introduced before the signing of the Treaty).

Member States rejected the narrow definition of the remit and the *Discussion Paper* had to be withdrawn. The then audiovisual Commissioner, Marcelino Oreja, undertook a further effort. He made clear that: 'the funding of public broadcasting is entirely subject to the rules of competition…[and]…funding of public television by the member states does not distort competition in the common market to the detriment of the common interest' (Oreja, 1998).

He also appointed a High Level Group on Audiovisual Policy whose report (European Commission, 1998) specifies the relevant principles on which the funding of public broadcasting should be based. These are:

- The funding of public broadcasting should respect the principle of proportionality, going no further that what is strictly necessary to fulfil the public service and be provided under conditions of complete transparency.
- Public funding should be used solely for fulfilling the public service remit, as defined by each member state.
- When a public service broadcaster receives funding from sources other than the public sector to carry out its public service remit, and this broadcaster is involved in purely commercial activities (i.e., which go beyond those defined as part of its public service remit), it must keep separate accounts.
- Public activities should primarily be funded from public sources. Use of advertising should remain secondary.

Meanwhile, the Commission started ruling on some of the complaints, usually finding in favour of public service broadcasters.[6] Moreover, in May 2000, the Commission adopted a decision that granted an exemption from normal antitrust law to the rules of the European Broadcasting Union (EBU) governing the joint acquisition and sharing of broadcasting rights for sports events in the framework of the Eurovision system. The exemption is valid until 2005.

However, some the complaints were left pending and private channels sued the Commission before the European Court of First Instance (CFI) for failure to act in accordance with its obligations.

Finally, in November 2001, the Commission released a Communication on the application of State aid rules to public service broadcasting. It is, for the time being, a definitive stand on the issue, stating the need for a clear definition of the remit (while stating that a 'wide' definition, practically encompassing everything that a PSB broadcaster puts on the air could be acceptable), for formal entrustment of the public service mission to a particular broadcaster or broadcasters, the need for transparency (including dual accounting, so that public funding cannot be used to finance or cross-subsidise commercial activities), and independent supervision. It also noted that state aid should not exceed the net cost of the public service mission, taking into account other direct or indirect revenues derived from the public service mission. Also, the Communication states that the existence of State aid for PSB broadcasters in a particular country cannot be assumed automatically, but must be established on a case-by-case basis.

This allowed the Commission to start clearing up its backlog of cases and at the end of 2003 it issued rulings saying that the cases of public funding in Spanish, Italian, Portuguese and French public broadcasters were in line with state aid requirements.[7]

However, private broadcasters are not letting the matter rest there. They continue to make complaints to the European Court of Justice. Also, in March 2004, the leading private media associations, Association of Commercial Television, European Publishers Council and Association Européenne des Radios, released a White Paper (2004) entitled *Safeguarding the Future of the European Audiovisual Market*. The White Paper concludes that years of over-funding and under-regulation of public broadcasters have undermined the competitiveness of the television industry as well as adversely affecting multi-channel television, TV programme production, radio broadcasting, internet content and the press.

They also accuse the European Commission of taking over ten years to deal with some of the complaints against public service funding. This delay was compounded by: (a) inadequate financial transparency in publicly-funded broadcasting, and (b) the failure of EU member-states to properly define the remit of publicly funded broadcasters in receipt of state aid, which has resulted – in the view of the private sector – to 'an unprecedented level of market distortion'. The private media associations contend that publicly funded broadcasters have benefited and will benefit from:

- Forecast growth in state aid to European publicly funded broadcasters of 4.8%, more than 20% ahead of forecast GDP growth over the period 2001–2004.
- Lack of independent regulation: over half of Europe's publicly funded broadcasters do not fully comply with the independent regulation requirement set out by the European Commission on the application of state aid rules to public service broadcasting.
- The option to capture commercial revenues in addition to state aid, something not permitted in other liberalised sectors according to the EU Treaty and articles 87 and 86.2.

Therefore, they call on the EU Member States with publicly funded broadcasters who collect advertising in addition to state aid to initiate the process of migration to a single-funded model and to implement correctly, and in an impartial manner, the existing competition as provisioned by the EU Treaty as they have been applied to other sectors with a significant public sector element.

It remains to be seen what effect the private broadcasters' pressures will have. It is unlikely to change the EU's approach and is, in fact, seen by some as an expression of the private sector's frustration and helplessness in the face of development of EU policy, which has largely gone against its wishes. Nevertheless, private media owners may be more effective in influencing policy at the national level, and if EU Member States change their approach, the EU itself would no doubt duly follow. A first result, however, is that public broadcasters have faced increased scrutiny concerning the financing of their operations, especially their digital ventures. The last investigation (March 2005) of the European Commission on the funding of public broadcasters was in Germany (ARD and ZDF), in the Netherlands (NOS) and in Ireland (RTE).

The Digital Challenge
European television is on the eve of digitalisation, so public service broadcasters have to face an additional challenge in both audience and funding, since the entry of a plethora of digital channels will further fragment the audience and decrease public broadcaster's advertising revenue. Analysts believe that in the new digital environment public broadcasters may witness a further decrease in their audiences, which will certainly pose questions about the legitimacy of their licence fee.

In the digitalised television environment, a new challenge for public broadcasters is to evolve in a way that allows them to continue to serve though their traditional transmission infrastructure, while taking advantage of opportunities in the new media universe. In effect, the digital age poses a certain number of threats and challenges to public broadcasters (Molsky, 1999, pp. 19–20):

> The introduction of digital television means *more costs* in the short and medium term as public broadcasters purchase new equipment, to make investments in infrastructure and continue to operate older equipment, due to their public service remit, until an eventual analogue switch-off. The numerous services launched by private companies, which do not have similar obligations, will erode further the position of public broadcasters, and hit their audience shares and commercial revenues.

The *growing cost of programmes,* such as films and sports, is also adversely affecting the public broadcasters' financial position. This is due to the intense competition from private broadcasters. The result is a high increase in programme prices and has forced public broadcasters either to try to outbid them for the remaining programmes – directly affecting the financing and production of other programmes – or to lose these and see their viewing share and advertising revenue drop even lower.

Public broadcasters need to allocate considerable amounts of money to convert to digital (infrastructure investment), where most of their spending in general goes into programming, with what are essentially stagnant revenues. Moreover, this leads the public broadcasters to establish new channels, which do not necessarily generate significant income.

The difference for public broadcasters in comparison to private media groups is that their income (especially the licence fee) is not only static, but, as we have seen, cannot be easily used for digital ventures. However, public broadcasters are responding to challenges. Almost all the public broadcasters of Western Europe have adopted digital strategies (see chapter 7). Public broadcasters can also rely on a certain number of significant assets, such as (Molsky 1999, pp. 21–22):

■ Their legacy since they have developed a 'brand' and, as a result, have often secured a loyal following. In contrast to their private rivals, who are the targets of take-overs and mergers, or constant adjustments, public broadcasters benefit from a degree of stability.
■ They offer a broad choice of programming to the widest possible audience. They also produce quality programmes.
■ They are generally popular, often commanding the largest audiences in most countries; they are often critical to the success of new digital platforms.
■ They generally offer a comprehensive service at a very reasonable cost to viewers.

Although these assets may have a positive result for public broadcasters, it is unclear whether they can benefit from them. In fact, the private media associations, in the above noted White Paper (2004), accuse public broadcasters that in so doing, they 'lever their dominant market position and well-known brand to rapidly attain market leading positions'.

The EU is on record as stating that the European and national regulatory frameworks should allow public broadcasters to take advantage of the new developments and opportunities of the digital era. In the UK, the Communications White Paper considers that public service broadcasting will continue to play a key role in the digital future, and perhaps, a more important role than in the past (White Paper, 2000, pp. 47–8). On the other hand, the British government in February 2000 rejected the BBC's request for a supplementary £24 digital licence fee, and instead increased the licence fee from April 2000 by £3 (£104 per year). This was significantly less than the £10–£15 increase that some analysts had predicted. The increase in the licence fee will provide the BBC with an extra £200 million a year, but the Corporation had asked for an extra £700 million. The licence fee will be raised by 1.5 % year above inflation for the period 2000–2007, which will make it worth £700 million per annum by 2006–2007. This arrangement certainly causes problems for the BBC's digital strategy. The BBC has had to sell one of its divisions, BBC Technology, in order to obtain funds to finance digital development. Barry Cox (2004), the British government's digital television adviser, has pointed out that in the digital era the BBC should start to pave the way for a new kind of public service broadcaster, which maintains its production base but is funded by voluntary subscription rather than compulsory tax. The BBC has replied that in this case its channels would be made available only to people who could afford to pay (about £13 per month or £156 per year), it would lead to a loss of consumer welfare, and those who did subscribe would be paying more for a narrower range of services (BBC 2004, p. 115).

This is just one example of the policy and regulatory approach to the future of PSB in the digital era. On the whole, European countries assign an important role to PSB broadcasters in the transition to digital terrestrial broadcasting and digital switchover and make sure that they are assigned multiplexes by law, in order to profit fully from new opportunities.

Concluding remarks

The funding and consequently the future of the public broadcasters will depend on whether they justify their legitimacy and whether the political climate will favour them. In effect, as in the past, the establishment and the survival of public service broadcasters will be more than a historical contingency. In the 21st century, their role will depend on several important factors: individual countries' media legislation, EU legislation and individual national policies. The speed of introduction of both digital television and the various interactive services will also be an important determinant.

The recent trends in some countries of replacing the licence fee by state grants or public funds or a kind of income tax may not pose any problem for the future of the public broadcasters as long as they ensure diversity of content, broad public access and, consequently, broad public support. In other words, public broadcasters have less to fear than their private counterparts, as long as they remain popular and seek to offer good value for money. As Molsky has noted (1999, p. 174), 'they are a recognised and familiar brand, and often remain the leading operators in their home markets'. Only in cases where public broadcasters lose their public, and consequently political support, would these new ways of funding, or even the old system of licence fees, cause an incremental problem. In other words, if public funds, grants or the licence fee become unjustifiable, then the public broadcasters will have to turn to advertising. But if dual funding for public broadcasters is now disputed, what would the reactions be in the case where advertising took on a prominent role in their income, especially when advertising revenue for the majority of European public broadcasters, as a share of total income, remained relatively static over the period 1992–95?

Nevertheless, the abolition of the licence fee is not easy. It is unlikely that a government will decide to abolish the licence fee in an era in which politicians are made to feel uncomfortable by the increased power of the private media and their owners. Moreover, one could say that the fact that private broadcasters protest against the dual funding of public broadcasters indicates that they are much less stable that their public counterparts. Politicians and the EU publicly support public broadcasters. But, political decisions frequently change. It is also often overlooked that the Protocol on public broadcasting annexed to the Amsterdam Treaty is mainly a political decision and public broadcasters continue to function in a hostile neo-liberal environment (see also Collins, 1998, p. 371). On the other hand, it is still the prerogative of the member states to define the public service remit. In effect, most states have not done so, and the prevailing policy is imprecise.

Still, what primarily worries public broadcasters is not the European Union or their governments but the challenges of the digital era. For example, a combination of the development of digital and pay-TV may lead to unknown results with regard to the future of public service broadcasters as we know them. In the best case, the licence fee revenues are likely to remain flat in real terms, reflecting growing public spending constraints in the downward pressure on the licence fee, compounded by the increasingly competitive digitalised environment. Public broadcasters may gradually enter a fiscal crisis, which will force them to cut costs and reduce their programming budgets in order to adapt to the new situation. This will also affect the quality of their programming, leading to a 'vicious circle' of declining audiences and, consequently, decreasing legitimacy of the licence fee. To fulfil their role and mission, public broadcasters need to be a major force in their national audiovisual landscape, and they must cater for all sections and groups of their society with, in particular, quality mass-appeal programming. If they become under-funded they will struggle to meet their public programming remit, and this in turn may call into question their right to public funding.

On the other hand, public broadcasters have a long tradition and reflect the democratic, social and cultural principles and needs of the European societies, and therefore occupy a special place in these societies. It is not a coincidence that, despite strong competition, public service broadcasters have been able to retain the licence fee system, provoking the rage of their private competitors. Moreover, public television has not been made unnecessary by digital transmission. 'On the contrary new technology strengthens the need for public control because it reinforces the factors that limit competition' (Curran, 2002, p. 204).

In either case, however, public broadcasters have entered a new era with an unpredictable future. It is up to them to justify their goals, mission and structure in the digital era.

Notes
1. Public broadcasters that carry no advertising and fund their public service activities mostly from licence fee revenue are the BBC (United Kingdom), Sveriges Television-STV (Sweden), Danmark's Radio –DR (Denmark). YLE of Finland could also be included in this category, as it can carry advertising only when covering major – and very expensive to buy – sports events, so public income represents about 94.5% of its revenues
2. According to the EAO, the amount of the licence fee varies considerably from 156.5 euros per inhabitant in Switzerland to 6 euros per inhabitant in Turkey. Among the countries with the fastest growth were Sweden (+69%), Germany (+59%) and Britain (+56%). European countries to have experienced a substantial increase in licence fee income between 1990 and 2000. By and large, the vast majority of Europeans paid an average of 190 euros in 2000 as licence fees, though the rate of licence fee evasion varies from country to country.
3. Meanwhile, the Conservative Party has sponsored the publication of a report *Beyond the Charter. The BBC after 2006* (Broadcasting Policy Group, 2004) which states that the future of PSB in the UK is threatened; radically different ways of delivering it are required; the structure and policies of the BBC do not serve the best interests of the creative community and a new structure would release the creative flows in the industry and resolve long-standing complaints of anti-competitive behaviour by the

BBC. Accordingly, the television licence fee should be steadily reduced from 2007 onwards, and gradually replaced by a combination of subscription and indirect public funding. It should be abolished completely when analogue television transmission is switched off. In future, the BBC should be regulated by consumer power, creative and commercial competition and a new institutional structure. In 2003/4, the annual amount of the licence fee was £121, generating an income of £2.8 billion.

4. There were also other reasons. First, a steadily growing number of citizens evaded payment of the licence fee. Secondly, only 50% of the proceeds from this source went to PSB, while the other 50% was treated by the Treasury as ordinary tax revenue. This was misleading, as people thought that the full amount of their licence fee went to the public broadcaster.

5. DG IV (1998) *Application of Articles 90, paragraph 2, 92 and 93 of the EC Treaty in the broadcasting sector. Discussion paper.* Brussels.

6. For example, in February 1999, the Commission approved the financing from public revenues of the two German public interest channels Der Kinderkanal and Phoenix, adopting the position that the transfers are compatible with the EC Treaty since they allow for public service remits of their public broadcasting. Moreover, in September 1999, the European Commission approved the financing from public resources of BBC News 24. It found that transfer of funds collected from licence fees to this thematic channel is compatible with the EC Treaty because it allows for public service remits for public broadcasting

7. See IP/03/1686 of 10/12/2003 and IP/03/1399 of 15/10/2003.

References

BBC 2004 *Building public value; Renewing the BBC for a digital world.* BBC: London. (Available at: http://www.bbc.co.uk)

Brants, Kees and Karen Siune(1992) 'Public service broadcasting in a public of flux', p. 101–115 in Karen Siune and W. Tuetzschler (eds.) *Dynamics of Media Politics; Broadcasts and Electronic Media in Western Europe.* London: Sage.

Brants, Kees (2004) 'The Netherlands', pp. 145–156 in M.Kelly, G. Mazzoleni and D. McQuail (eds) *The Media in Europe, The Euromedia Handbook.* London: Sage,.

Broadcasting Policy Group (2004) *Beyond the Charter. The BBC after 2006.* London: Premium Publishing.

Collins, Richard (1998) 'Public service broadcasting and the media economy; European trends in the late 1990s', *Gazette*, 60 (5), pp. 363–76.

Cox, Barry (2004) *Free For All? Public service television in the digital age.* London: Demos.(Available at: http://demos.co.uk)

De Bens, Els (2003) 'The Future of public service broadcasting in Belgium: opportunities and impediments', pp. 207–222 in P.Donges &.M. Puppis *Die Zukunft des Öffentlichen Rundfunks.* Köln: von Harlem Verlag,.

Curran, James (2002) *Media and Power.* London: Routledge.

Etzioni-Halevy, Eva (1987) *National Broadcasting Under Siege: A Comparative Study of Australia, Britain, Israel, and West Germany.* Basingstoke: Macmillan.

European Audiovisual Observatory (EAO) (2000) *Statistical Yearbook 2000, Television, Video and New Media in Europe.* Strasbourg.

European Audiovisual Observatory (EAO) (2002) *Yearbook 2002: Film, Television, Video and Multimedia in Europe*, Vol. 1: Economy of the European Audiovisual Industry,

European Audiovisual Observatory. Strasbourg.

European Commission (1998) *The Digital Age: European Audiovisual Policy.* Report from the High Level Group on Audiovisual Policy chaired by Commissioner Marcelino Oreja, Brussels: October.

European Commission *Communication of the Commission on the Application of the State Aid rules to Public Service Broadcasters,* Brussels, 15 November 2001 EC 320/11.

Hallin, Daniel C. and Stylianos Papathanassopoulos (2002) 'Political clientelism and the media: Southern Europe and Latin America in comparative perspective'. *Media, Culture and Society,* 24(2), pp. 175–198.

Holtz-Bacha, Christina. (2002) *A vicious circle; the difficult position of public broadcasting in Germany,* paper presented at the RIPE @ 2002 Conference, 17–19 January, Finland.

IP RTL Group (2003) *Television 2002. European Key Facts.*

Molsky, Norman (1999) *European Public Broadcasting in the Digital Age.* London: FT Media and Telecoms.

Norcontel Ltd (in association with NERA, *Screen Digest* and Stanbrook and Hooper) (1998) *Economic Implications of New Communication Technologies on the Audiovisual Markets.* A study commissioned on behalf of the European Commission. Brussels: Commission of the European Communities.

Oreja, Marcelino. (1998) Address to the Spanish Parliamentary Subcommittee on the RTVE (Spanish Broadcasting Corporation). Madrid, 11 December.

Papathanassopoulos, Stylianos (2002) *European Television in the Digital Age, Issues, Dynamics and Realities.* Cambridge: Polity Press.

Traquina, Nelson (1995) 'Portuguese television: the politics of savage deregulation'. *Media Culture and Society,* 17 (2), pp. 223–38.

Traquina, Nelson (1998) 'Western European broadcasting, deregulation, and public television: the Portuguese experience'. *Journalism and Mass Communication Monographs,* 167.

White Paper (2004) *Safeguarding the Future of the European Audiovisual Market,* A White Paper on the Financing and Regulation of Publicly Funded Broadcasters, Association of Commercial Television, European Publishers Council and Association Européenne des Radios, Brussels, March 2004.

White Paper (2000) *Communications White Paper.* London: Department of Trade and Industry/ Department of Culture, Media and Sport. Available at: http://communicationswhitepaper.gov.uk

7

PUBLIC SERVICE BROADCASTING AND NEW TECHNOLOGIES: MARGINALISATION OR RE-MONOPOLISATION

Minna Aslama and Trine Syvertsen

The new media have drastically transformed the broadcasting environment. Although specific situations in individual countries differ, the new media revolution manifests itself everywhere in Europe in four distinct areas: technology, the market environment, consumer behaviour and regulation (c.f., EBU, 2002, pp. 6–13, cf. also Wood, 2002; Dahlgren, 2000; Syvertsen, 2004a).

As important actors in the European media marketplace public broadcasters are very much part of these developments. The major technological and economic transformations nevertheless pose challenges to their current and future positions. One key question concerns the *centrality* of public broadcasting institutions in the years to come: are the new technological and economic developments likely to lead to a *marginalisation* of public broadcasting, or is it more likely that the public broadcasters will be allocated a more central position and may, indeed, 'crowd out' other operators (Collins, 2002)? A related question concerns the *distinctiveness* of the public broadcasters' content and services. Is there evidence that public broadcasters are using the opportunities presented by digitalisation and new technologies to develop more distinct and innovative content, or is it more likely that the strategies of public broadcasters will be indistinguishable from those of commercial organisations?

In this chapter, three aspects of media policy that are crucial for the future position of public broadcasters will be discussed. Firstly whether public broadcasters are allowed or encouraged to include new media such as *the Internet* as part of their services, secondly *how digital terrestrial television,* the most debated digital platform, is being developed and encouraged by policy-makers and governments, and thirdly what *new forms of content* public broadcasters are allowed or encouraged to develop. In short: To what degree are policies developed that will allow and make possible for public broadcasting institutions to evolve into multimedia organisations, using the new technologies to continue and renew the public service tradition?

Broadcasting Policies: Trends and Measures

As Table 1 illustrates, there exists a catalogue of possible responses that policy-makers have at their disposal when dealing with the issue of public broadcasting and new technologies:

Given the ambiguous stand of the EU (e.g., Näränen, 2003), policy makers in different countries have responded differently to the challenges posed to public broadcasters.

Table 1: Public broadcasting and new technologies: possible policy responses

Policy response	Explanation and examples
Allow	Public broadcasters are *allowed* to enter new distribution platforms and develop new services. Broadcasters are allowed to develop new forms of content, for example in the form of niche channels or new forms of multimedia or interactive content.
Oblige	Public broadcasters are *required* to take part in certain activities or distribute their services on certain platforms. The justifications for introducing such obligations may be, for example, that such services are crucial to combat the digital divide or further industrial policy goals such as a rapid transition to the information society.
Restrict	Public broadcasters are *restricted* from entering certain distribution platforms, employ certain business models, or develop certain services. The justification for such limitations may be, for example, that such services are incompatible with the broadcasters' public service remit or that public broadcasters are distorting competition by entering new areas.
Support	Public broadcasters are given special *support,* for example in the form of grants, financial incentives or increased licence fees, to develop new services and enter new platforms. The political justification may be, for example, that such services are crucial to realise cultural, social or industrial goals.
Protect	Policies are developed to *protect* public broadcasters, their investments, their positions, and/or their possibilities to enter new platforms. A form of protection may for example be to develop digital terrestrial television platforms, so that public broadcasters may have privileged access to a digital distribution network. Other measures may include policies to protect public broadcasters' right to attractive content.

While some have encouraged, obliged or supported endeavours to develop new services and enter new platforms, others have reacted more hesitantly or passively, or have introduced restrictions on what public broadcasters are allowed to do with new media. The following discussion demonstrates the main dilemmas and approaches.

Public Broadcasting and the Internet: Encouraged or Constrained?

European public broadcasters are increasingly utilising the Internet and mobile media. Radio stations available via the Internet have proven to be successful endeavours (Fontaine & Le Borgne-Bachschmidt, 2001). All the members of the European Broadcasting Union are present on the Internet and a great majority has teletext operations. Some 40% of them were already active in mobile media in 2001 (Mournier & Drumare, 2001). However, there is a great variation in what is being developed. While the BBC, for example, views the Internet as a true content provider, with commercial services included, the French and Hungarian broadcasters utilise it mostly as a public relations vehicle and a support for its traditional programming. In the globalising media market place national differences still prevail, due to different amounts of resources and differing legal provisions regarding the public service broadcasters and the new media.

The uneven development is partly caused by variations in financial resources and strategic capacity. Many of the smaller European broadcasters, particularly in Eastern and Central Europe, have only a small staff and no standard organisational structures for their new media and multimedia activities. There is much uncertainty about how important the Internet will become as a supplement (or as a threat) to broadcasting, and this creates insecurity about whether the business models developed for the Internet and on-line media will make them profitable investments. Commercial enterprises are anticipating that new forms of finance, such as e-commerce, on-line merchandising and on-line advertising will make them less dependent on traditional advertising (Roth, 2002). These same possibilities are, in principle, open to public broadcasters but, in order for these organisations to exploit such new forms of revenue, new policies or liberalisation of existing regulations may be necessary. It seems that the same questions arise as when commercial broadcasters entered the public service-dominated radio and television market: can those sites be separate commercial entities in which advertising plays a significant part (Hills & Michalis, 2001)? And should public broadcasters be allowed to use public funds, for example from licence fees, to develop services for the new media?

While many national governments and regulators have so far taken a passive stand towards the involvement of public broadcasters in new media, there are signs that the issue is becoming more controversial. An EBU survey shows that half of the funding for mobile services offered by member organisations is acquired by commercial revenues (mainly advertising and sponsorship), whereas the share of commercial funding in Internet activities constitutes one third of total funding (Mournier & Drumare, 2001). While policy-makers in some countries are keen to see these figures grow, others are introducing more restrictive regulations. The situations in Germany and Britain stand out as contrasting examples of the different policy approaches that have been developed thus far (Roth, 2002).

In Germany, the public broadcaster ARD is allowed to pursue on-line activities, but only services that complement their programmes. On-line sponsorship and advertising is prohibited, and there is considerable pressure to prevent the broadcaster from using public funds on the internet. In Britain, by contrast, the BBC has a massive web presence, with the government's approval. In 2000 the BBC site was divided into a public site and an advertisement-funded commercial site, but there are ongoing debates as to whether advertising should also be allowed on the public site.[1] Following complaints about cross promotion between television and the Internet services, some restrictions have nevertheless been imposed. In 2004 the BBC decided to shut down five of its websites in response to government review: it concluded that part of the BBC's web presence was having an adverse impact on commercial providers of competing services (Phillips, 2004). In general, however, the government has encouraged the BBC's on-line developments, commercial activities and partnerships included

The policy differences between Britain and Germany are paralleled in other regions. Even within the culturally homogenous Nordic region, policy approaches to the issue of public broadcasting on the Internet vary greatly. The Norwegian public broadcaster NRK obtained the right to transmit advertising on the Internet and teletext in 1999, and since then the two have become important advertising media and marketing outlets for the broadcaster (which has no regular advertising). In Sweden and Finland, the public broadcasters SVT and YLE are allowed to launch Internet activities, but strict restrictions apply on collaboration with commercial partners and funding: advertising and/or sponsorship is not allowed in any of the new technology services. The Danish case is in-between and reflects the dual situation of television: Parallel to the rules governing the television channels, no advertising is seen on the DR web sites, while ads are permitted for TV2's Internet activities.

To summarise, it appears that most public broadcasters are *allowed* to enter the internet, but that in several cases *restrictions* apply as to how profoundly they may exploit new media. More restrictions may be imposed as the new medium matures; it appears that restrictions are being imposed in several countries regarding advertising and/or sponsorship on the Internet (see the appendix by Marcel Betzel in the present volume; see also Betzel 2003). Restrictions are, however, only one barrier to entry.

The other side of the coin is whether the public broadcasters are actively encouraged or *obliged* to enter new markets, and whether their efforts are *supported* legally or financially. In the Greek case, for example, the state broadcaster ERT is allowed to develop new technologies and programmess, but in practice, any such decision needs the financial support of the government since the broadcaster has not the financial resources.

Generally, *encouragement* or support has not been forthcoming for the involvement of public broadcasters in the Internet and mobile media. As a consequence, the less affluent public broadcasters have had fewer opportunities to develop new services.

Public Broadcasting and Digital Television Platforms: Taking Charge or Tagging Along?

The key issue pertaining to new technologies and public service broadcasting has been digital television (DTV). For public service broadcasters, the core concern is the same as with all new communication technologies: how to avoid marginalisation in a situation where new distribution platforms, controlled by other operators, are increasing their presence. To protect their future position, public broadcasters have encouraged policy makers to develop terrestrial networks or introduce regulations against so-called walled gardens and proprietary technologies.[2] For public broadcasters there is also the choice of whether to enter cable and satellite platforms operated by others, as some of them have done,[3] or to reserve their content for platforms where they have more control, such as digital terrestrial television.

On the European level, policy responses have so far been hesitant. It seems that nationally there is a mixture of cultural policy and economic policy goals behind the drive to establish terrestrial television platforms. The following arguments are present in several countries, although the emphasis may differ:

Table 2: Arguments in favour of establishing digital terrestrial television networks

Arguments	Explanation and examples
Combating the digital divide	Digital terrestrial television is seen as a vehicle to get everybody on-line regardless of age, gender and educational differences. Born (2003, pp. 773–774) argues for example that the British government wanted to establish terrestrial networks as a means to foster social inclusion and political activity. Coppens (2003, p. 152) writes that the main purpose of the Flemish VRT was to respond to the government call to combat the digital divide, and grant all citizens 'equal opportunities to be part of the new information society'.
More rapid transitions to the information society	Establishing digital terrestrial networks is seen as a tool to further broader industrial policy matters, such as advancing the country or region into a fully-fledged information society. In Finland, for example, the emphasis was on developing the country as a leading information society corresponding to the advanced role of mobile communications in the Finnish economy (c.f. Castells & Himanen, 2003, also Brown & Picard, 2004). Corcoran (2002, p. 55) places the plans for DTT in Ireland within the government's 'ambitious plans to exploit the benefits of the information society'.
A more cost-effective infrastructure and analogue switch-off	Since digital distribution is less expensive than analogue distribution, terrestrial networks are seen as a way to save money on public broadcasting in the long run. In some countries, Britain among them, the argument was also that the state would make money on selling off radio spectrum that was no longer in use (Collins, 2002). The goal is thus to bring about the eventual switch-off of analogue

Arguments	Explanation and examples
	transmission networks to release spectrum for alternative uses (Brown & Picard, 2004).
Mobile distribution	The fact that terrestrial digital television was the only TV platform that could offer mobile distribution was held as an important argument in Norway (Syvertsen, 2004a).
Create competitive markets	Since digital and cable operators have already established digital networks, the argument has been that terrestrial networks are crucial to introduce more competition. Collins states that one of the purposes of the British government was to create competitive markets (Collins, 2002, see also Born, 2003). Also, in Norway, Spain, France and Italy the potential to generate increased competition in the national market was cited as important (Brown & Picard, 2004, Syvertsen, 2004a).
National regulation of digital broadcasting	Digital terrestrial broadcasting leaves national policy-makers with more control over digital television. Corcoran (2002, p. 53) argues that in the Irish case this argument was
	pronounced. Indeed, the key document was 'very tightly framed within the discourse of the nation'.
Regional broadcasting	The promotion of regional and special interest programming was cited as an important reason for digital television in Germany (Brown & Picard, 2004). Also, in France channel capacity has been reserved for regional broadcasting (SOU, 2004, p. 132).
Protect public service broadcasting	Since digital terrestrial television is more easily regulated, establishing terrestrial networks may be seen as a way to protect public service television. This argument was very pronounced in Norway (Syvertsen, 2004a, p 192), but also emphasised in countries such as Britain (Collins, 2002, p. 9).

The difficulties associated with the switchover imply that digital television will evolve along different paths in different countries, Transition periods from analogue to digital broadcasting are expected to be quite long in many countries. One estimate is that digital television will reach 80 million European households by the end of 2007, and that satellite will remain the prominent digital platform, accounting for some 40% of the market. Some public broadcasters may have real difficulties going digital at all. The Greek broadcaster ERT holds a license for a digital platform, but this platform exists on paper only as there are insufficient resources to fund the switchover. In Hungary, digital satellite television is well under way, with more than 80 television programmes, but national public service programmes and the national commercial programmes of terrestrial broadcasting are not part of the offer; there are no definite plans for a terrestrial platform. In Ireland, the public broadcaster was 'squeezed out' in the political deliberations, and in

2002 there was no sign of the DTT platform that had legally been provided for in a broadcasting bill a few years earlier (Corcoran, 2002, p 63).

Also, the regulatory frameworks established for public broadcasting and digital terrestrial television vary greatly country by country. In some countries the public broadcasters are seen as crucial vehicles to combat the digital divide and further the information society. These institutions are therefore *obliged* to take part in certain activities. Contrary to the case of the Internet and of mobile media, many public broadcasters also seem to be *supported* financially to develop digital television. In Germany and the U.K., for example, the annual fee for the PSB was raised to accommodate the costs.

In other countries, public broadcasters are *allowed* to enter digital platforms, but do not receive particular encouragement or sufficient economic support to do so. This is the case, for example, in Greece and Hungary. More specific *requirements* and *restrictions* also apply in some cases. In some countries minimum limits for geographical coverage are imposed. In Austria, PSB activity, apart form the two terrestrial TV channels, has to be outsourced to a subsidiary company (EPRA, 2004).

To sum up, in many cases public broadcasters have been granted technical and financial resources to play a leading role in digital terrestrial television. The development of a terrestrial digital platform is also seen as a way of *protecting* public broadcasters. Indeed, an analysis by the European Platform for Regulatory Authorities concludes that 'when the proactive approach of the PSB meets a regulatory model that assigns a leading role to the PSB, the DTT seems to find a favourable context to develop' (EPRA, 2004).

The Digital Opportunities: Distinction or Commercialisation?
We have observed that public broadcasters in many countries seem to be supported and encouraged to enter the digital era. But what about the content of the services that the broadcasters are developing? To what degree are public broadcasters using the new opportunities to produce new forms of content and address new audiences? To what degree are policies being developed to encourage and support new forms of content and modes of address?

Two strategies in particular stand out for public broadcasters in the digital environment: the development of thematic or target channels, and so called enhanced television, that is, content with additional services. As Hujanen (2004) notes, the point of departure for the digital transition to many public service television broadcasters, from the BBC to the German ARD, the Swedish SVT, and the Finnish YLE, seems to be the following: they simulcast existing analogue channels and add new thematic ones to their digital channel bouquet. Most of the new channels seem to avoid challenging commercial competitors head on, as they focus on informational and educational genres. Neither, however, is there much evidence that a substantial amount of original programming is produced for the thematic channels. Among the thematic channels on offer are news and current affairs channels, children's channels[4], and various cultural and educational services.[5] In Sweden and Italy, sports channels are either planned or included in the public service portfolio (Jutterström, Söderberg & Björk, 2004).

Although the new digital channels are certainly extending the public service output, many worry that the development towards thematic channels may be detrimental to public broadcasting. Thus, Hujanen (2004) claims that generalist channels should remain an essential feature of the public service digital supply and that this is necessary if public service broadcasters are to act as a factor of social cohesion.

The second main strategy is enhanced television, i.e. content coupled with additional services. These may include communicative features (chats), entertainment (voting or participation in games from home) and transactions such as TV shopping (Orava & Perttula, 2004).[6] Interactive possibilities are more relevant for some public service programming; where news and weather, sportscasts, studio discussions, reality programmes, game shows and advertisements are 'ITV-ready', dramatic content is much more difficult to enhance (Gálik, 2002). This may lead to some forms of programming being prioritised at the cost of others.

In the early days of digital communication, some public service broadcasters opted for daring explorations in order to try out interactive possibilities. In Norway, the NRK put on a show called *Forfall* ('Decay') in 2001, where a well-known performance artist and broadcaster was locked into a shop-front window with the mission of decaying as much as possible (mentally as well as physically) in a week. In Finland, YLE broadcast an interactive drama series for a month in 2000 and later the show was transformed into an installation that became a part of a new media art exhibition. In both cases, one of the purposes was to try out off-broadcasting-time possibilities (OBT) and the combination between different functionalities such as TV, radio, phone, SMS, the Internet and chat. This kind of experimental content could not be easily imagined as a part of commercial programme and strategy development and, in general, public service has opted for less avant-garde strategies when new services are made permanent. Later applications include more prominent use of mobile phones and SMS messages as supplements to programmes or as basis for programmes of their own, in both NRK and YLE (Beyer et al, 2004). Syvertsen (2004b) distinguishes between serving the public as citizens, audiences, customers and players/participants, and claims that public broadcasters are predominantly using the digital opportunities to serve the public as audiences and customers, rather than as citizens and participants.

The European Broadcasting Union (2002, p. 40) argues that the traditional idea of universality may need to be rethought in the new era – not just universality of the *contents* as manifested in the traditional generalist channels, but also universality across the full portfolio of *services*, some of them specialised or tailored for specific audiences. The EBU seems to want it all: it maintains that the elements of the public service content-strategy in a digital environment should include (1) full scale and distinctively public service content and programming; (2) traditional generalist channels also in new multimedia environments; (3) new elements in existing concepts; and (4) new interactive services, as well as services for the on-demand environments (EBU, 2002, pp. 17–18).

In the current phase, it seems unclear what kind of universality will be achieved and what exactly the new technologies will imply regarding a potential renewal of the content. This depends partly on the policy and regulatory framework: are the public broadcasters obliged or enabled to do something new? It appears that content regulations imposed on digital channels of public broadcasters are rather limited. The remit of the Flemish eVRT is merely to guarantee the user access to accurate, reliable and quality information, entertainment and services based on VRT-products and products from third parties. Coppens (2003, p. 155) claims that the remit is vague and unimpressive, and even less clear for the digital than for the analogue services. In some countries, most notably in Scandinavia, there are requirements concerning cultural programming, subtitling for the deaf and the amount of programming time that may consist of repeats, but the programme requirements are nowhere very strict. In Greece, the remit for regulation for digital television states that 25% of the licence programming should be in Greek; that 30% should be either dubbed or subtitled; and that controllers of five or more channels should allocate one for parliamentary coverage (Iosfides, 1998/99). In a majority of countries, however, digital theme channels are not even defined in the legal remit (see the paper by Marcel Betzel in the present volume; see also Betzel, 2003).

Many analyses of digital television tend to end with the same conclusion: that the transition from analogue to digital amplifies rather than reduces the need for content regulation. Regulation in the form of *quotas* and general remits is not sufficient, and may even be counterproductive as it encourages media companies to spread the resources thinly instead of investing in original productions (c.f. Corcoran, 1999). Generally, the boom in digital channels is turning content and talent into scarce and expensive goods, and the problem in the future may be to fund the regular services, and not just the new ones. EU regulations do not seem to rule out the possibility that public broadcasters may develop pay-TV channels in order to obtain new revenue, but the exclusivity of the services could lead to claims that the public service is failing universality.

It is still too early to identify a clear pattern regarding content regulation for digital services. In most countries the emphasis is on establishing services and building up a customer base for the digital media. From this point of view, content regulation is considered counterproductive. So far there appears to be little evidence that public broadcasters are using the digital opportunities to develop more distinct content and new ways of addressing the audience and neither is there much political encouragement or demand that they actually do so.

Conclusions: Marginalisation or Remonopolisation

We have suggested that new technologies may pose a threat of marginalisation for public broadcasters in the market-driven situation. Yet, as depicted in this chapter, the multifaceted transformations due to new technologies suggest multiple risks and uncertainties, as well as evoke different policy reactions nationally. Three scenarios that have been put forward in Danish policy debates – *The Sea of Information, The Digital Lagoons and The Media Islands* – poignantly illustrate the magnitude of the unpredictability of the situation (Jauert 2003, pp. 198–199):

The Sea of Information scenario gives the dominant position to the Internet as the most individual and interactive medium. Contents are then produced and distributed with an infinite number of providers. *The Digital Lagoons* (also known as the gatekeeper scenario) places a few global companies that are active across the media and technologies in charge of the whole media chain. They control everything from copyrights to set-top boxes and programme subscriptions.

These two scenarios imply a strong possibility of marginalisation of publicly funded and nation-bound public service institutions. The third scenario of the *Media Islands* suggests however, that public broadcasters may retain a more dominant position. The lack of demand for interactivity and of investments in technology makes it difficult for new services to earn a return, and consequently, the media landscape may not change as much as many of the prophets of the new media revolution have claimed. Indeed, it seems that many players in the field, from public broadcasters themselves to politicians, scholars, and intra-governmental bodies such as the Council of Europe (2004), believe, at least implicitly, in the third scenario and are convinced that public service broadcasting is worth investment and support, even and especially in the new media era. As one market analysis proposes, channel proliferation and increased competition for audiences may lead to content-regulation focusing on a decreasing number of channels and the role of publicly funded broadcasters becoming more – not less – important (Datamonitor, 2002).

It might be, then, that the actual situation in most countries resembling the *Media Islands* scenario is creating political will and policies that, instead of marginalisation, advocate a kind of remonopolisation of public service. Collins (2002, p. 11), for instance, argues that the BBC's new position may be seen as a 'threat to competition, diversity and pluralism'. The Government uses the BBC to achieve its industrial policy goals – it is a more flexible instrument than private operators, but the result may be that the BBC may 'crowd out' other operators in the public service market, for example in this instance, alternative arts and history channels. Current must-carry rules for public broadcasting makes the situation worse, since this leaves no incentive for cable operators to include other specialist channels.[7] Concern about re-monopolisation is voiced also in other countries, but carries less weight in smaller markets. For instance, the Flemish digital policy provides public broadcaster VRT with a terrestrial monopoly, but this is not called into question as VRT already has a monopoly on analogue TV (and 95% of the households are connected to cable) (Coppens 2003, p. 154). While the segmentation and diversification strategy may work well in large television markets, it may not work with smaller European public service broadcasters where more populous neighbours are rolling out digital television.

This chapter has shown that, as the EU leaves many aspects of public service to the individual nations, a variety of approaches in developments and accompanying policies regarding the new media era will continue to take shape in different countries. This is not unusual, as public service broadcasting has been defined in a multitude of ways and taken different forms in the past. Accordingly, what can be predicted for the new media era is that the fundamentally nation-bound characteristics of public service broadcasting will remain and take shape in a variety of forms between marginalisation and re-monopolisation.

Notes

1. The public site (http://www.bbc.co.uk) is the most visited non-portal site outside the U.S. (Roth 2002).

2. One of the European-wide issues is the unwillingness of the EU to impose regulation concerning standards for digital television transmission and reception. This has resulted in different standards for satellite, cable and terrestrial transmissions and, accordingly, in the need for viewers to acquire different set-top boxes. Consequently, digital satellite operators are employing proprietary and non-interoperable standards in order to 'lock in' their existing subscribers (Brown & Picard, 2004, p 6).
3. For example, while it has been the policy of NRK and BBC to be available on all platforms, the Hungarian and Finnish public service broadcasters are not available on digital satellite.
4. The BBC offers channels for both pre-school and older children.
5. The Swedish SVT, together with the educational broadcasting service UR, is, as at 2004, planning to launch a 'Knowledge Channel'; in Britain and Italy the BBC and RAI both have special channels for documentaries and culture, and the Finnish YLE *Teema* combines educational, cultural and science programming.
6. Regarding interactive services, two models seem to be emerging: walled gardens and enhanced television. The latter is the alternative of public broadcasters. Each model includes e-mail, electronic programme guides, limited Internet browsing, the ability to interact with programmes in real time and voting on programme content (Corcoran 2002).
7. Se Collins' (2002, pp. 12–13) list of the BBC's anti-competition actions.

References

Betzel, M. (2003) *Programme performance of public service broadcasting and its mission in the digital age.* Unpublished paper, EPRA.

Beyer, Y., G.S. Enli, A.J. Maasø & E.Ytreberg (2004) 'Small talk makes a big difference: recent developments in interactive, SMS-based television'. To be published in *Television and New Media*, forthcoming.

Born, G. (2003) 'Strategy, positioning and projection in digital television: Channel Four and the commercialisation of public service broadcasting in the UK', *Media, Culture & Society*, Vol. 25:6, pp. 773–799.

Brown, A. & R.Picard (2004) *The Long Hard Road to Digital Television in Europe.* Working Paper presented in the 6th World Media Economics Conference, HEC Montreal, Canada, May 12–15, 2004.

Castells, M. & P. Himanen (2003) *The Information Society and the Business Environment: The Finnish Model.* Oxford: Oxford University Press,.

Collins, R. (2002), '2002 – digital television in the United Kingdom', *Javnost: The Public*, Vol. 9:4 pp. 5–18.

Coppens, T. (2003) 'Digital public broadcasting in Flanders: Walking the tightrope', *Telematics and Informatics*, Vol. 20:2, pp. 143–159.

Corcoran, F. (1999) 'Towards digital television in Europe', *Javnost: The Public*, Vol. 6:3, pp. 67–85.

Corcoran, F. (2002) 'Digital television in Ireland: local forces in a global context', *Javnost: The Public*, Vol. 9:4, pp. 49–66.

Council of Europe, (2004) *Recommendation 1641 (2004) Public service broadcasting.* The Parliamentary Assembly of the Council of Europe.

Dahlgren, P. (2000) 'Key trends in European Television', pp. 23–34 in J. Wieten, G. Murdock & Dahlgren P. (eds.) *Television Across Europe. A Comparative Introduction.* London, Thousand Oaks & New Delhi: Sage Publications.

Datamonitor (2002) *Changing Regulation for Digital and Interactive TV*, Datamonitor Analyst Report.

Datamonitor (2003) *Digital and Interactive TV Markets: Service Development and Uptake to 2007,* Datamonitor Analyst Report.

EBU (2002) *Media with a purpose. Public Service Broadcasting in the digital era.* The Report of the Digital Strategy Group of the European Broadcasting Union.

EPRA, (2004) *Final Report* of the Working Group on Digital Terrestrial Television in EPRA Countries. June 2, 2004.

Fontaine, G. & F. Le Borgne-Bachschmidt (2001) *Objectives, organisation and funding of public service broadcasting,* Council of Europe/IDATE – Institut de l'audiovisuel et des telecommunications en Europe.

Gálik, M. (2002) 'Value added services on digital television platforms', *Javnost: The Public,* Vol. 9:4, pp. 67–74.

Hills, J. & M. Michalis '(2001) 'The internet: A challenge to public service broadcasting?' *Gazette,* Vol. 62:6, pp. 479–493.

Hujanen, T. (2004) 'Implications for Public Service Broadcasters', pp. 57–84 in A. Brown & R. Pickard (eds.) *Digital Television in Europe.* New Jersey: Lawrence Erlbaum Associates.

Iosfides, P. (1998/99). 'Regulating Digital TV: The Greek Experience', *International Journal of Communications Law and Policy,* Vol. 1:2 Printed from Internet: http://www.ijclp. org [07.08.03].

Jauert, P. (2003) 'Policy Development in Danish Radio Broadcasting 1980–2002. Layers, Scenarios and the Public Service Remit' pp. 187–203 in G.F. Lowe & T. Hujanen (eds.) *Broadcasting & Convergence: New articulations of the public service remit.* Gothenburg: Nordicom.

Jutterström, C., L.Söderberg, & C. Björk (2003) 'Digital in Sweden – Takes up the challenge', in *DIFFUSION Online.* 2003/44. Printed from Internet: http://www.ebu.ch/en/union/ diffusion_on_line/index.php?display=EN [10.09.04].

Mournier, P. & X. Drumare (2001) *The Internet and Multimedia Activities of EBU Members,* unpublished presentation, EBU Strategic Information Services (SIS).

Näränen, P. (2003) 'European Regulation of Digital Television. The opportunity lost and found?' pp. 57–68 in G. F. Lowe, & T. Hujanen, (eds.) *Broadcasting & Convergence: New articulations of the public service remit.* Gothenburg, Nordicom.

Orava, J. & M. Perttula (2004) *Interactive digital TV in Europe.* E-Content Report 7. ACTeN. Printed from Internet: www.acten.net [10.09.04].

Phillips. L. (2004) *BBC closes 5 websites as review criticises online activity,* 06/07/2004. Printed from Internet: www.dmeurope.com [10.09.04].

Roth, A (2002) *The thin line – PSBs Online,* presented at the RIPE@2002 Conference, Finland, January 17–19, 2002. Quoted with the permission by the author.

SOU, (2004) *Nytt regelverk för marksend digital-TV,* Statens offentliga utredningar 2004:39. Stockholm, SOU. Printed from Internet: www.regeringen.se/sb/d72048/ a/12626 [19.09.04].

Syvertsen, T. (2004a) *Mediemangfold. Styring av mediene i et globalt marked.* Kristiansand: IJ-forlaget.

Syvertsen, T. (2004b) 'Citizens, audiences, customers and players – a conceptual discussion of the relationship between broadcasters and their publics1, *European Journal of Cultural Studies,* Vol. 7:3, pp. 363–380.

Wood, D. (2002) 'Bits 'R' Us. New economics and approaches for digital broadcasting', *EBU Technical Review.* January, 2002.

8

LOOKING TO THE FUTURE

Karol Jakubowitcz

In the preceding chapters of this part of the book, we presented major policy dilemmas concerning public service broadcasters in Europe – both in general terms (Chapter 5) as well as in particular key areas: remit (Appendix to Chapter 5), financing (Chapter 6) and PSB access to, and use of, the new technologies (Chapter 7).

The purpose has been to see whether national and international media policy does indeed provide an answer to how PSB should readjust to changing circumstances, and what sort of service is expected of PSB today and will be in the future. And the main question was whether policy-making has delivered, or indeed is capable of delivering, a new concept of PSB suited to the conditions of the 21st century.

Before we attempt to draw conclusions from the examination of these issues in the preceding chapters, and to look into the future, one more question suggests itself: is there anything left to defend? In other words, has the oft-mentioned 'dumbing down' of PSB[1] or the 'programme convergence' of public and commercial broadcasters deprived the former of any distinctiveness in the broadcasting landscape? As Marcel Betzel (Appendix to Chapter 5) argues, legislators and regulators certainly expect PSB to be distinctive and different from commercial broadcasting (see Peeters et al., 2004, on different interpretations and criteria of PSB distinctiveness). However, have they been able to meet that expectation, given that they operate on highly competitive markets? After all, as reported by the European Audovisual Observatory (2004), in January 2004 there were more than 3000 television channels in the then 15 member states of the EU alone, of which PSB channels were a clear minority:

■ 38 public service channels with a licence for national coverage by analogue terrestrial transmission;

- 2 mixed ownership (public/private) channels with a licence for national coverage by analogue terrestrial transmission;
- 43 privately-owned channels with a licence for national coverage by analogue terrestrial transmission;
- 21 commercial packagers (digital platforms) distributing channels to end-users (cableoperators and DTT operators are not included here);
- 75 publicly-owned channels with national coverage through cable, satellite or DTT distribution;
- 702 privately-owned channels with national coverage through cable, satellite or DTT distribution,
- 218 channels (public or private) targeting non-national markets (including channels targeting markets outside the EU). Alternatively, 162 'dedicated channels' can be identified in the European Union, that is channels conceived for a specific country but established in another country;
- Around 1,900 channels with regional or local coverage, of which 62 are also accessible via satellite, meaning that they are *de facto* national or pan-European;
- 162 regional or local windows in national programming schedules.

Despite heavy competition, most public service channels retain their distinctiveness, as will be shown briefly below.

Quantitative Distinctiveness

Most public service channels maintain what might be called 'quantitive' distinctiveness in terms of the prevalence of different types of content, as shown by a comparison with private channels in selected countries (France, Iceland, Italy and Poland):

PSB companies are: France 2 and France 3 (France); RUV (Iceland), RAI (Italy), TVP (Poland). Private companies are TF1 and Canal+ (France), Stöð2 (Iceland), Mediaset (Italy), Polsat, TVN, TV4 and Canal+ (Poland).

However, quantitative distinctiveness more often refers to the range and diversity of content. A McKinsey (2004) study of public service broadcasting around the world (Australia, Canada, France, Germany, Italy, Japan, Netherlands, New Zealand, Spain, Sweden, U.K. and U.S.) shows that programmes in 'PSB genres' (i.e. cultural, religious, news, factual or children's programming) are similarly prominent in most of the countries under study – 34–44% of content broadcast is in a 'PSB genre'. A comparison of the breakdown by programme genre of PSB and commercial television channels in Finland confirms this tendency.

PSB clearly manifest greater diversity of programme genres and greater emphasis on news and information, cultural and educational programmes (both non-existent on commercial channels), children's programmes, sports and less on fiction and entertainment.

Figures for Norway display a similar tendency as those for Finland, as shown in Table 3.

Table 1: Comparison of programme contents on PSB and private television channels

	Fiction and Entertainment		News and Information	
	PSB	PRIVATE	PSB	PRIVATE
France	38%	69.3%	42.5%	13.7%
Iceland	39%	55%	24%	15%
Italy	43%	75.1%	26%	16.8%
Poland	43.1%	74.8%	22.9%	8.8%
Average	39%	68.5%	25.3%	13.8%

Source: Bruck, Dörr, Cole, Favre, Gramstad, Monaco & âulek, 2004, based on the Yearbook of the European Audiovisual Observatory, 2003.

A general comparison of output by genre can help reveal the marked differences between public and private broadcasters. Most television programmes classified as factual, information, education, culture, etc., can be considered as high social-value genres. In mixed funding systems, like France and Germany, the percentage of output comprising these genres by public service broadcasters is more than double that of private competitors; in pure licence fee-funded markets, like the UK, where this output is particularly high, owing to the public service obligations of some of the private channels, their combined output of high social-value genres is greater than elsewhere; and, for example, in Spain, where public service broadcasters are more dependent on advertising, the output of these genres is 60 per cent higher for the public service broadcasting channels.

Table 2: Shares of programme genres by television channel in 2002 (%)

	PSB Channels		Commercial Channels	
	TV1	TV2	MTV3	Nelonen
News	9	5	7	5
Current affairs	21	10	16	1
Factual programmes	14	16	3	4
Cultural programmes	6	2	0	0
Hobbies/personal interests	3	7	4	4
Sports	7	20	8	12
Domestic fiction	2	1	5	1
Foreign fiction	13	14	30	44
Movies	6	7	9	15
Children's programmes	6	9	5	4
Educational programmes	13	1	0	0
Entertainment programmes	2	6	13	11
Other	0	2	0	0

Source: Aslama, 2003.

Table 3: Programme genres on Norwegian channels in percent of total offer (2001)

	PSB	Commercial channels	
	NRK	TvNorge	TV3
News	19	5	0
Information	22	7	1
Culture and education	14	2	0
Child programmes	8	0	10
Drama	20	74	58
Entertainment	10	10	9
Sport	8	0	2
Other/TV-shop	0	1	19
Total	**101**	**99**	**99**

Source: Syvertsen (2002, p. 45), Norsk tv-meter-panel/Gallup.
Note: All categories are balanced to the closest whole number. 'Culture and information' include art/culture/media, music, nature, religion/philosophy, science and education. 'Other' includes pause programme and unspecific programmes. As for TV3 most of this programme category includes TV-shop.

Figure 1 Comparison of overall television output of 'high social-value genres' – 2002.

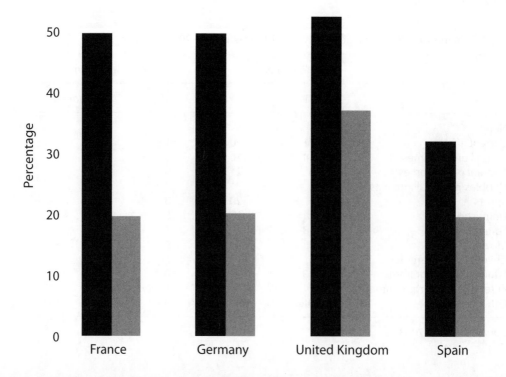

Source: EBU, 2004a.

In the EU-15, high social-value programming in television (genres like education, factual, arts, news and information) represents on average 51% of the total broadcast hours for the main television channels of public service broadcasters. If thematic channels are added, the figure rises significantly. In public service radio, more than 100 music and culture channels reach a potential audience of 300 million with high-quality programming making a particular contribution to cultural diversity.

Over the past few years, public service broadcasters have also constantly increased their total broadcast output and depended less on foreign acquired content. Own-production increased in percentage terms as well as in absolute value against acquired programmes, and remains high. Figures for the EU-25 are similar. This constitutes a high stimulus for national production. In many countries, without a public service broadcasting commitment to own production national production would be virtually non-existent.

Acquired includes purchased and pre-purchased, defined as follows. Purchased: made by an external service and the broadcaster then buys the rights to broadcast it (e.g. feature films). Pre-purchased: the rights are bought before the production is made. Exchange: a production exchanged either live, deferred or in material form between broadcasting organisations (including Eurovision, etc). Re-versioned: an acquired programme that has been altered in some way to make it more suitable for the local market (includes dubbing, editing, subtitling, etc.).This high level of non-acquired programming creates strong levels of investment in domestic production and supports national audiovisual industries across Europe.

Quantitive distinctiveness may also be reflected in the origin of programming, e.g. 'domestic' (i.e. local, national and European) programming as against programming imported from outside Europe. According to European Commission (2004), the

Figure 2 Public television broadcasters' shares of own production vs. acquired in the European Union: 2001–2002

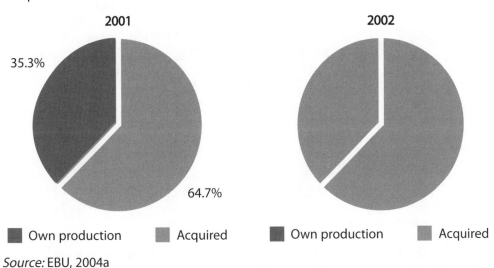

Source: EBU, 2004a

proportion of European productions by public service channels is consistently higher than that of private channels. The data provided in the Annex to the Communication also shows that public service broadcasters have consistently surpassed the quota for European works produced by independent producers.

In the digital era, efforts to achieve quantitative distinctiveness also lead to the development of a portfolio of programme services (satellite or digital terrestrial), seeking to extend the range of content and serve different needs more fully. The BBC, for example, now operates five different types of programme services:

■ Mainstream services (BBC 1 and BBC 2, BBC Radio 2, Radio 4 and Radio Five Live and bbc.co.uk).
■ Audience-targeted services (BBC Radio 1 and 1Xtra, BBC Three, CBBC and CBeebies, BBC Asian Network): focused on audience groups, defined by age or ethnicity.

Table 4: European television production of top PSB and commercial broadcasters in the five largest markets (% 2002)

Germany		Italy	
ARD	88.1	RAI 1	75.5
ZDF	87.2	RAI 3	64.7
——————		RAI 2	61.0
Sat1	72.2	——————	
RTL	72.0	Canale	559.7
Spain		Rete 4	58.1
TVE1	75.4	Italia 1	45.3
TVE2	58.5	**United Kingdom***	
——————		BBC1	81.0
Tele5	57.3	BBC2	81.0
Antena 3	55.6	——————	
France		ITV	80.0
France 2	79.8	Channel 4	72.0
France 3	74.6	ITV2	59.0
——————		Channel 5	55.0
TF1	65.1		
M6	63.6		

Source: European Commission, 2004.

* In the UK all broadcasters have public service obligations, so the distinction is between publicly- and commercially funded television channels.

- Special-interest services (BBC Radio 3, BBC Four, BBC News 24, BBC Parliament, Five Live Sports Extra, 6 Music, BBC 7, some bbc.co.uk services): offering added value through deeper, extended, more specialist content in particular genres.
- Specific services for the nations, regions and localities of the UK (BBC Scotland, BBC Wales, BBC Northern Ireland, BBC English regional television, BBC local radio, Where I Live websites).
- International services: the BBC's global news services – BBC World Service radio, BBC World and bbcnews.com

Public service broadcasters in other countries have adopted a similar strategy: RAI in Italy now has six television channels, in Germany ARD offers 17 different programmes in its digital bouquet while ZDF has ten, Swedish Radio offers a portfolio of seven digital services and Danish Radio offers ten DAB services (cf. EBU, 2004b).

Qualitative Distinctiveness
Qualitative distinctiveness refers to a variety of features of PSB programming. The management contract of the Flemish PSB broadcaster, VRT, refers to a number of forms of quality that its programming should display:

- *Functional quality* refers to the programme supply as required by the television remit: 'a programme mix of information, culture, home-produced drama, light entertainment, sport and contemporary education';
- *Public quality* – ability to reach the entire Flemish population
- *Ethical quality* – the public broadcaster understands its emphasis on impartiality and veracity.
- *Operational quality* is covered by the VRT's guidelines on programme-making and efficiency.
- *Professional quality* refers to the internal quality control of both radio and television in cooperation with the VRT's own internal affairs department.

Some of these forms of quality are double-edged. For example, the requirement to reach the entire population of the country may in some circumstances be counterproductive, as it may lead to lowering of standards in order to boost ratings.

Quantitative distinctiveness should also manifest in differences of approach and depth of treatment of the issues between PSB and commercial stations. One example is provided by the coverage of politics in Germany (see Holtz-Bacha, 2003).

A study, undertaken in the middle of the 1990s, analysed the public affairs programming of two public and three commercial stations in Germany. With regard to the 'issue agenda' and the 'structure of the actors', both systems at that time presented clearly distinct content. Compared to the public stations, the commercial competitors concentrated more on issues from everyday life, events in the entertainment and media industry, as well as sensationalism. By condensing the issues in two categories, with politics/economy/culture on the one side and human interest issues on the other, a clear difference in the journalism at the commercial and the public stations becomes obvious.

The same is true for the structure of actors. Political actors have a better chance of appearing on the public programmes while private actors are seen more frequently on commercial programmes. Not surprisingly, there is also a contrast between both systems in terms of the level of reference of the issues: Public stations prefer events and issues that affect society as a whole or refer to a particular level of reference, meaning institutions or problems with effects for particular groups of society. Commercial stations deal preferably with issues referring to an individual, private level.

Finally, the dramaturgical presentation of issues on public and commercial TV shows differs. Emotional mood was used as an indicator here. In general, the shows on both systems were dominantly characterised by objectivity and matter-of-factness. However, where emotions could be detected, negative emotions like fear and sorrow were more frequently found than positive emotions like joy and compassion. Again, these emotional components appeared more often in the commercial than in the public programme services.

At the most general level, qualitative distinctiveness between PSB and commercial stations should stem from the very purpose and remit of those two types of broadcasters. The BBC's (2004) document *Building public value: Renewing the BBC for a digital world* clearly seeks to set PSB apart from commercial broadcasting in precisely those terms, with far-reaching consequences for its entire programming.

This approach defines PSB not only in terms of programme content but also by (1) how public service broadcasters define its audience and its needs and interests; (2) a definition of PSB's role on a competitive market; (3) in terms of the role of PSB as a social institution with certain characteristics (especially broadly understood autonomy) indispensable for its proper functioning.

Without going into more details, it is the definition of the audience and its needs that should be one of PSB's major distinguishing characteristics, and the foundation for its programme goals. Public service broadcasting properly so called perceives its audience as composed of whole human beings, with a full range of needs and interests (as citizens; members of different social groups, communities, minorities and cultures; consumers; and seekers of information, education, experience, advice and entertainment), also seeking to broaden their horizons and enrich their lives.

Programming created in this spirit continues to attract audience attention and recognition, as shown by the fact that – as reported by McKinsey & Company (2004) – in every country examined in its study, 31–42% of viewing is of television 'PSB genres'. Also Bruck, Dörr, Cole, Favre, Gramstad, Monaco & Culek (2004), using data from the European Audiovisual Observatory *Yearbook* for 2003, note that public television channels still command important audiences at the national level, in the majority of countries, of around 30–45%, while some countries show a much larger market share of audiences in public television (i.e. Croatia at 87%, Denmark at 70%), and some much smaller (Turkey at 8%, Greece at 10% and Lithuania at 12%).

The important thing is that public service broadcasters' audience shares have held more or less steady over the past 8 years, when there has been an explosion of multichannel broadcasting in many countries.

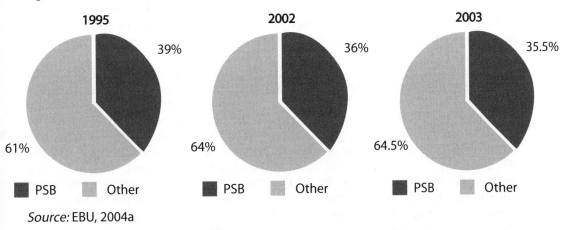

Figure 3 Public service broadcasters' audience shares in the EU: 1995–2003

Source: EBU, 2004a

Table 5 shows the audience shares of PSB television and radio stations in selected European countries in 2003.

Table 5: Audience shares of PSB organisations in 2003 (all channels; %)

Country	Television	Audience Share	Radio	Audience Share
Germany	ARD+ZDF	44.2	ARD (total)	55.6
UK	BBC	38.3	BBC	51.9
France	France 2+3+ 5	39.5	Radio France	22.2
Italy	RAI	44.9	RAI	18.1
Spain	TVE	30.6	RNE	23.4
Netherlands	NOS/NPB	35	NOS	33
Belgium Fr.	RTBF	18.7	RTBF	34.7
Belgium Fl.	VRT	37.6	VRT	80.7
Austria	ORF	51.7	ORF	82
Portugal	RTP	28.8	RDP	9.9
Ireland	RTE	40.7	RTE	43
Sweden	SVT	40.5	SR	66
Denmark	DR	33.6	DR	68
Finland	YLE	43.8	YLE	51
Norway	NRK	43.6	NRK	59
Poland	TVP	54.5	PR	26
Czech Rep.	CTV	29.7	CR	26.9
Hungary	MTV	17.5	MR	29
Estonia	ETV	24.1	ER	38.7
Slovakia	STV	24.9	SK/SR	40.7
Lithuania	LNRT	12	LRT	23

Source: EBU (2004c). Audience shares are those of the total programme offer of each station, potentially including satellite or digital terrestrial channels.

Policy Responses to PSB Evolution and Needs

On the basis of the foregoing, we can say that, yes, there is something left to defend: PSB – though weakened and suffering from an identity crisis – in most cases retains a powerful position on the broadcasting scene and enjoys strong audience support.

On the other hand, as Chapters 6, 7 and 8 show, there has been no uniform policy response to the dilemmas inherent in determining the future of PSB. European public policy *vis-à-vis* PSB has long been internally contradictory in that PSB 'is expected to do better than the private channels in embodying the public service ideal of which it is no longer allowed the monopoly … and in order to achieve this it is expected to adopt a mode of operation which no longer distinguishes it from the commercial channels … So it is expected to be similar and different at the same time' (Atkinson, 1997, p. 25). The resulting confusion may account for the PSB organisations' uncharacteristic timidity and uncertainty in making their case. As Betzel shows in the appendix to Chapter 5, legislators and regulators appear to be fairly united in their determination to promote the public service remit. While supporting the 'All-Embracing' PSB model, they also show a preference for a 'less is more' policy, seeking to restrict the remit to the key elements which demonstrate the public and distinctive nature of PSB. As noted by Betzel, the following elements can be observed all over Europe, however rarely does the remit in a country embraces all these aspects:

- Universality of content, understood as both universality of basic supply on generalist programmes as well as programmes specialised or tailored for specific audiences;
- Universality of access, a clear presence on all significant relevant media and platforms, including the online and on-demand environment;
- Basic journalistic standards, editorial freedom and independence from both political ties and commercial parties;
- High quality of programmes and services to constitute a benchmark of quality and professionalism.

This shows that policy-making, as far as the PSB remit is concerned, has not gone beyond standard formulae and has been incapable of addressing the dilemmas of the current era, as outlined in Chapter 5.

On the other hand, as shown in Chapters 7 and 8, there is much less unanimity as concerns funding and the new technologies.

One extreme in the current debate is represented by Italy which – in the 'Gasparri' and 'Frattini' laws – has:

- upheld the system of far-reaching government control of public service broadcasting;
- framed the conflict of interest issue in such a way as to allow Silvio Berlusconi, as Prime Minister, to continue both owning MEDIASET (the dominant commercial television broadcaster) and to control RAI;
- allowed continued concentration of the media;
- and launched the process of privatisation of RAI, which in the first instance amounts to its renationalisation.

Also Denmark has launched the privatisation of TV2, a public service broadcaster.

Perhaps the other extreme may be represented by the United Kingdom once the BBC Royal Charter renewal process is over. This is indicated by the stance taken by OFCOM, the regulatory body, which has announced that in its view 'The BBC should continue to be the cornerstone of public service broadcasting. A strong and independent BBC is essential for successful PSB in the UK, and should continue to be properly funded by the TV licence fee'. OFCOM does want to see greater BBC commitment to 'pure PSB'[2] and to use PSB in the digital age to 'fill the gap that will be left in the market'. However, it notes at the same time that PSB is to make 'full use of new technology and distribution systems' (by no means a commonly accepted policy, as is clear from Chapter 8). It also recognises, crucially, that growing competition on the market, as digital technology leads to an explosive growth in the number of channels, will mean that commercial broadcasters will provide *less* 'high social value' content, rather than *more*. Hence the stress on maintaining the BBC more or less unchanged and indeed to create a 'Public Service Publisher', a new entity, funded by additional money, in order to:

■ operate as a small commissioning and publishing organisation, using public funds to encourage creative ideas for all visual electronic media, such as broadband, from a range of producers;
■ commission (award contracts to) independent producers to provide programmes for specific priority areas;
■ make sure its new content is effectively promoted, advertised and made widely available using all the major distribution systems; and
■ make sure that all its activities reflect our proposed PSB purposes and characteristics.

Such sharp differences of approach to PSB are typical and clearly result from differing policy approaches. McKinsey&Company (2004) has identified three broad intervention approaches to public service broadcasting:

■ *Minimalist*: There is no regulation of the genre or quality of programming broadcast by commercial channels. Public funding is under $30 per head. Examples include Italy, New Zealand, Portugal, Spain and the U.S.
■ *Cultural exception*: Regulation compels commercial broadcasters to produce particular types of programming, often on the basis of maintaining a national identity. Public funding is under $30 per head. Examples include Australia, Canada and France.
■ *Broad PSB intervention*: Regulation requires commercial broadcasters to show particular types of programming. Public funding is over $50 per head. Examples include Germany, Netherlands, Sweden and the U.K.

A similar picture emerges from a comparative review of content regulation (ITC, 2002).

There is a clear difference here between countries with a non-interventionist approach, and those, like France, which clearly intend to guide the content providers towards specific goals (centred on the promotion of specific national cultural elements). A group of countries, including Germany, Finland and Sweden, have quite substantial commitments to the objectives of regulation but are moving away from rules based tools

Figure 4 Regulatory framework by country

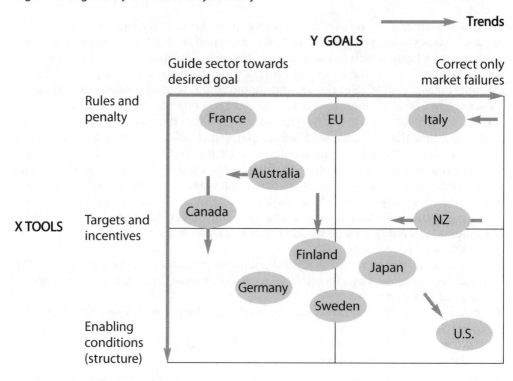

Source: ITC, 2002.

towards reliance on structural interventions only, for example, by funding public service output. The UK, the ITC added, would appear towards the bottom left of the matrix, with substantial policy goals for the sector but an increasing reliance under new legislation on industry structures and incentives and a reduction in regulation based on rules and penalties.

Given these differences, it is impossible today to be sure that European governments will indeed be willing and able to take a clear stance on the future of PSB and the ways it should adjust to survive and prosper in the 21st century.

Accountability Systems

European countries appear to share a common approach in one area: imposing stricter accountability systems on PSB organisations. Under increasing pressure to justify their policies *vis-à-vis* PSB, governments and regulators do so in keeping with the spirit of the times:

The core of the contract can remain. The state *offers certain privileges* to some channels, and in return each channel provides something of worth beyond that which the market alone would provide The BBC is the most privileged ... *In return* the nation has on the whole been well-served.' (Tessa Jowell, U.K. Minister for Culture, Media and Sport, 2002; emphases added.)

Thus, the terms of the debate appear to be reversed. PSB – until now seen as a dedicated organisation created to perform a service and (at least in theory) assured of institutional and financial guarantees required for the purpose – is today portrayed as an organisation which for some unspecified reason is offered certain 'privileges' and must show its 'gratitude.' This is certainly a form of government response to growing pressure from the commercial sector and from the sceptical public – and indeed from the European Union – for more objective and quantifiable criteria for assessing PSB performance.

Accordingly, as noted by Coppens (2004),

- In several countries service contracts, signed between the broadcaster and the government for a limited period of time and stating what the PSB objectives are, have been introduced. In such a service contract, the broadcaster is asked to meet certain performance goals, laid down in so-called performance indicators [3];
- These performance indicators (PI) form the second element of the new PSB-policy. Although all service contracts contain some performance indicators, the PI's can also be found in other documents, drafted by the broadcasters themselves, such as yearly statements of commitments or promises. Performance indicators are quantitative or qualitative targets the broadcaster must meet within a fixed time, either each year or over the duration of the contract or licence.
- Lastly, the public broadcasters faced new accountability mechanisms scrutinising their performance and – in some cases – attaching PSB-performance with financial consequences. The idea of performance analysis is now firmly embedded in the new PSB-policy, even though the variety of several schemes to assess PSB's performance is high.

All this can be seen as part of an evolution of PSB from an 'Autonomy model' to a 'Controlled Service model' and consequently from self-regulation by public service broadcasters to a greater role of external bodies in evaluating PSB performance within a system which ties financing to well-defined performance commitments and strategic as well as business plans (Svendsen, 2002).

'Contracts' take the form either of outright licences to broadcast, e.g. in the Netherlands (see 'Special: Concession Policy Plan 2000–2010 – Making a Difference', 2000), or indeed of contracts or authorisations of some sort (e.g. France, the Flemish Community of Belgium).

One can say that the more recent legislation concerning these 'contracts' is, the more attention is paid to the financial aspects of the fulfilment of programming obligations and generally of the operation of the PSB broadcaster. For example, while French PSB broadcasters have traditionally been bound by *cahiers des charges*, defining their programme obligations, amendments to the Freedom of Communication Act No. 86–1067 of 30 September 1986 adopted in 2000 also provided for 'agreements in respect of objectives and means' (*contrats d'objectifs et de moyens*) to be concluded by the government for 3 to 5 years with each PSB company. A financial accountability system has also been created as concerns observance of the agreement[4]

Another case in point is the 5–year 'management contract' concluded between the Flemish Community of Belgium and the Flemish Radio and Television Company (VRT). Under Article 15 of the *Decree for the transformation of the BRTN into a public sector public limited company* (1997), the contract specifies 'special terms and conditions for the granting of financial means for the performance of the duties of a public service charged with fulfilling the task of public broadcaster' and regulates (1) measurable objectives; (2) objectives concerning personnel management and financial policy, especially the generalised introduction of cost accounting for programmes; (3) the calculation of the financial package required for the performance of the duties of a public service; (4) the publishing before 1 June of the following year of an annual report evaluating the implementation of the management contract during the previous year; (5) the measures to be taken should a party not fulfil the obligations it has entered into under the terms of the management contract.

In addition to specifying all these matters in considerable detail, the 2002–2006 management contract also devotes specific attention to innovative media projects, including development of a multimedia e-service platform in Flanders. It said it wanted the VRT to ensure that reliable electronic services were available to everyone. Under the terms of the new management contract, e-VRT will develop a software service platform (ASP), set up a MPEG research programme for the Flemish audiovisual sector and launch a Digital Home Platform trial project. The Flemish government has already allocated additional resources to finance the Digital Home Platform and the MPEG research project.

This shows that a contract may, depending on the circumstances, be either regressive or progressive in nature. Where the intent is to create for a government an alibi that it is enforcing a clear definition of the remit and cost-effectiveness on a PSB broadcaster and the approach is bureaucratic, the effect may be to stifle the broadcaster. Depending on the more general context, a contract may also be part of a general system of government and political control of the PSB broadcaster, depriving it of editorial autonomy and institutional independence required for the proper performance of its obligations. Where the approach is more enlightened, the contract may point the way to the future.

Conclusion
In 1991, when he was receiving the Man of the Year Award in Cannes, Silvio Berlusconi said:

> Public television is dying. All broadcasting activity will pass into the hands of the private sector in the next ten years. Commercial television enhances democracy, strengthens the economy and with the money gained improves programme quality.

That was certainly an ideology-driven and self-serving prediction. More to the point, it has not come true.

No uniform policy approach to the dilemmas faced by PSB in the digital age has emerged at the European level. Nor is it ever likely to. Like every social institution, PSB has always been shaped by national traditions and preferences – ideological, political, cultural and economic. Nevertheless, it is clear that, despite the ideological shift described in Chapter 5, public service broadcasting has retained a strong position and is slowly evolving to respond to the challenges of the Information Society. As awareness of the fact that the PSB remit will not be made redundant in the conditions of content abundance (as was noted by OFCOM in the report cited above) becomes more widespread, chances are that models of delivering it being developed by more advanced countries today will be emulated elsewhere.

A conference on 'The Key Role of Public Service Broadcasting in European Society in the 21st Century' organised by the Dutch Presidency of the EU in September 2004 adopted conclusions which are worth citing in part:

- It is essential that public service broadcasters are able to reach all sectors of society. To ensure universal access, a relevant mix of new and traditional media platforms is needed. The remit for public service broadcasters should therefore be independent of the delivery method.
- The activities of public service broadcasters are integral to the European Union's goal 'to become the most competitive and dynamic-based economy capable of sustainable growth with more and better jobs and greater social cohesion'. Public service broadcasters should drive innovation. Developing a high-quality range of services will stimulate growth in knowledge-based economies, enabling related objectives such as life-long learning.
- Public service broadcasters play a crucial role in fostering cultural diversity across an enlarging European Union. They stimulate communities to discuss, thus creating greater social cohesion with deeper mutual understanding.
- Concentration of media ownership within the European Union is undesirable. Public service broadcasters enhance media pluralism, with a mix of quality, broad-based programmes, as well as specialised content.
- Secure funding for public service broadcasting is essential. It should be written into law, at both the national and European level. This is vital to ensure that public service broadcasters serve the democratic, social and cultural needs of all societies, in accordance with the Amsterdam Protocol.
- All Member States need to ensure that their public service broadcasters are editorially independent of political influence. They must have the necessary resources to fulfil their public service obligations.
- Public service broadcasters have a duty to demonstrate their value to society within their respective states.
- The remit of public service broadcasters should be properly defined while at the same time it should provide flexibility to enable broadcasters to adapt to new developments.

These conclusions have no formal standing, but they do signify a growing awareness that the challenges of the 21st century require new thinking and new models of delivering a public service in broadcasting and all other forms of public communication. Sooner or later this will deliver practical results.

* * *

This chapter has been developed, in part, on the basis of information and reports provided by members of Team 2 of the 'Changing Media-Changing Europe' programme of the European Science Foundation: Minna Aslama and Kaarle Nordenstreng (Finland), Els de Bens (Belgium), Christina Holtz-Bacha and Winfried Schulz (Germany), Ildiko Kovats (Hungary); Ralph Negrine (U.K.), Stylianos Papathanassopoulos (Greece), Trine Syvertsen and Vilde Schanke Sundet (Norway).

Notes

1. OFCOM has, for example, noted the following weaknesses in British PSB: '(i) A risk-averse approach is reducing innovation and marginalising the specialist content - arts, current affairs, education, religion - that audiences tend to value less; (ii) Range within some genres has narrowed for example in drama where soaps now account for 55% of the output while the proportion of new drama titles has declined steadily over the past five years; (iii) And in factual, where factual entertainment such as reality shows and docusoaps have displaced more serious factual programming' (Richards, 2004). Similar developments can be found in many countries.

2. It states for example that 'Our phase 1 report identified 'copycat' programming, the BBC screening similar programmes to those on other channels, and competitive head-to-head scheduling against other channels (such as screening EastEnders at the same time as ITV1 screen Coronation Street or Emmerdale), as particular concerns. [...] In future, the BBC should consider whether Hollywood blockbusters and other expensive 'bought-in' programmes couldn't be provided equally well by commercial broadcasters, such as ITV1' (OFCOM, 2004).

3. Coppens (2004) notes that the system of service contracts was introduced in the 1990s in Belgium, Italy, Portugal and Sweden and in recent years was extended to Denmark, France and Ireland, following a national and/or European debate on PSB-policy. Other countries such as the UK or the Netherlands might follow this trend in the coming years.

4. These agreements are drawn up in consultation with the boards of directors of each PSB company, which then oversee their implementation. The chairman of France Télévision submits a report each year to the commissions with responsibility for cultural affairs of the Assemblée Nationale and the Sénat concerning the performance of the company's agreement in respect of objectives and means. Each year, at the time of the vote on the Finance Act, the Parliament, based on a report by a member of each of the finance commissions of the Assemblée Nationale and Sénat with the powers of a special rapporteur, authorises the collection of a tax named licence for right to use based on television receivers and approves the allocation of public funds allocated to the licence application account between the companies France Télévision, Radio France, Radio France Internationale, France Overseas Network, the company Arte France and the Institut national de l'audiovisuel. Additionally, a government report on the situation and management of public sector institutions must be attached to the finance bill.

References

Aslama, M. (2003) *Suomalainen tv-tarjonta 2002*[Finnish television supply 2002]. Helsinki: Liikenne- ja viestintäministeriön julkaisuja. [Ministry of Transport and communications]

Atkinson, Dave (1997) 'Public Service Television in the Age of Competition', in Dave Atkinson, Marc Raboy (eds.) *Public Service Broadcasting: the Challenges of the Twenty-first Century*. Reports and Papers on Mass Communication, No. 111. Paris: UNESCO.

Bruck. Peter A., Dieter Dörr, Mark D. Cole, Jacques Favre, Sigve Gramstad, Maria Rosaria Monaco, Zrinjka Peru‰oko âulek, (2004) *Transnational media concentrations in Europe*. Report prepared by the AP-MD. AP-MD (2004) 2 rev 5. Strasbourg: Media Division, Council of Europe.

Coppens, Tomas (2004) *Fine-tuned or out-of-key? Instruments for measuring PSB-performance*. Paper delivered at the RIPE@2004 Conference, Copenhagen and Aarhus.

EBU (2004a) *The European Broadcasting Union's Contribution*, Conference on 'The Key Role of Public Service Broadcasting in European Society in the 21st Century' organized by the Dutch Presidency of the EU, Amsterdam, September 2004, http://www.ebu.ch/en/union/under_banners/EBU_contribution.php

EBU (2004b) *EBU Members' company profiles*. Geneva.

EBU (2004c) *EBU Members' Audience Trends 1992–2003*. Geneva.

European Audiovisual Observatory (2004) *Transfrontier Television in the European Union: Market Impact and Selected Legal Aspects*. Background Paper prepared by the European Audiovisual Observatory for a Ministerial Conference on Broadcsting, organised by the Irish Presidency of the European Union. Dublin & Drogheda 1–3 March 2004.

European Commission (2004) Sixth Communication on the application of Articles 4 and 5 of Directive 89/552/EEC 'Television without Frontiers', as amended by Directive 97/36/EC, for the period 2001–2002. COM(2004) 524 final, Brussels.

Holtz-Bacha, Christina (2003) 'Of Markets and Supply. Public broadcasting in Germany', pp. 109–122 in Taisto Hujanen, Greg Lowe (eds.) *Broadcasting and Convergence: New Articulations of the Public Service Remit*. Gothenburg: NORDICOM.

ITC (2002) *Comparative Review of Content Regulation*. A McKinsey Report for the Independent Television Commission. London: Independent Television Commission.

Jowell, T. (2002) Speech at the Westminster Media Forum, 12 March 2002.

McKinsey & Company (2004) *Review of Public Service Broadcasting Around the World*. London, http://www.ofcom.org.uk/consultations/current/psb2/psbwp/wp3mck.pdf.

OFCOM (2004) *Ofcom review of public service television broadcasting. Phase 2 - Meeting the digital challenge*. Plain English Summary. http://www.ofcom.org.uk/consultations/current/psb2/pes/?a=87101

Peeters, A., L. d'Haenens & J. Bardoel (2004) *Defining Distinctiveness In Search of Public Broadcasting Performance and Quality Criteria*. Paper delivered at the RIPE@2004 Conference, Copenhagen and Aarhus.

RICHARDS, E. (2004) *OFCOM Review of Public Service Broadcasting*. Speech to Westminster Media Forum, http://www.ofcom.org.uk/media_office/speeches_presentations/ richards_ 20040525?A=87101.

Svendsen, Erik Nordahl (2002) *The Regulation of Public Service Broadcasting, An EPRA Inquiry*. Paper presented during the 16th meeting of the European Platform of Regulatory Authorities. Ljubljana, 24–25 October.

Syvertsen, Trine (2002) 'Fjernsyn' i Bjørnstad, in *Medienorge 2002._Fakta om norske massemedier*

9

MEDIA GOVERNANCE STRUCTURES IN EUROPE

Karol Jakubowicz

Introduction

Nothing can beat the World Summit on the Information Society (WSIS) in Geneva (December 2003) for symbolism and 'High Noon' drama as far as 'culture v commerce' media policy showdowns are concerned. From that point of view, it was a classic. It was also an object lesson in global governance, its mechanisms and driving forces.

Complex organisations, such as the UN, can be interpreted as political systems, and therefore as battlefields of competition for hegemony and leadership (for an extensive discussion of the EU from this point of view, see Richardson, 2001)[1]. A major role can be played by problem definition: whoever defines the problem under discussion can then control the process – set the agenda, determine policy framing and formation, develop solutions, etc.

In this case, the idea to hold WSIS was initiated by the ITU in 1998 (Utsumi, 2002). In 2001, the UN General Assembly agreed that the ITU – rather than, for example, UNESCO (also a potential candidate in view of its strong communication and informatics sector and a history of involvement in information and communication issues on a global scale) – should take the lead role in its preparation. Given the technological and free-market orientation of the ITU, that was a significant decision in terms of international agenda-setting and policy-making. It meant that 'the predominant view at the Summit [would be] one that envisions the information society as a world apart, pertaining to the digital realm, whose main challenges are to ensure connectivity – especially in the global South – and to establish a favourable environment for investments and operation of the electronic market' (Burch, 2004).

'Commerce' had thus originally gained the upper hand. However, 'culture' counterattacked. UNESCO launched a major drive (with regional 'Regional Pre-Conferences for the World Summit on Information Society' held on every continent) to frame the approach differently[2]. For example, UNESCO countered the monolithic vision of 'the Information Society' with the concept of 'Knowledge Societies', stressing both the diversity of social, cultural and linguistic frameworks, and the fact that what matters is not information as such, but the resulting knowledge assimilated and used by societies.

Moreover, the WSIS was officially a tripartite Summit, including governments, civil society and the private sector, the latter two with observer status, but with the right to make written and oral submissions. Civil society organisations, grouped in part around the Campaign for Communication Rights in the Information Society (CRIS), 'insisted on broadening the agenda to include such themes as human rights, open access to information and knowledge, free and open source software, literacy, education and research, cultural diversity, attention to those with special needs, and a gender perspective' (Burch, 2004). They ultimately adopted their own declaration *Shaping Information Societies for Human Needs*: using the plural as acknowledgement of the pluralistic composition and needs of mankind, and stressing that Information Society should serve people and not only markets.

The battle for problem definition and policy formation at WSIS was fought on a global scale and involved a great number of stakeholders of every description. To mention just one more example, the fact that originally the 'traditional' media were to be excluded from consideration at WSIS led to the holding of a World Electronic Media Forum in Geneva as a side event to WSIS. It was dedicated to highlighting the contribution of broadcasting and broadcasters to the Information Society, as well as the present and future opportunities of media in the Information Society, with particular reference to the key role of media and television, universal access to information, freedom of expression, cultural diversity, economic development, social cohesion and education. As with UNESCO, the danger perceived in the original problem definition that left the media out of account spurred all of the world's broadcasting unions, in an historical first, to agree on a common platform to be submitted to the Summit[3].

The final result of this battle – an unhappy last-minute compromise (despite three Preparatory Conferences) between 'commercial', 'cultural', 'human rights' and 'political' perspectives in the form of a 'Declaration of Principles' and an 'Action Plan' – can satisfy no-one: 'The Declaration establishes a foundation of common goals among participants. It is not a selective foundation: the list encompasses nearly every human-rights related theme supported by the UN, including goals like alleviating poverty, expanding education, combating AIDS, promoting environmental sustainability, and advancing peace. In fact, the list is so far-reaching that no single message or clear set of priorities emerges' (Bridges, n.d.). As a result, 'most actors in the WSIS process will be able to find language in the final documents that they can use as support for their agendas …. But many other issues are absent or inadequately dealt with and overall there is little coherence' (Burch, 2004).

This case study of global governance suggests a number of conclusions. First, the number of stake-holders in any policy-formation process has grown enormously. In view of this, Keane (2001) describes the current situation at the global level as a case of 'New Medievalism:' a mélange of political and legal structures and a clutter of nation states and regional and local governments; intergovernmental agencies and programmes, as well as intergovernmental structures with sectoral responsibilities like the WTO; and the International Court of Justice and other global institutions seeking to enforce the rule of law. This hotchpotch system of global governance also includes global accords, treaties, and conventions; policy summits and meetings; and new forms of public deliberation and conflict resolution like truth commissions that have a global impact. These interacting and overlapping neo-medieval structures, says Keane, are undoubtedly having the effect of slowly eroding both the immunity of sovereign states from suit and the presumption that statutes do not extend to the territory of other states.

Second, governance involves a more complex, differentiated and diffuse systems of decision- and policy-making and control than is the case with the institutions and functions associated with 'traditional government': governance refers to the *process* of governing (i.e. collective problem solving in the public realm) and to interaction between participants in this process (cf. *E-governance. Democracy, technology and the public realm*, n.d.) rather than to the institutions and agencies which make up government. As a result, any policy and the regulatory frameworks created in this process result from an interplay of divergent forces, seeking to achieve a workable compromise between their different interests and goals. Any pre-conceived ideas guiding the formal policy-maker (government or parliament) will, as likely as not, be changed or modified in the process. Thus, among the structural prerequisites of the ideal type of governance is the existence of countervailing forces of roughly equal power, none of which is capable of winning exclusive control over policy-making or government, or of pursuing its own objectives without regard for other participants in the process.

Third, as in the case described above, the process of 'governance' is often dedicated, or leads in the final analysis, to the formulation of policy or legislation. In this light, it can usually be seen as a contribution to, and a corrective of (but also, in some cases, as substitution[4] for), traditional 'government', democratising the process of decision-making, but ultimately producing standard legal or policy texts, to be implemented and enforced by government or administration in its traditional form.

And fourth, governance may often fail to produce a clear-cut result, compounding the complexities of globalisation and the difficulties of global policy-making and implementation. The participation of many stake-holders and overlapping policy-making and regulatory venues, requiring extensive and prolonged negotiations, coordination and mutual adjustments, may itself ultimately result in a tendency to streamline global governance, so as to reduce strains and difficulties resulting from the present 'neo-medieval' situation.

Globalisation and Global Governance

Giddens (1997, p. 3) defines globalisation as:

> The intensification of world-wide social relations which link distant localities in such a way that local happenings are shaped by events occurring many miles away, and vice versa. This is a dialectical process because such local happenings may move in an obverse direction from the very distanciated relations that shape them. Local transformation is as much part of globalisation as the lateral extension of social connections across time and space (see also Featherstone, 1990; Waters, 1995; Bauman, 1998; Riggs, 2000)

Giddens is right to point to the dialectical (in fact internally contradictory) nature of the process. Otherwise, it could hardly be understood in its full complexity. In terms of media studies, the effect is that 'glocalisation' has been proposed as a framework for the study of international communication (Kraidy, 2003).

Anheier, Glasius and Kaldor (2003, p. 6) distinguish a number of types of globalisers, reflecting the preferences and positions on globalisation of actors and organisations, as well as of political parties, governments and individuals. These are: supporters, regressives, reformers and rejectionists.

'Regressive globalisers' are individuals, groups, firms, or even governments (the US government is specifically mentioned in this respect) that favour globalisation when it is in their particular interest and irrespective of any negative consequences for others. The emergence of regressive globalisation or indeed of the rejectionist position (as represented by religious and nationalist, or indeed populist groups and movements) can be seen as an element of 'local transformation' unfolding in response to globalisation as such. However, the authors note that the rise of regressive globalism, as for example in the case of religious and nationalist militant groups, may reverse the process in general. The rise of anti-immigrant parties and the entry of 'tough' language on asylum-seekers and integration in Europe and Australia, the pursuit of an 'America first' policy by the US Administration, and the rise of communal politics in many other parts of the world suggest that 'anti-cosmopolitan' values may now be in the ascendant (see also Delbrück, 1993, on renationalisation as a countervailing force of globalisation and internationalisation).

This is noted also by Keane (2001, p. 39): 'Borderless exchanges also produce strong political reactions in favour of the local and national, for instance among losers who react to their dis-empowerment resentfully by taking revenge upon others, sometimes cruelly, guided by ideological, uncivil presumptions like xenophobic nationalism.' Such groups favour nation-state thinking; yet they organise transnationally and indeed are growing both as a reaction to the insecurities generated by globalisation and because they are able to mobilise by making use of the new global media and funding from Diaspora groups – also in order to make political capital out of the fear (whether justified or not) of gobalisation and its effects among their political constituency.

A system of global governance is slowly emerging in response to globalisation. Nation-states are tending to lose their capacity to control their own societies. They compensate this loss of control partly by implementing international and supranational regimes. Dahl (1999) describes 'international governments' (i.e. international organisations) as systems of decision-making by political and bureaucratic elites that operate with a very high degree of autonomy, within limits set by charters, treaties, or other international agreements. In his view the extent of 'delegation of authority' to international policy elites goes beyond any acceptable threshold of democracy, since the means for holding domestic bureaucracies accountable to democratically elected leaders are far stronger and more extensive than the means for holding international governing elites accountable. And the capacity of the interests they effect by their decisions to react and modify the decisions of domestic government are, in his judgment, far greater than in the case of international organisations.

Coleman and Porter (1999) add that to the extent to which globalising processes, whether economic, ecological, military or cultural, transcend usual territorial boundaries, they challenge democratic self-governance in three ways: (1) because of the mismatch between economic markets and political boundaries, whereby increasing economic interdependence on the global scale undermines national sovereignty and the accountability of political leaders; (2) because of the technical expertise required to engage in global governance, reducing citizen access to, and comprehension of, the decision-making process; (3) and because of private authority, wielded by growing private sector, which supplants the political decision-making process.

Different future scenarios of global democracy are proposed in the literature, as Keane (2001) suggests: (1) a transnational democratic legal order, a community of all democratic communities, something resembling a global *Rechtsstaat*; (2) a complex international system of nominally sovereign, democratic states that are the voting members in a variety of international forums; or (3) a new compromise between these two options: a cosmopolitan process of democratisation through which citizens gain a voice within their own states and in sites of power among their states (as in Held's concept of 'cosmopolitan democracy;' see Held, 1997)

It may be said that the rise of a 'global civil society' (Anheier, Glasius & Kaldor, 2001; 2003) somewhat modifies the view of 'global governance' as described by Dahl. Kaldor, Anheier and Glasius (2003, p. 4) define 'global civil society' as the sphere of ideas, values, organisations, networks, and individuals located primarily outside the institutional complexes of family, market, and state, and beyond the confines of national societies, polities, and economies. They also emphasise the normative implications of the concept:

> Global civil society is also about the meaning and practice of human equality in an increasingly unjust world … It is also about searching for, and developing, new forms of civic participation and involvement in a globalising world; it is about finding and giving 'voice' to those affected by old, new, and emerging inequities in the broadest sense, and providing a political and social platform for such voices to be heard. Global civil society is about civic engagement and civic-mindedness in a transnational, potentially global sphere; it is about private action for public benefit however defined.

This could be said to apply to civil society action with regard to WSIS. A theoretical foundation for such action is provided by Nanz and Steffek (2003). They view global governance from the perspective of a 'deliberative' theory of politics as a framework of social and institutional conditions that facilitate the expression of citizens' concerns and ensures the responsiveness of political power. Democracy is regarded here as intrinsically enhancing the legitimacy of government or governance because it ensures the (procedural) conditions for a high quality of the decision-making process with respect to regulatory choices.

This contributes to the emergence of a 'global public sphere', seen by the authors as a communicative network where different (national and sectoral) publics partially overlap. A global public sphere will hardly be as all-encompassing and unitary as national ones, but rather the ensemble of overlapping (national/sectoral) public communication about the same (sometimes very specific) issue or problem. In this respect, the prime task of international civil society lies in its capacity to enable stakeholders of global governance to make informed judgements and choices.

In this view, civil society comprises all those social actors (public or private) that seek to influence political deliberation about public norms by means of argumentation. Global governance regimes are understood here as sites of public deliberation and cooperative inquiry, involving a variety of social actors (government officials, experts, NGOs, stakeholders etc.) with diverse (national/sectoral) perspectives on a certain issue. Fostering extended deliberation among those actors over the nature of problems and the best way to solve them, participatory arenas produce a pool of (transnationally) shared arguments which contribute to the emergence of a global public sphere

Taking the World Trade Organisation as an example, Nanz and Steffek portray a system of 'deliberative participation' at the global level in the following way:

Table 1: Elements for promoting public deliberation about world trade policy

Issue	WTO actions	Civil society actions
Exposing world trade governance to public scrutiny	Dissemination of official information. Providing documents, Internet access, press releases	Dissemination of critical information. Informing press, national parliaments, grass-roots groups
Bringing stake-holder concerns into the WTO	Organisation of outreach meetings; granting speaking time to NGOs; obliging state representatives to justify decisions taken	Participation in meetings with officials and state representatives. Debating political proposals among civil society groups
Empowering disadvantaged groups of stakeholders	Technical training of developing country representatives	Providing critical expertise to state representatives and non-state actors

Source: Nanz & Steffek, 2003, p. 22.

Organised civil society is thus to play the role of a 'transmission belt,' a discursive interface between deliberative processes within international organisations and an emerging transnational public sphere. First, civil society organisations can give voice to citizens' concerns and channel them into the deliberative process of international organisations. Second, they can make internal decision-making processes of international organisations more transparent to the wider public and formulate technical issues in accessible terms.

Needless to add, terms such as 'global civil society' or 'global public sphere' are contested by other scholars (Keane, 2001; Keohane, n.d.; Dahlgren, 2003, Tomlison, 1994). While overambitious and theoretically largely unfounded, these terms do, however, point to nascent forms of global arrangements reminiscent of their name-sakes at the national level.

Global Policy-Making in Communications
At the risk of considerable oversimplification, global policy-making in the communications field can be seen, from one point of view, in terms of a conflict between different sets of contrasting values and policy objectives. Winseck and Cuthbert (1997) present it as a struggle between 'limited' and 'communicative' democracy, with the former clearly in the lead. The tension between was reflected during WSIS, with civil society organisations clearly supporting 'communicative democracy'[5].

Venturelli (1998; n.d.) has a broader view of global policy-making in this area as a conflict between liberal internationalism and cultural and information rights, again with the former much more capable of influencing actual policies being pursued. Put differently, this could be seen as a 'globalisation vs. anti-globalisation' conflict. In the media sector, we are witness to a 'free flow vs. cultural diversity' battle.

In terms of the 'commerce vs. culture' perspective, three broad and distinct basic arguments can be identified in the globalisation debate concerning the audiovisual sector and the broader field of cultural industries:

- One favours complete liberalisation of trade in audiovisual goods and the inclusion of audiovisual in the services negotiations, in which case the audiovisual sector would not be treated as being any different than trade in any other kind of commodity or service.
- This position is generally not accepted among European countries, which are predominantly (this goes especially for members of the European Union where this is the official common policy; see European Commission, 2003) in favour of the second argument, i.e. that the audiovisual field holds a special position because of its cultural value and should therefore be granted a privilege and an exemption from total liberalisation (which if applied to the audiovisual sector would preclude measures in support of audiovisual industries, i.e. subventions). The second argument is linked to the wish to avoid 'Americanisation' or 'globalisation' of culture and the loss of European national/regional cultural values.
- There is also a third position which goes beyond the protection of the audiovisual field at the national level by using the 'cultural exemption' in trade agreements, and

seeks the creation of an international instrument for the protection of cultural diversity as such. This argument is broader than just the audiovisual field and centres on the issue of cultural diversity, which is defined to include all forms of artistic and cultural expression including popular culture, traditional knowledge and practices and linguistic diversity (cf. the UNESCO 'Universal Declaration on Cultural Diversity' or the Council of Europe's 'Declaration of the Committee of Ministers on cultural diversity'). The third position is at present converging around the idea of a draft Convention on Cultural Diversity whose elaboration, originally launched by the International Network on Cultural Policy (INCP), is to be completed by UNESCO. This convention is seen as a possible future tool to protect and support diversity in the media field as well.

From another point of view, the distinguishing feature of global communications policy-making today is that policy is no longer 'made' at any clearly definable location, but across a range of sites. The entire process of globalisation, technological change and ascendance of neoliberal political economy (Herman & McChesney, 1997; Wilkin, 2001) has been marked by important shifts in power relations between major actors: international organisations, nation states, stateless conglomerations of corporate capital, civil society, etc. Internationalisation and globalisation of media markets, together with transfrontier broadcasting, promote the coexistence in those markets of different policy-making and regulatory structures, as well as legal frameworks, potentially at cross-purposes with one another. Even more importantly, however, these structures additionally come under the impact of a variety of other forces – social, political, economic, technological and cultural – that may disrupt and change the entire framework of reference within which policy used to be formulated and pursued. The global media order is the ultimate result of the interplay of these forces.

Specific policy issues, such as copyright or rules governing property transactions, migrate from one level to another, often typifying the flashpoint of conflicts between jurisdictions. 'Policy' has responded to these processes, in recognition of its own diminishing usefulness and effectiveness, i.e. by initiating a process of deregulation which helps set the stage for governance. As a result, Raboy (2001, p. 12) has pointed out, 'we need a new paradigm for media policy, appropriate to the geopolitical and technological context in which we are now living'.

That paradigm will be difficult to develop, given the fluid situation now prevailing in global policy-making. An illustration of what this means in practice is provided by an overview of the global ICT policy environment (see Implementation Team ..., 2002), consisting of a few groups of actors:

- Principal Players: ITU, WTO and ICANN;
- Supporting Institutions: World Bank Group, World Intellectual Property Organisation (WIPO) and UNESCO;
- New Fora and Actors: (i) NGOs (concerned with promoting the development of ICT-based networks and services, or focused on the use of ICTs to promote sustainable economic, social, cultural and political development); (ii) Business community organisations (BCOs), including national chambers of commerce whose main interest

is in promoting policies, regulations and practices that encourage trade and investment between countries, as well as task forces and roundtables that address emerging global issues of policy, regulation and development from a private sector perspective; (iii) Hundreds of private sector fora (PSFs) that have been established by ICT enterprises to develop international standards for ICT technology, networks and services; (iv) Legions of academics, researchers, policy advisors and regulatory practitioners who engage in ongoing public discussion, debate and analysis of the basic principles that should guide decision-making on international ICT issues.

When ITC policy themes are cross tabulated with policy issues and global venues for their consideration and resolution, the result is as follows:

Table 2: Global ICT Policy Themes, Issues and Venues[6]

Policy theme	Policy issues	Global venues
Convergence and Digitalization	Wireless and Radio Spectrum Allocation (New Services, Harmonisation Frequency Bands, etc.)	ITU
	Universal Access and Interoperability – (Bottlenecks, Essential Facilities, Anti-Trust, Emerging Standards, etc.)	ITU, IETF, W3C, WTO, GBDe
	Common Identifiers (Domain Names, ENUM, Object Identifiers, etc.)	ICANN, IETF, WIPO
	Regulatory Reform (Redefining Regulatory Spheres, Converged Agencies, etc.)	Various, including the World Bank and IMF
Networked Economy	Consumer Protection (Cross Border Redress and Dispute Resolution, Jurisdiction, etc.)	OECD, ITU, WIPO, UNCITRAL, GBDe
	Electronic Contracts and Signatures (Authentication, Standards, Model Laws, etc.)	UNCITRAL, IETF, W3C, OECD
	Intellectual Property (Copyright, Trademarks, ISP liability, etc.)	WIPO, ICANN, WTO
Global Information Society	Network Security (Cybercrime, Hacking, Critical Infrastructures, etc.)	ICANN, ITU, OECD
	Language and Cultural Diversity (Multilingual Domain Names, Content Diversity, etc.)	ICANN, WIPO, ITU, UNESCO
	Market Conditions (ICT for Trade, Pricing, Affordable Inputs, Credit, Taxation, etc.)	WTO, UNCTAD

Source: Implementation Team …, 2002.

This situation provides evidence to support Kleinwaechter's (1998) view of the emergence of a new 'trilateralism' in global communications negotiations and policy-making, i.e. the involvement of governments, industry and citizens in the process. Long before WSIS in 2003, the ITU changed its constitution in the early 1990s to admit a new category of members: representatives of the private sector. Previously an intergovernmental organisation (with 190 Member States in 2002), it became a 'bilateral' organisation, involving some 650 non-governmental Sector Members. Its treaties provide an international legal framework for cooperation between governments, the private sector, and other actors. According to Kleinwaechter (1998, p. 75), there has been a significant power shift within the ITU from governments to private-sector representatives 'who will dominate it in the [21st] century'. He detects the same process at the WTO and WIPO, noting that 'while national governments still play a crucial role in the drafting of legal principles, all three bodies have opened their doors – with different degrees – to non-governmental members, mainly from the private sector'.

With time, 'bilateralism' became 'trilateralism', as evidenced by the G7 Ministerial Conference on Global Information Networks (Bonn, 1997), which adopted three declarations: a Ministerial Declaration, an Industry Declaration, and a Users' Declaration, or indeed by WSIS. (see also Richardson, 2001, for an analysis of policy-making within the EU from this point of view).

Preparations for the Tunis stage of WSIS in 2005 are taking this a step further with 'trilateralism' turning into 'quadrilateralism', as a new partner has been added to the list. In addition to governments, industry and civil society, also international organisations (especially those in the UN system) have been invited to join the preparatory process and to take part in the Summit alongside the others.

This process, notes Kleinwaechter, could lead to a totally new system of global regulation of information and communication. Industry, government and users have a lot of common interests, but also different priorities: a return on investment for the industry; stability and security (and taxes) for the government; and costs, trust and human rights for the users.

Yet another important feature of new global communications policy-making is the changing nature of policy and regulatory instruments applied at present. This has to do both with the nature of technologies being regulated and the regulatory process itself.

On the one hand, new forms of media, and especially new technologies, require a different regulatory approach, based much more on self-regulation, co-regulation or 'regulated self-regulation' (see e.g. *Proceedings of the Information Seminar* ..., 1999; Schulz & Held, 2001; Nikoltchev, 2003) than traditional broadcasting. Secondly, and equally importantly, 'trilateralism' has produced 'a search for a new type of agreement among a variety of different partners with different legal status who try to combine the positive elements of a regulated system, like stability, with the flexibility of a non-regulated environment' (Kleinwaechter, 1998, p. 76). The norms which result from this process are very often defined as voluntary principles that are not binding under international law. However, Kleinwaechter points out, the binding power of these voluntary principles is very often higher than that of a legally binding norm: while institutions can survive a decision of a court, they risk disaster and disappearance if they violate the voluntarily agreed rules of the market. The benefit of such voluntary principles is that they can more easily be changed or amended if the environment changes.

On the other hand, there arises the question of the democratic legitimacy of such voluntary principles and of accountability for their non-observance. This observation is made by Raboy (1998, p. 68) who points out that the emerging global regulatory system in communication is a harbinger of a future system of world governance: 'Left unchecked, it will have enormous implications for the future of democracy and human rights, insofar as it is based on political decision-making at a level where there is no accountability, the recognized autonomy of private capital and [often] the formal exclusion of the institutions of civil society. In terms of international relations, it extends the dependency of the technologically-less-developed parts of the world. As a social project, it locates human development as a potential benefit of economic investment, rather than as the principal goal'.

Classifying Global Media Governance Actors

A number of criteria may be applied in developing typologies of these actors.

Raboy (2001) proposes to group them according to their place in the global system:

- **global organisations**, encompassing bodies that have traditionally been part of the United Nations family such as the International Telecommunications Union (ITU), UNESCO, and newer ones such as the World Trade Organisation (WTO). Most politically-constituted 'nations' belong to these organisations, through their official government authorities. Procedures are nominally meant to be inclusive but are actually restricted to government representation. Regarding communication, this sector has been strongly marked by the power shift in recent decades from organisations dedicated to communication and cultural issues such as UNESCO or the ITU to those focusing on commercial or trade issues such as the World Intellectual Property Organisation (WIPO) and the WTO.
- **multilateral exclusive 'clubs'**, such as the OECD and the G8, which collectively exercise enough economic clout to influence the globe without having to deal directly with lesser economies politically. More streamlined, and thus more efficient, than more cumbersome global organisations like the WTO, these clubs can at the same time afford to put forward a more generous public discourse while promoting specific projects (such as the 1995 Global Information Infrastructure project or the 2000 Okinawa Charter on Global Information Society). They currently serve as the main testing-ground for pro-business proto-global policies, with the extremely important caveat that their decisions are binding on no one and not accountable.
- **regional multi-state groupings**, the most important being the EU and NAFTA, each of which represents a distinct model: the first an economic union with a political agenda; the latter a trade zone which nominally has no political ambition. The difference means the EU can elaborate common policies in the name of the general community,

while NAFTA-type regimes can only constrain the policy-making range of member states. The previously mentioned EU protocol on public broadcasting stands, at this time, as the only living example of a transnational cultural policy that supersedes economic imperatives.

■ regardless of their weakened condition, **nation states** continue to be the main site of communication and cultural policy-making. Cultural policy agencies in countries such as Canada and France have been fighting rearguard actions against the constraining effects of global trade agreements their countries have themselves signed. There is an increasing recognition of the need to bring these issues to global fora as a basis for legitimating the continuation of national sovereignty in cultural matters on an equal footing with trade rules. National governments that wish to do so can still actively regulate important aspects of domestic broadcasting and telecommunication industries, sustain public cultural institutions and subsidise national cultural production. But the extent to which this can continue will require agreement at a higher level.

■ the **transnational private sector** has organised itself to achieve representation in official fora. No longer merely restricted to lobbying, transnational corporations and their associations are increasingly present at the tables where policy decisions are made. Groups such as the Global Business Dialogue for e-commerce and the Global Information Infrastructure Commission, speaking for the forty or so largest corporations in the IT sector, have become a powerful force in setting the global communication policy agenda, especially with respect to Internet, e-commerce and new media issues.

■ less resourced and generally more distant from the centres of power, **civil society organisations** are less present in policy debates, but culture and communication is becoming – like the environment before it – one of the rallying points of grassroots mobilisation. Global associations such as AMARC (community radio), Vidéazimut (video) the Association for Progressive Communication (Internet users), and Computer Professionals for Social Responsibility now represent alternative media producers worldwide, while umbrella groups such as the Global Communication Network and the Platform for Democratic Communication are burgeoning.

■ finally, amid all this bustle, cutting edge issues such as Internet regulation are increasingly **'transversal'** in that they cut across sites of clear-cut jurisdiction.

This is typified by controversies surrounding the creation in 1998 of ICANN (the Internet Corporation for Assigned Names and Numbers) and its subsequent development.

At the same time, important issue clusters regarding transnational media and universal themes, such as the right to communicate, can be said to be **'homeless'** in that they are not being dealt with systematically anywhere.

A different typology of these actors could be proposed, in line with the primary objectives they pursue. Among institutionalised actors, we can distinguish those which are oriented towards:

■ political goals (UN, OSCE);
■ economic goals (WTO, OECD, UE);

- technical (and market-oriented) objectives (ITU);
- socio-cultural goals (UNESCO);
- protection of copyright and other rights (WIPO);
- representing regulatory authorities (European Platform of Regulatory Authorities – EPRA);
- representing the interests of particular types of media operators (EBU, Association of Commercial Television – ACT),
- pursuit of certain values (Council of Europe, NGOs like Article 19);
- research (European Institute for the Media, European Audiovisual Observatory).

Of course, in some cases there are no clear-cut differences between different types of objectives, or some actors pursue a range of different objectives. Obviously, the impact these actors have is different and depends on their placement in the convergence configuration. The most obvious reason for their varying importance is the sort of objectives they pursue and the nature of their powers.

'Hard' objectives are those which have to do with law, the economy, technology, etc.

'Soft' objectives, by contrast, relate to the pursuit or protection of certain values, ideas and ideals.

Different types of organisations are established to pursue these kinds of objectives:

- 'Hard' objectives are the domain of organisations with at least legislative/regulatory powers, and sometimes also executive and administrative powers;
- 'Soft' objectives are the domain of standard-setting organisations which may, if at all, adopt binding legal instruments only in the form of collective agreements among their members (e.g. the European Convention on Transfrontier Television adopted within the context of the Council of Europe).

These two types of actors are complemented by industrial and other lobbies (e.g. EBU, ACT, etc.) and NGOs representing a variety of concerns and interests. Some of them can be quite effective: e.g. the EBU has been an important player in EU debates on public service broadcasting, including the adoption of the Amsterdam Protocol and the development of the Commission Communication on the Application of State Aid Rules to Public Service Broadcasting. On the other hand, commercial broadcasters appear to have prevented the exemption of public service broadcasting from the EU competition rules.

Research institutes have little impact on the process of governance, but provide the information and analyses exploited by various actors in this processes.

Some of these actors can themselves be regarded as case studies of governance. This could be said of the European Union whose media (or audiovisual) policy, as noted above is certainly not the product of a single and unified Community vision of the sector. Instead it must be regarded as a result of a hard won compromise between both Member States and rival power centres within the institutions. The shifting balance of power between them produces the twists and turns of EU audiovisual policy, sometimes more oriented to culture, at other times with more stress on commerce (see Prosser, Goldberg & Verhulst, 1998). One example of this is the EU's policy *vis-à-vis* public service broadcasting. The European Commission was originally determined to apply a much stricter, market- and competition-oriented approach to PSB, only to have to change its approach under pressure from member states and acknowledge its importance in terms of satisfying the democratic, social and cultural needs of each society and of preserving media pluralism (Jakubowicz, 2004).

Appendix: media governance actors on the European Scene

Given the great multitude of media governance actors in Europe, we can only mention a small selection of the most influential ones.

Intergovernmental Bodies and Organisations

The various international organisations in Europe approach media issues from quite different perspectives. For example, whereas the Council of Europe and the OSCE pursue an approach dedicated to protection of human rights and democratic values, the European Union is known for its economic and technological approach.

European Union

The European Union, now composed of 25 countries, is the key European organisation in terms of media policy.

The EC Treaty established the Community institutions, notably the Council of Ministers, the European Parliament (EP), the Commission and the Court of Justice of the European Communities, and it confers legislative, executive and judicial powers in prescribed fields upon them.

The EU's approach to the media industry has proceeded from the fact that:

> Under the Treaties, the Community has no independent mandate to shape the area of the media. Rather, the legal bases are 'horizontal', in other words they are designed to achieve general objectives of the Community, especially the completion of the internal market ... Community policy in the area of the regulation of media content is thus essentially ... governed and limited by the internal market objective of freedom of movement for goods (including newspapers and magazines, for example) and services (including radio and television broadcasts). ... It must regulate those matters that are necessary for the completion of the internal market, but may not regulate anything else (Reding, 2002, p. 7).

Nevertheless, the EU's policies have had a major impact on European media, in that they have ranged over the following areas:

- Development of the regulatory framework for television, Information Society services and electronic communications;
- Development of support mechanisms at a European level promoting the growth of the audiovisual industry and the production and distribution of European audiovisual works;

- Elaboration of common technical standards to promote integration; preparing the technological and regulatory foundations for the transition of the European audiovisual sector into the digital area;
- The issue of ownership and the impact of cross-media concentration, including control of mergers and acquisitions to protect competition on the media market;
- The external dimension of the Community's audiovisual policy, including trade negotiations within the WTO and other organisations.

Within the European Commission, the Directorate responsible for audiovisual policy is the Information Society and Media Directorate-General. Previously, audiovisual policy was part of the Education and Culture Directorate-General, but in the Barrosso Commission, it was moved to what was previously the Information Society Directorate-General, so that the new DG could bring together all three aspects of modern day electronic communications – in the fields of broadcasting, computer networks and of electronic communication services. This is symptomatic of the EU Commission's approach to the media primarily in terms of their economic role, in recognition of the fact that all sectors of economic activity depend heavily on information and communication technologies.

Accordingly, the DG's role is officially described as:

- Promoting a European Information Society (IS) founded on innovation, creativity and inclusion.
- Supporting innovation by stimulating the competitiveness of the ICT sector and by promoting the widest and most effective take-up of Information and Communication Technology (ICT).
- Fostering creativity by encouraging the growth of new and emerging markets particularly in the areas of media and digital content.
- Encouraging inclusion by assisting widespread access to ICT and use of ICT-based services for both citizens and businesses.
- Bringing the Information Society (IS) closer to people and to businesses by raising the visibility and impact of IS and media policies at EU and Member State level.

From this point of view, it is interesting to look at the internal structure of the DG. It is composed of the following directorates:

- Directorate R: Resources
- Directorate S: General Affairs
- Directorate A: Audiovisual, Media, Internet
- Directorate B: Electronic Communications Policy
- Directorate C: Lisbon Strategy and Policies for the Information Society
- Directorate D: Network and Communication Technologies
- Directorate E: Content
- Directorate F: Emerging Technologies and Infrastructures
- Directorate G: Components and Systems
- Directorate H: ICT for Citizens and Businesses

In addition, several other Directorates-General also have communications-related responsibilities, though each operates from a rather different perspective:

- DG for External Relations which represents the EU at G8 and World Trade Organisation meetings, dealing with such issues as the convergence of the communications sector, intellectual property rights and the liberalisation of communications services.
- DG for Enterprise and Industry;
- DG for Competition which plays an important role in the prevention of anti-competitive agreements and actions including monopolies and mergers, issues of great importance in relation to the recent development of the media industries.

Finally the DG for the Internal Market has an interest in the liberalisation of audio-visual markets and which originally produced *Television Without Frontiers: Green Paper on the establishment of the common market for broadcasting, especially by satellite and cable* COM(84) 300, May 1984, which set the scene for the major actions taken by the then EEC in relation to the audio-visual industry.

With so many different Directorates-General potentially involved, the potential for inter-institutional conflict is considerable (see e.g. Harcourt, 1998).

The European Parliament has a Committee dealing with questions relating to information and the media: the Committee on Culture, Youth, Education, the Media and Sport. It has had an important role in the initiation of media policy, being mainly concerned with the promotion of European integration, emphasising cultural as well as market aspects, and it has continued to play a significant role right up to and including the 1997 revision of the Television Without Frontiers Directive. It has also had a strong interest in public service broadcasting.

The European Court of Justice has heard several cases over the years, including prior to the implementation of the Directive, directly and indirectly involving the provision of audiovisual services or aspects thereof. These include cases establishing the basic competence of Community action in relation to the media and those interpreting the Television Without Frontiers Directive and shaping its implementation.

In addition to the institutions discussed above, the Treaties create one form or another.

Council of Europe

The Council of Europe is a standard-setting organisation in the area of human rights, and in the media field; this extends in particular to the role of the media in a democratic society, freedom of political speech and criticism of government, and a watchdog role of the media (for a review of the Council of Europe's stance and policies on the media, see Karaca, 2003).

The Council has long been concerned with audiovisual policy and regulation. Media in general, and audiovisual media in particular, are understood to be, on the one hand, aspects of general human rights (freedom of expression, balanced by the right to a private life) and, on the other, indispensable means for promoting and protecting democratic societies through the dissemination of information and the formation of public opinion. Article 10 of the Convention on Human Rights and Fundamental Freedoms, taken together with the Declaration on the Freedom of Expression and Information adopted by the Committee of Ministers on 29 April 1982, have been described as a 'veritable European media charter'. The case-law developed by the European Court of Human Rights on the basis of Article 10 is Europe's major legal *acquis* in this field, a body of law of utmost importance (see *Case-Law Concerning Article 10 of the European Convention on Human Rights*, 2000).

On the CoE Secretariat side, media activities are dealt with by the Media Division, operating within the Directorate of Human Rights. The Media Division supports the work of the Steering Committee on the Mass Media (or CDMM), composed of representatives of all member states and setting. Its mandate is to:

■ Develop European cooperation on means of public communication with a view to further enhancing freedom of expression and information in a pluralistic democratic society, as well as the free flow of information and ideas across frontiers,
■ To this effect, work out concerted European policy measures and appropriate legal and other instruments to address the issues raised notably by the functioning of means of public communication in a democratic society, in particular their impact on human rights and democratic values; to develop activities which advance the goals of democratic security and cultural cohesion and pluralism in a pan-European perspective;
■ Monitor the implementation by member States of the non-binding instruments prepared under its authority;
■ Prepare the European Ministerial Conferences on Mass Media Policy and to ensure their follow-up on the basis of the relevant decisions of the Committee of Ministers;
■ Various specialist, expert committees meet under its general auspices.

The 7th CoE Ministerial Conference on Mass Media Policy (Kiev, March 10–11, 2005) called for the Committee's name to be changed to Steering Committee on the Media and New Communication Services, in order to extend its mandate to the ICTs and Information Society, and to enable it to develop policies for human rights protection also in these areas.

A number of conventions have been adopted under CoE auspices. The Committee of Ministers has adopted a large number of non-binding recommendations, which add up to an important body of European standards on various issues related to the media. Monitoring of observance of freedom of expression standards by member states, conducted by the Secretariat, as well as by the Parliamentary Assembly of the Council of Europe, has contributed to raising standards of human rights protection in this area in Europe.

Organisation for Security and Cooperation in Europe
The Organisation for Security and Co-operation in Europe (OSCE), which co-operates closely with the Council of Europe, categorises audiovisual media matters as an aspect of the democracy and democratisation of European states. The OSCE's Office of

Democratic Institutions and Human Rights has compiled a thematic database: OSCE Commitments with respect to the media.

The OSCE established in 1992 the position of the High Commissioner on National Minorities. The successive Commissioners have issued a number of guidelines and recommendations on the protection of minority rights in the media and have intervened with governments and media organisations in this sphere in many OSCE countries.

At the end of 1997 a new organ, the OSCE Representative on Freedom of the Media, was approved and its mandate agreed upon. Based on OSCE principles and commitments, the Representative is to:

- observe relevant media developments;
- advocate and promote full compliance with relevant principles and commitments;
- assume an early-warning function and concentrate on a rapid response to serious non-compliance with OSCE principles and commitments;
- address serious problems caused by obstruction of media activities and unfavourable working conditions for journalists; and
- support the Office for Democratic Institutions and Human Rights in assessing the conditions for the functioning of free, independent and pluralistic media before, during and after elections.

Stability Pact for South Eastern Europe
The Stability Pact was created at the EU's initiative in 1999 'to foster peace, democracy, respect for human rights and economic prosperity in order to achieve stability in the whole region'. It is the first serious attempt by the international community to replace the previous reactive crisis intervention policy in South Eastern Europe with a comprehensive, long-term, conflict prevention strategy, involving the creation of a secure environment, the promotion of sustainable democratic systems, and the promotion of economic and social well being. The structure and working methods of the Stability Pact are modelled on the CSCE process. A special feature is that, at Regional and Working Tables, representatives of South Eastern European countries are, for the first time, on an equal footing with those of international organisations and financial institutions in advising on the future of their region and in setting priorities concerning the content of all three working areas.

Organisationally, the Stability Pact relies on the Special Coordinator. His most important task is to bring the participants' political strategies in line with one another, to coordinate existing and new initiatives in the region. The Special Coordinator chairs the most important political instrument of the Stability Pact, the Regional Table. There are three Working Tables, which operate under the Regional Table: Democratisation and Human Rights; Economic Reconstruction, Co-operation and Development; Security Issues (with two Sub-Tables: Security and Defence, and Justice and Home Affairs).

The European Commission and World Bank were appointed to coordinate the economic assistance measures for the region. They jointly chair a High-Level Steering Group in which the finance ministers of the G8 countries and the country holding the EU presidency work together with the representatives of international financial institutions and organisations and the Special Coordinator.

The EU undertakes to draw South Eastern Europe 'closer to the perspective of full integration … into its structures', including eventual full membership. As a contribution to the Stability Pact and an interim step towards membership, the European Union set up a new generation of Stabilisation and Association Agreements. These are aimed at the five South Eastern European countries which so far had no contractual relationship with the EU, i.e. Albania, Bosnia-Herzegovina, Croatia, FYR Macedonia and Serbia and Montenegro.

Stability Pact Partners.
The countries of the region:

Albania, Bosnia-Herzegovina, Bulgaria, Croatia, FYR of Macedonia, Moldova, Romania and Serbia and Montenegro

The European Union Member States and the European Commission

Other countries: Canada, Japan, Norway, Russia, Switzerland, Turkey, USA

International organisations: UN, OSCE, Council of Europe, UNHCR, NATO, OECD

International financial institutions: World Bank, International Monetary Fund (IMF), European Bank for Reconstruction and Development (EBRD), European Investment Bank (EIB), Council of Europe Development Bank (CEB)

Regional initiatives: Black Sea Economic Co-operation (BSEC), Central European Initiative (CEI), South East European Co-operative Initiative (SECI) and South East Europe Co-operation Process (SEECP)

European Radiocommunications Office
The European Radiocommunications Office (ERO) is the permanent body for European spectrum management, i.e. the allocation and assignment of spectrum frequencies. The functions of the ERO are defined in the ERO Convention and include a role in the long term planning of the radio spectrum, liaison with national frequency management authorities, coordination of research studies and consultation with interested parties on specific topics or parts of the frequency spectrum. In addition, the ERO assists the European Radiocommunications Committee (ERC) in carrying out its numerous activities. The ERC is one of three committees that form the European Conference of Postal and Telecommunications Administrations (CEPT), the regional regulatory telecommunication organisation for Europe. The ERC is concerned with the development of policy on radiocommunications issues which includes the coordination of frequencies and administrative and technical matters relating to the regulation of radio in Europe. The ERC is also responsible for preparing the European proposals and positions for conferences of the International Telecommunications Union (ITU) dealing with radiocommunications.

European Platform of Regulatory Authorities (EPRA)

EPRA was established in April 1995, to enable regular and informal meetings of representatives of European independent regulatory broadcasting authorities. As the European Institute for the Media provides the Secretariat, meetings tend to be coordinated with EIM's Television and Film Forum. The meetings are used to exchange information, interpretations and applications regarding common issues of national and European media regulation.

European Audiovisual Observatory

The European Audiovisual Observatory was set up under CoE auspices in 1992 to enhance the transparency and availability of information on the audiovisual industry in Europe. It operates under an extended partial agreement of the Council of Europe. Apart from its specific information provision services and publications, it is arguably the most complete repository of data on all media organisations and institutions – public and private – in Europe, or relevant for Europe.

European Broadcasting Union

The European Broadcasting Union was established in 1950 and is of course a non-governmental organisation. Originally, it aimed to assist the solution of common legal and technical problems of European public service broadcasters. It is the world's largest professional association of national broadcasters, especially following a merger with the EBU on 1 January 1993 of the International Radio and Television Organisation (OIRT) (the former association of Socialist Bloc broadcasters). It has active members in European and Mediterranean countries and associate members in 30 countries elsewhere in Africa, the Americas, and Asia. In the course of its development, mechanisms for exchanging programmes and news have been developed. Four categories currently exist: Eurovision Network Services; Eurovision News Exchanges; Eurovision Programme Exchanges; and Euroradio. The legal sector's activities relate mainly to issues of copyright law and lawmaking, such as the acquisition of rights, lobbying on behalf of its members in European and global institutions and facilitating contractual access for non-members to the Eurovision Network.

Collaboration exists between the EBU and the European Group of Television Advertising (EGTA set up in 1974) which is an association made up of 28 sales houses or commercial departments of TV channels from 22 countries which are members of the EBU. EGTA concerns itself with analysing and lobbying on all matters to do with television advertising and has recently, in conjunction with the EBU, put the European Interactive Guide to TV Sponsorship on-line, thus facilitating all the information available on sponsorship in 40 countries and 79 channels.

Association of Commercial Television

The EBU has a counterpart organisation, Association of Commercial Television (ACT), representing the commercial sector's interests in such areas as advertising and e-commerce; intellectual property; competition and public sector broadcasting; media ownership; audio-visual policy; new services; protection of minors; sports. It seeks to promote, and lobby for, the interests of the commercial sector in all major European organisations, including the EU, the CoE, WIPO, the European Advertising Tripartite and the Advertising Information Group as well as with the European Services Forum. Members of ACT include Antena 3, Spain; Antenna TV, Greece; BSkyB, UK; Canal+, France; DSF, Germany; ITV, UK; M6, France; Mediaset, Italy; Mega Channel, Greece; MTV-Oy, Finland; Premiere, Germany; ProSieben, Germany; RTL Group, Luxembourg; Sat 1, Germany; Sky Italia, Italy; Sogecable, Spain; Telecinco, Spain; TV 3, Ireland; TV 4, Sweden; Vlaamse Media Maatschappij, Belgium.

Association Européenne des Radios/Association of European Radios (AER)

Association of European Radios (AER) is a Europe-wide trade body representing the interests of over 4,500 private/commercial radios stations in eleven EU Member States, Switzerland and Romania. AER's main objective is to develop and improve the most suitable framework for private commercial radio activity. AER constantly follows EU actions in the fields of media, telecommunications and private radio transmission in order to contribute, to enrich and develop the radio sector. Furthermore, AER intends to promote the diffusion and the use of new technologies in radio transmission (in particular, the DAB system – Digital Audio Broadcasting). AER encourages co-operation between its members and with other European radio stations and associations, in order to preserve and develop freedom of speech, freedom of enterprise, private initiative and the protection of listeners.

AER actively tries to contribute with its presence in Brussels to the European Institutions' working process (European Commission and European Parliament, in particular) and the Council of Europe. AER is currently an observer in the WIPO (World Intellectual Property Organisation), and a member of the World DAB Forum, AIG (Advertising Information Group) and EASA (European Advertising Standards Alliance).

AER is composed of private radio national associations whose target is to promote private radio broadcasters' interests in Europe and to offer technical assistance to its members. Today, AER is represented in Denmark, Finland, France, Germany, Greece, Italy, Portugal, The Netherlands, Spain, Sweden, Switzerland, Romania (as Associate Member) and the UK.

Members of AER include : AERC – Asociación Española de Radiodifusión Comercial, Spain; APR – Associação Portuguesa de Radiodifusão, Portugal; ARCA – Associatia Romana de Comunicatii Audiovizuale, Romania; EIRA – Athens Independent Radio Station Association, Greece; CRCA – Commercial Radio Companies Association, UK; KOMM – Foreningen Af Kommercielle Lokal Radio & TV-Stationer, Denmark; NVCR – Nederlandse Vereniging voor Commerciele Radios, The Netherlands; RNA – Radio Nazionali Associate, Italy; RU – Radioutgivareföreningen, Sweden; SRL – Suomen Radioiden Liitto Srl Ry, Finland; SRGP – Syndicat des Radios Généralistes Privées, France; SRN – Syndicat des Réseaux Radiophoniques Nationaux, France; VPRT – Verband Privater Rundfunk und

Telekommunikation eV, Germany; VSP/ASRP – Verband Schweizer Privatradios/ Association Suisse des Radios Privées, Switzerland).

European Publishers Council

The European Publishers' Council (EPC) is a high level group of Chairmen and CEOs of leading European media corporations actively involved in multimedia markets spanning newspapers, magazines, Internet and on-line database publishing; many EPC members also have significant interests in private television and radio.

The EPC is not a trade association, but a high level group of the most senior representatives of newspaper and magazine publishers in Europe. The EPC was founded in January 1991 with the express purpose of reviewing the impact of proposed European legislation on the press, and then expressing an agreed opinion to the initiators of the legislation, politicians and opinion-formers. It is pledged to do everything it can to promote the concept and operation of the Internal Market, which it believes is fully in the interests of Europe's citizens.

Publishers are in the information business and are major providers of the content of Europe's information highways. They consider themselves as key to the EU's growth and competitiveness as the integrated information industry becomes the largest single economic sector in Europe by the end of the century; they seek a coherent approach to legislation for the information industry. In their view, publishers must not be prevented by outdated or restrictive legislation from safeguarding their future prosperity and viability.

Members of EPC include: Agora, Poland; Axel Springer Verlag, Germany; Bonnier Group, Sweden; Burda Media, Germany; Daily Mail and General Trust, UK; De Persgroep, Belgium; De Telegraaf, Netherlands; Der Standard, Austria; Egmont Group, Denmark; Editoriale L'Espresso, Italy; Financial Times Group, UK; Gruner + Jahr, Germany; Grupo Prisa, Spain; Hachette Filipacchi Medias, France; Impresa, Portugal; Independent Newspapers PLC, Ireland; Lambrakis Publishing Group, Greece; News International, UK; Reed Elsevier, UK; Ringier, Switzerland; Rizzoli Corriere della Sera, Italy; SanomaWSOY Corporation, Finland; Schibsted, Norway; Société Ouest-France SA, France; Telegraph Group Ltd, UK; Trinity Mirror plc, UK; Verlagsgruppe Georg von Holtzbrinck GmbH, Germany; Vocento, Spain.

European Newspaper Publishers' Association ENPA

The European Newspaper Publishers' Association ENPA is a non-profit organisation currently representing some 3.000 daily, weekly and Sunday titles from 17 European countries. More than 91 million copies are sold each day and read by over 240 million people.

ENPA describes itself as working towards ensuring a sympathetic European legislative and economic environment, as these are indispensable conditions for the development of an independent newspaper industry. In particular, it is concerned with strengthening and defending the freedom of the press, both editorial and commercial, as fundamental rights. It is service-orientated and provides a comprehensive information network for its members and from which officials in the European Union and the Member States also can benefit, and aims to facilitate the exchange and transfer of know-how and ideas to its members and related organisations alike.

ENPLA affiliates European the following newspaper publishers' associations:

- VÖZ - Verband Österreichischer Zeitungen; Association Belge des Editeurs de Journaux – ABEJ; Belgische Vereniging van de Dagbladuitgevers – BVDU; Danske Dagblades forening; Sanomalehtien Liitto (Finland); Syndicat de la Presse Parisienne; Syndicat de la Presse Quotidienne Régionale; Bundesverband Deutscher Zeitungsverleger; Association Luxembourgeoise des Editeurs de Journaux; Athens Daily Newspaper Publishers Association; National Newspapers of Ireland; Federazione Italiana Editori Giornali; vereniging De Nederlandse Dagbladpers; Norwegian Media Business Association; Associação da Imprensa Diaria Portuguesa; Asociación de Editores de Diario Españoles; The Swedish Newspaper Publishers' Association; Schweizer Presse; The Newspaper Society (UK).
- Associated Members: DISTRIPRESS (Switzerland); Société Professionnelle des Papiers de Presse (France)
- Observers: Magyar Lapkiadok Egyesulete (Hungary); Polish Chamber of Press Publishers; Czech Publishers Association (UVDT); Eesti Ajalehtede Liit (Estonia).

European Advertising Standards Alliance
The EASA is a non-profit organisation which brings together national advertising self-regulatory organisations (SROs) and organisations representing the advertising industry in Europe. The Alliance represents the advertising industry on advertising self-regulation issues and promotes high ethical standards in commercial communications by means of effective self-regulation. Its general mission includes: the promotion and development of self-regulation; the support of existing advertising self-regulatory systems; the management and coordination of the Alliance's cross-border complaints mechanism to ensure that cross-border complaints – through a specific procedure – are resolved speedily and effectively; the provision of information and research concerning advertising self-regulation.

Currently 28 self-regulatory bodies (SRO's) are in Alliance membership. 24 of these are from 22 European countries and the other 4 are from non-European countries.

European Internet Services Providers Association
EuroISPA is the pan-European association of the Internet services providers associations of the countries of the European Union. EuroISPA is the world's largest association of ISPs. EuroISPA describes its mission as follows: to protect and promote the interests of Europe as a whole within the global Internet, securing for Europe a premier position in the key industry of the new Millennium; to help deliver the benefits of this new technology of liberation and empowerment to individuals, while at the same time meeting the legitimate concerns of parents and others responsible for the weaker members of society; to encourage the development of a free and open telecommunications market, something of great benefit to society as a whole but essential to the healthy development of the Internet; and finally, to promote the interests of our members and provide common services to them where these cannot be had elsewhere.

The following nine ISP associations are Members of EuroISPA:

■ AEPSI - Asociación Espanola de Proveedores de Servicios de Internet ; AFA – Association des Fournisseurs d'Acces et de Services Internet; AIIP – Associazione Italiana Internet Providers; ISPA Austria – Internet Service Providers Austria; ECO Forum – Verband der deutschen Internetwirtschaft; ISPAI – Internet Service Providers Association of Ireland; ISPA Luxembourg – Internet Service Providers Association of Luxembourg; NLIP – Branchevereniging van Nederlandse Internet Providers; ISPA UK – Internet Services Providers Association UK; LINX – The London Internet Exchange (Associate member)

NGOs, Civil Society Organisations

European Federation of Journalists
The European Federation of Journalists (EFJ) is created as a regional organisation within the framework of the Constitution of the International Federation of Journalists to represent the interests of journalists' unions and their members. The EFJ is Europe's largest organisation of journalists, representing about 280,000 journalists in over thirty countries. The EFJ campaigns for trade union rights within all the political institutions of Europe, including the European Union, the Council of Europe and the OSCE. In South-East Europe, the IFJ's Media for Democracy programme promotes independent trade unions and associations of journalists, reform of the legal environment, public service broadcasting, professional ethics through structures for self regulation, human rights and conflict reporting, and safety of journalists.

South East Europe Media Organisation
The South East Europe Media Organisation (SEEMO), an affiliate of the International Press Institute (IPI), is a non-governmental, non-profit network of editors, media executives and leading journalists from newspapers, magazines, radio, TV, Internet, new media and news agencies in the South Eastern European Region: Albania, Bosnia, Bulgaria, Croatia, FR Yugoslavia (Serbia, Montenegro, Kosovo/Kosova), Greece, Macedonia (FYROM), Moldova and Romania.

Notes
1. Harcourt (1998) offers a fascinating analysis, from this point of view, of internal struggle between various Directorates-General of the European Commission, for control of the media ownership issue when the matter was debated in the EU during the 1990, and thus for the ability to impose their own definition of the problem, to set the agenda of debate, propose their own policy instruments and solutions – and thus to win a battle in the constant competition among the DGs. The implication is that almost every important issue sets off such a struggle within the European Commission. And indeed, DG Information Society (with its free market orientation), in tandem with DG Competition and DG Internal Market, have in recent years overshadowed DG Education and Culture (with its cultural approach) in determining the orientation of the EU's media and communications policy.
2. The Europe Region conference (Mainz, 27–29 June 2002) issued a Mainz Resolution in which participants agreed on the following principles as regards acces, for example: '(a) Matters related to access are not limited to technological infrastructure, but concern as well equally the cognitive, economic, and physical dimensions, resources

of the Information Society; (b) Access is fundamental in the Information Society. It is based on universal principles and on commonly agreed values, such as recognition of privacy in the use of information; respect for the right of others to information; willingness to sharing knowledge as a resource which will not diminish with usage; recognition, promotion and safeguarding of cultural and linguistic diversity in organizing access to information; promotion of empowerment and participation in the information society;(c) Generally acknowledged commercial interests in exploiting and profiting from knowledge and cultural resources should not compromise the primacy of the public interest'.

3. This 'Broadcasters' Declaration' expressed the conviction that public and private broadcasters will play a key in bringing about an information society in which all citizens are included and can participate and stressed their commitment and contribution to such fundamental values as freedom of expression, access to information, media pluralism and cultural diversity, and put forward the following principles and objectives: '1. Communications technology is not an end in itself; it is a vehicle for the provision of information and content; 2. Freedom of expression, freedom and pluralism of the media and cultural diversity should be respected and promoted; 3. The electronic media have a vital role to play in producing, gathering and distributing quality content within the information society; 4. Television and radio are crucial for ensuring social cohesion and development in the digital world; 5. Information should remain accessible and affordable to everyone'.

4. Kleinwaechter (1998, p. 78) notes that 'Industry does no longer 'influence' decisions which are made on the governmental level, but they take the lead and 'invite governments' to contribute to solutions, which will be under the control of global business'.

5. The CRIS campaign had been launched by the Platform for Communication Rights, a grouping of NGOs, formed in 1996, pursuing a strategy relating to communication and democratisation oriented to promoting the contribution of communication to the democratisation of society, and the democratisation of communication structures, institutions and processes.

6. The less known acronyms are: GBDe – Global Business Dialogue; W3C – World Wide Web Consortiou, IETF – Internet Engineering Task Force; UNCITRAL - United Nations Commission on International Trade Law.

References

Anheier, H., M. Glasius, & M. Kaldor (eds) (2001) *Global Civil Society 2001*. Oxford: Oxford University Press.

Anheier, H., M. Glasius & M. Kaldor (eds) (2003) *Global Civil Society 2003*. Oxford: Oxford University Press.

Bauman, Z. (1998) *Globalization: The Human Consequences*. Cambridge: Polity Press.

Bridges, M. (n.d.) *WSIS – Conference Hype or Lasting Change?* http://cyberlawharvardedu/ briefings/wsis

Burch S (2004) *Global media governance: Reflections from the WSIS experience Media Development, No 1*. wwwwaccorguk/modulesphp?name=News&file=article&sid=1485

Case-Law Concerning Article 10 of the European Convention on Human Rights_(2000) Strasbourg: Directorate General of Human Rights.

Coleman, W. D. & T. Porter (1999) *International Institutions, Globalization and Democracy:*

Assessing The Challenges. Paper prepared for the 11th Annual Meeting on 'Socio-Economics, Globalization and the Good Society', Madison, Wisconsin, USA, 8–11 July.

Dahl, R. A. (1999) 'The Shifting Boundaries of Democratic Governments' *Social Research,* Fall. wwwfindarticlescom/cf_dls/m2267/3_66/58118484/p10/articlejhtml?term=

Dahlgren, P. (2003) *Internet, Public Spheres and Political Communication: Dispersion and Deliberation.* Papers from MODINET's conference on Media Convergence, Mediated Communication, and the Transformation of the Public Sphere Oct 21st-22nd, 2003. wwwhumkudk/modinet/Calendar_aktiviteter/oktober/Peter_dahlgrenhtm

Delbrück, J. (1993) 'Globalization of Law, Politics, and Markets - Implications for Domestic Law: A European Perspective', *Indiana Journal of Global Legal Studies,* Fall: 1(1). http://ijglsindianaedu/archive/01/01/delbruckshtml#top

E-governance Democracy, technology and the public realm (nd) International Centre for e-governance, wwwicegovorg

European Audiovisual Observatory (2004) *Transfrontier Television in the European Union: Market Impact and Selected Legal Aspects.* Background Paper prepared for the EU Conference on the Impact of Transfrontier Broadcasting Services on Television Markets in Individual Member States, Dublin & Drogheda 1 - 3 March 2004. Strasbourg: Council of Europe.

European Commission (2003) 'Towards an international instrument on cultural diversity' *COM*(2003) 520 final Brussels.

Featherstone, M. (ed) (1991) *Global Culture Nationalism, Globalization and Modernity.* London: Sage.

Giddens, A. (1997) 'The globalizing of modernity', pp. 19–26 in A Sreberny-Mohammadi, D. Winseck, J. McKenna & O. Boyd-Barrett (eds), *Media in a global context A Reader.* London: Edward Arnold.

Harcourt, Alison (1998) 'EU media ownership regulation: conflict over the definition of alternatives' *Journal of Common Market Studies,* September.

Held, David (1997) 'Democracy: From City-states to a Cosmopolitan Order?' in R.E. Goodin & P. Pettit (eds) *Contemporary Political Philosophy: An Anthology.* Oxford: Blackwell Publishers.

Herman, Edward S. & Robert W. McChesney (1997) *The Global Media The New Missionaries of Global Capitalism.* London and Washington: Cassell.

Implementation Team on Global Policy Participation (2002) *A Roadmap: Global Policymaking for Information and Communications Technologies Enabling Meaningful Participation by Developing-Nation Stakeholders.* New York: G8 Digital Opportunity Task Force.

Jakubowicz, Karol (2004) 'A Square Peg in a Round Hole: The EU's policy on Public Service Broadcasting', *Journal of Media Practice,* 4(3), pp. 155–175.

Kaldor, M., H. Anheier & M. Glasius, (2003) 'Global Civil Society in an Era of Regressive Globalisation', in H Anheier, M Glasius & M Kaldor (eds) *Global Civil Society 2003.* Oxford: Oxford University Press.

Karaca, K. (2003) *Guarding the Watchdog – The Council of Europe and the Media.* Strasbourg: Council of Europe Publishing.

Keane, J. (2001) 'Global Civil Society?', pp. 23–47 in H Anheier, M Glasius & M Kaldor (eds) Global Civil Society 2001, Oxford: Oxford University Press,.

Keohane, R.O. (n.d.) *Global Governance and Democratic Accountability* wwwpolidukeedu/people/faculty/keohanehtml

Kleinwaechter, W. (1998) 'A New Trilateralism in Global Communication Negotiations? How Governments, Industry and Citizens Try to Create a New 'Global Communications Charter', *Javnost/The Public*, V(4), pp. 74–80

Kraidy, M.M. (2003) 'Glocalisation. An International Communication Framework?' *The Journal of International Communication*, 9(2), pp. 29–49.

Nanz, P. & J. Steffek (2003) *Global governance, participation and the public sphere.* Paper prepared for the 2003 ECPR Joint Session, Workshop 11: The Governance of Global Issues - Effectiveness, Accountability, and Constitutionalization Edinburgh (UK), 28 March – 2 April.

Nikoltchev S. (ed) (2003) 'Co-regulation of the Media in Europe', *IRIS Special*. Strasbourg: European Audiovisual Observatory.

Proceedings of the Information Seminar on Self-Regulation by the Media (1999) DH-MM (99) 7 Strasbourg: Directorate of Human Rights, Council of Europe.

Prosser, Tony, David Goldberg & Stefaan Verhulst (1998) *EC Media Law and Policy*. London: Addison Wesley Longman.

Raboy, Marc (ed.) (1998) Symposium: Global Media Policy. *Javnost/The Public*, V(4), pp. 63–105.

Raboy, Marc (2001) *National, Transnational and Global Approaches to Public Media*. Paper presented at a conference on 'Rethinking Public Media in a Transnational Era' Center for Media, Culture and History, New York University.

Reding, V. (2002) *The challenges facing a future European regulatory system for media and communications*. Speech/02/490 Medientage, Munich, 17 October. http://europaeuint/rapid/start/cgi/guestenksh?p_actiongettxt=gt&doc=SPEECH/02/490|0|RAPID&lg=EN

Richardson J. (ed) (2001) *European Union, Power and policy-making*. London: Routledge.

Riggs, F. W. (2000) *Globalization Key Concepts*. (http://www2hawaiiedu/~fredr/gloconhtm)

Schulz, W. & T. Held (2001) *Regulated Self-regulation as a Form of Modern Government Interim*. Report Hamburg: Hans Bredow Institute for Media Research at the University of Hamburg.

The Concept of Global Governance (n.d.) The Commission on Global Governance New York, wwwcggch/chap1html

Tomlison, J. (1994) 'Mass Communications and the Idea of a Global Public Sphere', *The Journal of International Communication* 1(2), pp. 57–70.

Utsumi Y. (2002) Report On Activities Leading To Prepcom-1 Document WSIS/PC-1/DOC/8–E, http:\\wwwituint/wsis

Venturelli, S. (1998) 'Cultural Rights and World Trade Agreements in the Information Society', *Gazette* 60(1), pp. 47–76

Venturelli S. (n.d.) *From the Information Economy to the Creative Economy: Moving Culture to the Center of International Public Policy*. Washington: Center for Arts and Culture. wwwculturalpolicyorg

Waters, M. (1995) *Globalization*. London and New York: Routledge.

Wilkin, Peter (2001) *The Political Economy of Global Communication An Introduction*. London: Pluto Press.

Winseck, D. & M. Cuthbert (1997) 'From Communication to Democratic Norms Reflections on the Normative Dimensions of International Communication Policy' *Gazette*, 59(1), pp. 1–20.

10

TOWARDS DEMOCRATIC MEDIA GOVERNANCE

Cees J. Hamelink and Kaarle Nordenstreng

This final chapter focuses on what is typically called 'policy' – the political, legal, economic as well as cultural terms of reference, which are seen to regulate the media in society. In fact, the theme of the ESF Programme team behind this book was first formulated as 'Media policy between culture and commerce' and it became shorter ('Media between culture and commerce') just as a matter of convenience during the working process.

Speaking of policy we are dealing with both values and management. On the one hand there are *normative positions* which implicitly or explicitly determine the socio-political role and objectives being served by the media. On the other hand there are *institutional arrangements* which direct the operation of the media to fulfil those roles and objectives. The concept of policy combines these normative and institutional aspects of regulation. It also combines the management by both public and private agencies. In recent years there has been a shift from state-centred policymaking to new forms of multi-actor governance.

In discussing the policies and governance of media one always counts on some premises and paradigms about the nature of society and the relations between society and media. A central premise is typically democracy – mostly taken at face value, without further examination. We shall begin by highlighting these contextual perspectives.

Media and society
Our starting point are the three basic levels or pillars present in any consideration of society: first, the *State* and related governmental institutions; second, the *Market* and

related property and commercial phenomena; thirdly, people and citizens, or the *Civil Society*, apart from the two preceding spheres. A graphical presentation of this articulation of society is as follows:

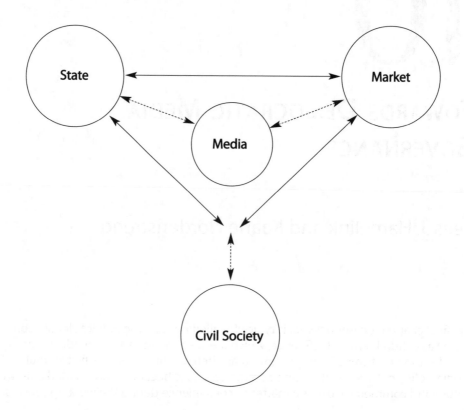

The figure is borrowed from the Norwegian social scientist and peace research pioneer Johan Galtung (1999) who places the media floating between the three pillars (he calls the Market pillar 'Capital'). In the history of European countries the media have first found their place close to both the State and the Capital, emerging out of late-feudal patronage and boosted by mercantile capitalism. With the rise of modern democracy and party structure, the media became part and parcel of the Civil Society, while broadcasting remained closely tied to the State. The second half of the 20th century has brought the media increasingly towards Capital-driven markets.

Like Galtung, we do not see market forces completely absorbing globalising society; we admit that there is burgeoning strength in the civil society with its new movements. Thus the media take a challenging place in a field of conflicts. The media are vital channels, not only for the Civil Society in relation to the State and Market, but also in communication between the State and Market in order to ensure a common public sphere and dialogue in society. If the media succeed in attaining a strong and independent position in this triangle, they could assume the status of a fourth pillar in the power structure of society.

There is another way of viewing media as the fourth element in a democratic society, based on the classic *separation of powers* in a political system as suggested by Montesquieu (Cohler et al., 1989). According to this conventional thinking, the Parliament chosen in general elections constitutes 'legislative power', while the government with all the ministries and other administrative agencies make up 'executive power', and the courts represent an independent 'judiciary power'. The media as an agent of independent journalism has been added to this picture as a 'fourth branch of government' (see, e.g., Powe 1991).

The same role for carrying out checks and balances of the three main branches of government has also been suggested for other institutions such as trade unions and new social movements, but the media still enjoy a special status in this respect, mainly due to the constitutional guarantees of freedom of information based on international law on human rights (Hamelink 1994). Lately, however, media themselves with their commercialisation and tabloidisation developments have been brought under a critical light, leading to proposals such as the establishment of a global media watch as a 'fifth power'. This proposal was made by Ignacio Ramonet, the editor of *Le Monde diplomatique*, at the Social Summit in Porto Alegre in 2003. The same idea is behind initiatives to set up a system of international media monitoring.

Obviously there are different types of media in any society and therefore it is misleading to speak of 'media' as a uniform concept. Nevertheless, one can analytically distinguish between different *media systems and models*, which may operate in a democratic society. Accordingly, Hallin and Manzini (2004) present three models: (1) 'polarized pluralist model' for the Mediterranean countries, (2) 'democratic corporatist model' for the North/Central European countries, and (3) 'liberal model' for the North Atlantic countries. A different typology is provided by McQuail in the latest edition of his canonic textbook (2005), based on normative approaches to the media leading to four models: (1) 'liberal-pluralist or market model', (2) 'social responsibility or public interest model', (3) 'professional model', and (4) 'alternative media model' (pp. 185–186).

While these are broad political models, which characterise the media, or part of the media, in a given country, one can distinguish also different *tasks and roles*, which the media perform in society. Christians et al. (2006) suggest four roles for the media based on their relation to the dominant political-economic powers on the one hand, and the citizens of the civil society on the other. These roles are (1) 'cooperative' for serving the power, (2) 'surveillance' for reporting the power, (3) 'facilitative' for serving the civil society, and (4) 'radical' for questioning the political system. Like McQuail's models above, these roles are offshoots of a normative theory of the media in a democratic context. In other words, all these roles and models are part and parcel of what is known as democracy, and they invite not only examination of the media as such but also the concept of democracy, and the whole media-society relationship.

Media policy

Media policy has mostly been understood to mean public and *official regulation* of the media – their ownership structures and terms of operation, which ultimately shape their content. Yet policy in this connection should not only be seen as official state activity but as a general aspect of regulation of communication at all levels. In addition to official regulation based on laws and administrative directives by the authorities there is also *self-regulation* by the media themselves – by owners and professionals, notably journalists with their codes of ethics. Moreover, a third level of regulation can be distinguished around the media: the *cultural and political traditions* that prevail in society and set a pervasive and often invisible frame of reference for the media to operate.

Obviously, some kind of media policy is operating at each of these levels. From a social scientific point of view, everything in society is being regulated in one way or another, and there are no areas of life that are totally free from any regulation. Hence concepts such as *deregulation* are somewhat misleading; what is at issue is mostly *reregulation* under new conditions.

It should also be noticed that media policy does not only refer to the regulation of different *mass media* but also *telecommunication,* which in the age of digitalisation embraces computers, databases, etc. Actually, convergence of different technologies and uses of media makes it impossible to separate media from each other. To mark this broader meaning the concept has typically been called 'communication policy', which is made up of media policy, on the one hand, and telecommunications policy, on the other. Both sides of policy have evolved out of technical and political needs to regulate communications, particularly since the introduction of telegraph and radio. Further needs for an overall regulatory approach came from the economic development of print media and advertising.

In their overview of the concept of media policy and its historical development Van Cuilenburg and McQuail (2003) single out three phases: (1) emerging communications industry policy from the mid-19th century until the Second World War, (2) public service media policy from the mid-1940s until the 1980s, and (3) a new policy paradigm since the 1990s. The ultimate goal of the first phase was efficiency; the second phase was driven by democracy, while the third phase pursues welfare in the political, social and economic spheres; the third phase also highlights the principles of freedom of communication, access to communication, and the dualistic concept of control and accountability. At all times communication policy has been driven by the idea of public interest with a distinctive national approach. Van Cuilenburg and McQuail place the origins of communication policies 'in the interaction between the pursuit of national interests by states and the operations of commercial/industrial enterprises. Both government and industry have sought mutual advantage by way of privileges, regulations and restrictions' (Ibid, p. 182).

The seeking of mutual advantage and the pursuit of national interests in the communication field has not always occurred under peaceful conditions in the spirit of consensus. On the contrary, it has typically been full of conflicts and confrontation – particularly so in the 1970s when the concept of communication policy made its break through among the political, professional as well as academic circles. As Herbert Schiller (1975) pointed out: 'The issues in the communication field take on increasing significance in the larger struggle to maintain or to change the total system. Accordingly, national communications policy-making may be regarded as a battleground of the contending forces in the social stage' (p. 90). While Schiller reminded us that 'class conflict has now moved into the communications-cultural sphere in an *explicit* way' (p. 82), he emphasised the strategic importance of communication policy as a way to maintain democratic control of what happens in the field.

Indeed, there was a widely held view among so-called progressive forces in the 1970s that communication policies serve a democratic cause, since they raise hidden structures to a public arena, both nationally and internationally. Political parties, media professionals, as well as academics, were invited to participate in articulating the existing and alternative policies – in a constructive way to be brought to the democratic process, starting with a debate in the Habermasian spirit and ending with decisions in the political machinery. For progressive academics this offered a welcome route to depart from the traditional quantitative path of logical positivism and to adopt a 'holistic framework' (Nordenstreng, 1977, p. 280).

On the other hand, there were also those advocates of communication policy who could not be classified as 'progressive' and 'democratic' – who sided rather with private corporations and conservative governments. As highlighted by their prominent representative Ithiel de Sola Pool (1974), these academics want to 'enter into the fundamental decisions about what the communication systems should be', but to approach 'issues in concrete analytic detail and not become engaged in old-fashioned verbal slogans' – the latter meaning such normative issues as 'social versus private ownership' and 'national sovereignty' (p. 9). In other words, Pool wanted to retain policy research within the 'administrative' territory instead of pushing it to the 'critical' domain.

In reality, both administrative and critical traditions were accommodated by the concept of communication policy as it evolved in the 1970s. A central platform in promoting and deliberating communication policies at that time was UNESCO (1972; 1976; 1979). A meeting of experts convened by UNESCO (1972) presented quite far-sighted perspectives: 'In "productivity", we witness, especially in the highly industrialised countries, a shift of emphasis from the production and distribution of "energy" to that of "information". The returns to be gained from viewing a nation's diverse communication activities as a whole, and projecting them into the future against the needs of society and the individual, are worth the effort, vital and urgent.' (p. 4)

Later, UNESCO's activity in communication policy was paralysed (in connection with the controversy around New World Information and Communication Order) and the paradigmatic approach in communication research was turned away from policy orientation (notably through a 'linguistic turn' towards Cultural Studies). Nevertheless, the notion of communication and media policy continued to lead its own life and by the turn of the millennium had even reached a new momentum, as demonstrated by authors such as the Euromedia Research Group (McQuail & Siune, 1998), David Hutchinson (1999) and Philip Napoli (2001).

Governance

In past decades strong pressures have emerged to shift the locus of decision making from public policymakers to forms of mixed public-private, semi-private and private intervention in the management of media issues as well as many other social affairs. Among other things, this implied a shift from cultural aspirations of public policymaking to the commercial interests of private managers. Such a shift represents a 'managerialist' approach to public administration, and it has been accompanied by another historical trend with an erosion of the traditional basis of political power and a diminishing role of the state. The concept of governance was first used to refer to these two trends, but later it became also to mean the trend away from a state-centred policy towards a more citizen-centred approach based on coordination and self-governance with different types of network and partnership relations. Thus the concept is increasingly known as *democratic governance*, and with the means of new information and communication technologies it has led to extensions such as 'democratic e-governance' (Anttiroiko, 2004).

Governance as a concept gained wide recognition with the 1995 report of the UN Commission on Global Governance. In *Our Global Neighbourhood* the Commission proposed that 'Governance is the sum of many ways in which individuals and institutions, public and private, manage their common affairs. It includes formal institutions and regimes empowered to enforce compliance as well as informal arrangements that people and institutions either have agreed to or perceive to be in their interest' (Commission, 1995, p. 2). The UNDP Human Development report of 1999 followed this direction and stressed that 'governance does not mean government' but 'the framework of rules, institutions and established practices that set limits and gives incentives for the behaviour of individuals, organisations and firms' (UNDP, 1999, p. 8). To this UNDP description should be added that governance should be understood as a process rather than as an institutional arrangement. The novelty of this process is that next to the representation of the public interest (as in the conventional political-administrative policymaking) the interests of other societal actors such as private industry, local communities and citizen's movements are also represented.

Precisely because of the broad conceptualisation of governance, the concept can be used in a variety of contexts. Among its many different uses in the current literature are the following:

- Governance is used by the World Bank and Western donor countries in the sense of *good governance*, which refers to the requirement for developing countries to demonstrate that their societies recognise democratic practices, respect human rights and the rule of law.
- With civil society organisations governance is popular as *global governance*, which refers to a global civil ethic as the basis for world management without government.
- In the business management literature governance is used as *corporate governance* which refers to the requirement of transparency in corporations towards the shareholders.
- In neo-liberal economic schools governance means *market governance*, which refers to the self-regulatory potential of market forces.

- Governance can mean *new public management,* which refers to a market-based system by which public institutions are managed as if they were private corporations.
- Governance means also *new coordination practices* through networks, partnerships and deliberative forums.

In the literature one finds conflicting views about governance. The common denominator though is that governance is seen as a process in which a variety of interests are coordinated through different forms of networks and forums. The preferred process may however be engineered along top-down managerial and institutional interests. By itself the governance process is not necessarily a democratic process. It is quite common to refer to governance processes as ways of managing critical issues in the public, private and semi-private spheres of modern societies. In past decades important shifts have taken place in the institutional arrangements for this management. New governance arrangements came about that involved a multitude of governmental and non-governmental agencies. In some arrangements governments retain the essential power of decision-making, while other stakeholders may be consulted, or be partners in debates, but state actors have the leadership and other actors are marginalised. In other arrangements the market forces of supply and demand are in control and only voluntary, self-imposed rules without enforcement mechanisms can intervene. Yet other arrangements are stakeholder-driven and imply forms of joint governance by all stakeholders, as in trilateral arrangements between states, commercial firms and civil society organisations.

Important developments in recent years are significant shifts from forms of local governance to national governance, but equally the delegation of political issue management from national levels to local communities and increasingly also the referral of decision-making on common affairs to supra-national agencies. Another crucial development is a shift from single-level public governance to multi-level forms of governance (often public/private arrangements) that involve national states, intergovernmental agencies, business firms and civil movements.

Governance on the national level can be described as a different way of managing national societies that emerged in response to the failure of conventional representative democracies and the need to accommodate the interests of new actors. Since on the international level there is no global government, the international community has begun to explore new forms of multi-stakeholder management of common issues.

In short, the idea of governance refers to 'changed views and conditions of government, which are characterised by transformation from hierarchies to networks, from command-and-control to initiate-and-coordinate practices, from control-orientation to developmentalism, and from state-centricity to multilevel governance' (Anttiroiko, 2004, p 28).

Governance and the media
Denis McQuail (2003) presents the notion of governance as particularly suited for the management of media issues: 'Governance has been described as "government without politics", which is especially apt in this case, since political interventions in the media are more sensitive than in other areas of policy' (p. 91). McQuail describes different forms of

media governance by using a formal/informal axis against an external/internal axis. This yields the following typology (p. 98):

	FORMAL	INFORMAL
EXTERNAL	Law and regulation	Market forces and relations Pressures and lobbies Public opinion review and criticism
INTERNAL	Management and financial control Self-regulation	Professionalism Organisational culture Norms and ethics

As McQuail observes, 'Media governance projects operate at several levels, ranging from the international to the local' (p 98). On the international level the issues are primarily technical, infrastructural, economic, and industrial. The lead agencies are the ITU (in particular the WARC), WIPO, and the WTO. An illustration of a key global governance issue concerns the management of the Internet. Most predominantly however, governance issues remain at the national level. As McQuail comments, 'The fulcrum of media governance remains the national level, since the nation state is still the main political unit and because most mass media still operate predominantly within the boundaries of the nation state' (p. 99).

For the purpose of this chapter media governance is defined as a *framework of practices, rules and institutions that set limits and give incentives for the performance of the media*. Admittedly, this definition leaves open the big question: Who/What is society?

The issue of media governance is quite complicated because media are both the object of societal governance as well as the key agents in the formation of images about governance in society. 'Governing is inconceivable without the formation of images', writes Kooiman (2003, p. 29). And he continues, 'In the governing process, images are the main frame of reference. Governing images and the way in which they are formed have an important, even decisive, influence on the unfolding of governing processes'. In democratic societies governing processes require a public sphere where those who govern and those who are governed can engage in dialogical communication about their respective images. In recent developments (both social and technological) communication in the public sphere has become increasingly 'mediated' and in this mediated interaction the media play a crucial role.

The complexity of media governance also results from the fact that media are located in civil society, but also operate in the market place, and are linked to state institutions. Moreover, the media as societal systems function simultaneously in economic, political, and cultural domains.

Media governance encompasses the governance of a professional group, of the commons, of productive processes, of content distribution, and of media-society relations. The range of this diversity implies that a diversity of governance measures is needed. Thus media governance will have to be a mixture of different governance modalities such as:

- *Self-governance* meaning that actors (like professionals in various domains) in societal processes manage their affairs in autonomous ways through processes of self-mobilisation and organisation. Implied questions are: In modern societies, can professionals – given their relations to state institutions and commercial business – be autonomous? Are self-governance instruments – such as professional codes of conduct – merely functional in keeping up appearances?
- *Cooperative governance* as in public-private partnerships. This refers to the management of societal issues through forms of collaboration among the actors involved.
- *Interventionist governance* in which the state shapes the framework (through modes of regulation, deregulation, reregulation, privatisation, liberalisation etc) within which other social actors can manage issues.

Media between culture and commerce

To add to the complexity there is also the observation that media governance is caught between culture and commerce.

With regard to media performance one finds such cultural aspirations as diversity of opinion, public participation, protection of the public sphere, and the spreading of science, technology and the arts. At the same time there are the commercial interests of opening and expanding markets, securing investments, unimpeded global trading, and protection of ownership rights.

Culture (as symbolic production) and Commerce represent different realms.

Culture represents:	Commerce represents:
Citizenship	Consumership
Human rights	Property rights
Politics	Markets
Public sphere	Privatisation
Spirituality	Materialism
Trust	Contract

In order to pursue this complexity the interaction between the realms of symbolic production and commerce should be analysed. We find the following dimensions:

- Media institutions are by and large commercial agencies.
- Most of their symbolic production is commodified.
- Symbolic production has gained considerable economic significance, to which, among others, the copyright business attests.
- Increasingly, symbolic production is commercially sponsored. This follows a long historical tradition of relationships between business patrons and the arts.

The key governance issue is how the domains of culture and commerce as well as their interaction should be managed. Traditionally, the issues emerging from the positioning of media as both cultural institutions and commercial ventures were managed through various forms of public and private policymaking. There were largely government policies through regulatory arrangements on national and regional levels and industrial self-regulatory measures. Is this still adequate or should – in view of the complexity of the dynamics between culture and commerce – a new form of transparent, participatory and socially accountable governance arrangement be developed?

Agreeing with McQuail's statement that 'Governance always involves some notion of a norm or standard, coupled with procedures of varying strictness, for enforcement'(2003, p. 91), we have to identify the leading standard for a governance arrangement and propose procedures for enforcement of that standard.

Normative standard
We propose that the normative guidance for media governance should be constituted by the notion of *communication rights*. This implies as the leading question: what characteristics should media governance have in order to most effectively protect communication rights? The questions that follow from this position are: what would be adequate enforcement procedures and how could multi actors be involved?

The societal management of complex and dynamic sub-systems – such as the media – requires a normative grounding that is supported by a wide public consensus. Given the specific European political history and the common European moral framework represented by both the Convention on the Protection of Human Rights and Fundamental Freedoms as and the Court of Human Rights (and its jurisprudence), it seems an obvious choice to seek normative guidance from the regional human rights regime.

Communication rights are those human rights – codified in international and regional human rights instruments – which pertain to standards of performance with regard to the provision of information and the functioning of communication processes in society. From these human rights provisions a set of specific communication rights can be developed that are based upon the key principles of freedom, inclusiveness, diversity and participation.

Freedom
The core of communication rights is proclaimed in Article 19 of the Universal Declaration of Human Rights: 'Everyone has the right to freedom of expression and opinion; this right includes the freedom to hold opinions without interference and to seek, receive and impart information and ideas through any media and regardless of frontiers.' This basic freedom is extended to international law in the International Covenant on Civil and Political Rights (Article 19), in other UN treaties, such as the Convention on the Rights of the Child (Article 13), and in all three main regional human rights instruments (Africa, the Americas and Europe).

Despite these guarantees, censorship remains a reality as humankind embarks on the 21st century. Political and commercial pressures on independent news reporting are ever-present and freedom of speech on the Internet is under serious threat in many parts of the world. It is therefore urgent that we renew the global commitment to freedom of information as 'the touchstone of all freedoms to which the United Nations is consecrated', as stated in United Nations General Assembly Resolution (59I), adopted at its very first session in 1946.

The right to freedom of expression is also increasingly under threat from significantly enhanced state and corporate powers to monitor and intercept communications around the world. It is crucial that the international community adopts robust rules and mechanisms to secure effectively the confidentiality of private communications.

Inclusiveness

International human rights treaties include many provisions purporting to guarantee inclusiveness, such as universal access to information and knowledge, universal access to education, protection of the cultural life of communities and equal sharing of advancements in science and technology. In the current global reality, however, large numbers of people are excluded from access to the basic means of communication such as telephony, broadcasting and the Internet. Access to information about matters of public concern is also unduly limited, and is also very unequal between and within societies. True commitment to inclusiveness requires the allocation of considerable material and non-material resources by the international community and national governments to overcoming these obstacles.

Diversity

Worldwide, existing forms of cultural, informational and linguistic diversity are seriously threatened. Diversity in all of these areas is as critical to the sustainability of the planet as the world's biological diversity. Communication diversity is crucial to democracy and political participation, to the right of all people to promote, protect and preserve their cultural identity and the free pursuit of their cultural development, and to sustainable development.

Diversity is needed at a number of levels, including the availability of a wide range of different content, diversity of ownership in the media and forms of access to the media that ensure that the views of all sectors and groups in society are heard.

Participation

International human rights stress the importance of people's participation in political processes, which from the perspective of communication rights implies the right to have one's views taken into account. In this context, the political participation of ethnic minorities, women and the marginalised is particularly important. Communication is essential to the processes of political decision-making. As the role of media in modern politics expands, this should not obstruct but rather support the broad participation of people in the political process through the development of participatory governance at all levels

Enforcement

Poor implementation remains the core weakness of the international human rights regime. For the development of a human rights culture it is essential that societies are constantly reminded of what significance they attach – in concrete socio-political and economic reality – to their formal human rights commitments.

In particular the case of communication rights deserves a permanent monitoring of actual conditions and likely trends. The state of these rights is an essential yardstick for the democratic quality of political systems, for the cultural sustainability of societies, and for the level of human security in the face of rapid technological development.

If it were possible to develop a reliable, consistent, valid and re-usable instrument for the assessment of country performance in the field of communication rights, this would be crucial tool for human rights advocacy. 'Evidence from the data, and arguments based on them, should stimulate human rights policymaking and legal reform. Nongovernmental organizations could use the findings to base or increase the impact of their critiques of governments, and as an advocacy tool to lobby for change and focus their activities as part of the epistemic community' (Watchirs, 2002, p. 728).

Multiple actors

Governments must be constantly reminded that they are legally required under the human rights treaties they have ratified to implement, promote and protect communication rights. Communication rights are the expression of fundamental needs. The satisfaction of these needs requires a strong political will and the allocation of considerable resources. Without the binding commitment to make such resources available, 'rights talk' only serves to deepen the global distrust of political institutions.

At the same time, full implementation of communication rights cannot depend only upon governments. Civil society also has a key role to play in terms of advocacy for rights, both in terms of monitoring and exposing rights abuse and in educating and popularising rights.

Encouraging and facilitating people to assert these rights through different types of social action, and to use them to realise the enormous potential of both the old and new technologies of media and communication, are vital tasks for all concerned people.

Interactive learning process

Media governance that is based upon the normative assumption of communication rights should be an interactive learning process. The key principles of this process should be:

- Legitimacy: all participating actors view each other mutually as acceptable parties.
- Accountability: all actors are prepared to disclose rationales for their public choices and take responsibility for the consequences of these choices.
- Interaction: the societal process through which actors co-regulate the public sphere is a permanent, dynamic, and iterative learning process with no fixed terminal point.

Interactive learning means that the parties involved learn from each other. Such learning should take place on a continuous and iterative basis among the professionals working in the media and representative bodies in the six domains. The state sets the regulatory environment in which such interactions can take place without undue interference from political and/or commercial interests. The ultimate goal of the process is to find an optimal balance of interests between public, commercial and civil sectors.

Governance aims in six domains

It can be argued that there are six specific domains where communication rights and the underlying principles are especially relevant and in need of a strong defence. These are: ethnicity, gender, children, the arts, journalism and citizenship. This choice may look rather arbitrary but its rationale stems from international human rights law. With regard to these domains the international community has adopted specific, and often binding, legal provisions. The enforcement of these provisions would be a major contribution to communication rights-inspired media governance in Europe.

The six domains suggest the following aims to be pursued:

- *Ethnicity*: realisation of the presence and participation of ethnically diverse social groups in the media and the production/dissemination of content relevant to a variety of ethnic representations.
- *Gender*: promotion and protection of the rights of women in terms of non-discriminatory representation and full participation in media decision-making.
- *Children*: promotion and protection of the rights of the child in terms of free speech, privacy protection and the production/dissemination of relevant content.
- *The arts*: realisation of the production/dissemination of a wide variety of artistic expressions and an intellectual property rights system that benefits all artistic production.
- *Journalism*: protection of editorial independence and promotion of professional accountability.
- *Citizenship*: the protection of the citizen's rights to free speech, to access to information, to the confidentiality of communication and the securing of ample public space.

There are serious obstacles that impede the realisation of these aims. Among these are the interests of the key economic and political players that do not match the radical erosion of the power of hegemonic forces that the respect for human rights inevitably entails. There is also the problem of a growing antagonism between state and citizens.

A fundamental change of direction is particularly difficult with regard to the domain of communication rights. There is a lot at stake, both politically ('war on terrorism') and economically ('neo-liberalism') that impedes a full realisation of these rights.

Crucial communication rights in many countries are currently suspended as part of the war on terrorism. The protection of cultural rights implies a rule on cultural exemption in word trade, which is not popular with the major trading parties. Intellectual property rights – a rapidly growing and profitable global business – are robustly enforced as trading rights and not as human rights. The commercialisation of knowledge impedes greater equality in access to and use of knowledge. Communication rights imply the preservation of public space, which is rapidly withering away worldwide.

Concluding questions

For the management of media performance in the European region this chapter has suggested the development of a form of governance that is multi-stakeholder, interactive and a reiterative learning process. The normative basis for this new governance model is constituted by the principles and standards of communication rights.

In order to realise a *European* media governance inspired by the standard of communication rights, it is necessary to confront some hard questions. Are there *European* media? Is there a *European* public sphere? Are there *European* citizens? Is there a *European* polity? Can transnational forms of media governance be democratic? If democratic citizenship means that people are part of a 'demos', is there a *European* 'demos'?

What does European media governance mean when there are no European media? There are primarily national media in the European region. We may wish that these media are governed through various mechanisms and procedures in accordance with the standard of communication rights, but to what extent can European governance institutions and rules facilitate this? There are in the European countries public spaces for political debate and public dialogue, albeit under threat of commercial take-over. What however can governance on the supra-national level do to diminish these pressures, and how can it preserve and even expand national public spheres? Can European media governance be democratic as long as no democratic European polity exists? Can European media governance be carried by a constituency of citizens as long as European citizenship has so little substantial significance for most people living in European countries?

All this, however, should not deter us from exploring future governance possibilities. It is to this exercise of assessing which type of media governance would offer the best chances for the protection of communication rights that the present chapter made some initial suggestions.

It should be realised however that, as long as the European region does not manage to establish a region-wide participatory politics and a real sense of supra-national citizenship, we will remain caught in conventional media policymaking, with a democratic, multi-stakeholder, responsive media governance as distant ideal.

The fundamental question is whether, when media are to play a role in local/national democracies, they can be governed by rules and institutions that are shaped and function at a great distance from the citizens in European countries. The often-cited European democratic deficit finds concrete expression in the low level of participation in elections for the European Parliament. In the most recent elections this was less than 25% of the citizens in the participating countries.

There is barely a democratic decision-making process on such essential matters as the control over vital resources or public services. The emerging Europe has a neo-liberal signature, is steered by market fundamentalism, in the politics of which the management of essential services (such as energy and water) is outsourced to private interests, and welfare-type social services are rapidly pushed away as too burdensome.

A similar process takes place with regard to the field of media, including public service broadcasting, which in many respects stands for the good legacy of European values. A voice of concern about this development was raised by the concluding conference of the research programme 'Changing Europe – Changing Media' in Nice in December 2004 – see the 'Nice Declaration (Appendix).

Is there an alternative?
In order to develop an alternative it is necessary to first of all break through the thinking that 'there is no alternative' ('TINA', Margaret Thatcher's leading principle) and that the current economic processes (e.g. the introduction and use of the Euro) and political processes (e.g. the EU expansion) are inevitable and irreversible. This myopic thinking poses serious threats for a peaceful European future. The European integration is not a TGV that could not be stopped and re-routed.

The recent rejection of the European constitutional treaty by citizens in France and the Netherlands demonstrates this very dramatically. The overwhelming 'no' vote in these countries and the likelihood of similar positions in other countries if more referenda were held, created a serious political crisis, but above all gives the space for democratic reflection on Europe's preferred future. Now there is time to take realistic stock of the present European condition and to wonder whether Europe – if guided by the market principles of privatisation and liberalisation – is able to solve the great social problems of crime, terrorism, drugs trading, migration, deteriorating social services, growth of poverty and widespread unemployment. Now the opportunity is offered to question whether Europe can replace the currently prevailing 'thin democracy' of liberal-representative politics with the 'strong democracy' (Barber, 2003) of participatory politics.

In this spirit also European media scholars have a momentum to act. They have kept a conspicuously low profile in the middle of recent developments. As a matter of fact, the media reform movements and their academic mentors are more visible in the USA than in Europe. For example, Robert McChesney (1999) and his 'Free Press' (www.freepress.net) provides impressive evidence about how democratic interests can be mobilised against current American mainstream. And Edwin Baker (2002) sets an exemplary model for scholarship in media law and policy by analytically showing how the market does not 'come close to providing people with the media content they want' (p. 114) and how democracy requires a structurally mixed media system and a degree of governmental intervention (pp. 283–284).

Europe needs a new Enlightenment in the sense of a new emancipation from irrational economic and political belief systems. The mass media are evidently key players in order to achieve this new consciousness They require more than anything else the strengthening of the diversity (in terms of ownership and content) of national media, the promotion of a great variety of local media, the improvement of high-quality training of media professionals, and the expansion of programmes of media education. The last requirement is possibly the most urgent issue. Without an educated, active and self-mobilising critical media audience, Europe will not get media that function on the basis of respect for people's communication rights!

The essence of sustainable politics is summed up by Schumacher's famous statement 'Small is beautiful'. Re-reading his book (1973) should be mandatory for everyone who thinks about Europe's future. Whereas the protagonists of the greater Europe may lead us into a conflict-laden future with ever less democracy, a Europe of small units that, with all their political, cultural and moral differences, manages to co-exist peacefully holds great promise. Small Europe, however, needs to develop in balance with the greater Europe of a supra-national human rights regime and effective enforcement machinery. Finding this proper political balance is critical to the future democratic governance of European media.

REFERENCES

Anttiroiko, A-V. (2004) 'Introduction to Democratic e-Governance', pp. 22–49 in M. Mälkiä, A-V. Anttiroiko. & R.Savolainen, (eds) *eTransformation in Governance: New Directions in Government and Politics.* Hersey, PA: Idea Group Publishing.

Baker, C.E. (2002) *Media, Markets, and Democracy.* Cambridge: Cambridge University Press.

Barber, B. R. (2003) *Strong Democracy.* Berkeley: University of California Press.

Christians, C., T. Glasser, D. McQuail, K. Nordenstreng, & R. White (2006) *Normative Theories of the Media: Public Communication in a Democratic Society.* Urbana: Illinois University Press (forthcoming).

Cohler, A., B. Miller, & H. Stone (eds)(1989) *Montesquieu: The Spirit of the Laws.* Cambridge: Cambridge University Press.

Commission on Global Governance (1995) *Our Global Neighbourhood.* New York, Oxford University Press.

Galtung, J. (1999) 'State, Capital, and the Civil Society: The Problem of Communication' pp. 3–21 in R. Vincent, K. Nordenstreng & M. Traber (eds) *Towards Equity in Global Communication: MacBride Update.* Cresskill: Hampton Press.

Hallin, D. and P. Mancini (2004) *Comparing Media Systems: Three Models of Media and Politics.* Cambridge & New York: Cambridge University Press.

Hamelink, C. (1994) *The Politics of World Communication: A Human Rights Perspective.* London: Sage.

Hutchison, D. (1999) *Media Policy: An Introduction.* Oxford: Blackwell Publishers.

Kooiman, J. (2003) *Governing as Governance.* London: Sage.

McChesney, R. (1999) *Rich Media, Poor Democracy: Communication Politics in Dubious Times.* Urbana, Ill: University of Illinois Press.

McQuail, D. (2003) *Media Accountability and Freedom of Publication.* New York: Oxford University Press.

McQuail, D. (2005) *Mass Communication Theory.* (5th Edition) London: Sage.

McQuail, D. and K. Siune, (eds)(1998) *Media Policy: Convergence, Concentration and Commerce.* London: Sage.

Napoli, P.M. (2001) *The Foundations of Communications Policy.* Cresskill, NJ: Hampton Press.

Nordenstreng, K. (1977) 'From Mass Media to Mass Consciousness', pp. 269–283 in G. Gerbner (ed) *Mass Media Policies in Changing Cultures*. New York: John Wiley & Sons,.

Nordenstreng, K. (2004) 'Media Monitoring: Watching the Watchdogs', pp. 343–352 in R.D. Berenger, (ed) *Global Media Go to War: Role of News and Entertainment Media During the 2003 Iraq War*. Spokane, WA: Marquette Books.

Pool, I. (1974) 'The Rise of Communications Policy Research', *Journal of Communication*, 24:2, pp. 31–42.

Powe, Jr., L.A. (1991) *The Fourth Estate and the Constitution: Freedom of the Press in America*. Berkeley: University of California Press.

Schiller, H.I. (1975) 'The Appearance of National-communications Policies: A New Arena for Social Struggle', *Gazette*, 21: 2.

Schumacher, E.F. (1973) *Small Is Beautiful: Economics As If People Mattered*. New York: Harper & Row.

UNDP (1999) *Human Development Report*. New York: Oxford University Press.

UNESCO (1972) Report of the Meeting of Experts on Communication Policies and Planning (Paris, 17–18 July 1972). Paris, Unesco document COM/MD/24.

UNESCO (1976) *Towards Realistic Communication Policies: Recent Trends and Ideas Compiled and Analysed*. Paris, Unesco Reports and Papers on Mass Communication No. 76.

UNESCO (1979) *National Communication Policy Councils: Principles and Experiences*. Paris, Unesco Reports and Papers on Mass Communication No. 83.

Van Cuilenburg, J. & D. McQuail, (2003) 'Media Policy Paradigm Shifts: Towards a New Communication Policy Paradigm', *European Journal of Communication*, 18: 2, pp. 181–207.

Van Heffen, O., W.J.M. Kockert & J.J.A. Thomassen (eds)(2000) *Governance in Modern Societies*. Dordrecht: Kluwer.

Watchirs, H. (2002) 'Review of Methodologies Measuring Human Rights Implementation', *Journal of Law, Medicine and Ethics*, 30: 4, pp. 716–733.

Additional resources used

Alston, P. (1999) Governance, *Human Rights and the Normative Areas*. Background paper for the *UNDP Human Development Report*.

Bache, E. (ed) (2004) *Multi-level Governance*. Oxford: Oxford University Press.

Bang, H. (ed) (2003) *Governance as Social and Political Communication*. Manchester: Manchester University Press.

Cliche, D., R. Mitchell, & A. Wiesand (2002) *Creative Europe. On Governance and Management of Artistic Creativity in Europe*. Bonn: ERICArts.

Curran, J. (2001) 'Media Regulation in the Era of Market Liberalism', pp. 216–232 in G. Philo & D. Miller (eds) *Market Killing*. London: Longman.

Desai, M. (1999) 'Global Governance'. Background paper for the *UNDP Human Development Report*.

Falk, R. (1995) *On Humane Governance*. Cambridge: Polity Press.

Hirst, P. (1999) *Globalization in Question: The International Economy and the Possibilities of Governance*. Cambridge: Polity Press.

Kleinwaechter, W. (2003) 'Global Governance in the Information Age', *Development*, 46: 1, pp. 17–25.

Kohler-Koch, B. & R. Eising (eds) (2000) *The Transformation of Governance in the European Union*. London: Routledge.

Kooiman, J. (Ed.) (1993) *Modern Governance: New Government-Society Interactions*. London: Sage.

Loader, B.D. (ed) (1997) *The Governance of Cyberspace*. London: Routledge.

Mueller, M.L. (1999) 'ICANN and Internet Governance: Sorting through the Debris of Self-regulation', *info* 1: 6, pp. 497–520.

Mueller, M.L. (2004) *Ruling the Root: Internet Governance and the Taming of Cyberspace*. The MIT Press,

Nayyar, D. (ed) (2002) *Governing Globalisation: Issues and Institutions*. Oxford: Oxford University Press.

O'Siochru, S. & B. Girard (2002) *Global Media Governance*. New York: Rowman & Littlefield Publishers.

Pierre, J. (ed) (2000) *Debating Governance, Authority, Steering and Democracy*. Oxford: Oxford University Press.

Prakash, A. & J.A. Hart, (ed.) (1999) *Globalization and Governance*. London: Routledge.

Raboy. M. (ed) (2002) *Global Media Policy in the New Millennium*. Luton: University of Luton Press.

Rosenau, J.N. and E.O. Czempiel (eds) (1992) *Governance without Government*. Cambridge: Cambridge University Press.

Biographies

Editor
Els De Bens is professor of media and communications studies at the university of Gent, Belgium. She is chairman of the Flemish Media Council and co editor of the European Journal of Communication. Her main research interests are media policy, media economy and new media developments.

Co-editors
Cees J. Hamelink is professor of international communication at the University of Amsterdam and professor for media, religion and culture at the Vrije Universiteit in Amsterdam. He is the editor-in-chief of the scientific journal *Gazette* and honorary president of the International Association for Media and Communication Research. He is the author of seventeen books on communication, culture and human rights.

Karol Jakubowicz, Ph.D., is Director, Strategy and Analysis Department, the National Broadcasting Council of Poland, the broadcasting regulatory authority. He is also Chairman of the Steering Committee on the Media and New Communication Services at the Council of Europe.

Kaarle Nordenstreng is professor of journalism and mass communication at the University of Tampere (since 1971). He has also been visiting professor in the universities of California, Maryland, Minnesota and Texas. His main research interests are mass communication theory, international communication, and media ethics. He has written or edited 30 book-size publications and over 400 scholarly articles and reports.

Jan van Cuilenburg is professor of communications policy at The Amsterdam School of Communications Research *ASCoR* of the University of Amsterdam, and chair of the Netherlands Media Authority, the regulatory authority for broadcasting in The Netherlands. Van Cuilenburg's current academic research focuses on the relationship between media competition, media innovation and media diversity.

Richard van der Wurff teaches media-economics and media strategy at the Department of Communication of the University of Amsterdam. He is researcher at The Amsterdam School of Communications Research *ASCoR* where he investigates the impacts of competition and concentration on media organization strategies and on diversity of media supply in various media markets. His current research focuses in particular on the consequences of online and intermedia competition for newspaper publishers and for the availability and diversity of news in society.

Authors

Ildiko Kovats is associate professor in communication theory at the Institute of Behavioural Sciences and Communication Theory, Budapest Corvinus University and formerly communication researcher at the Research Centre for Communication studies at the Hungarian Academy of Sciences, and at the Mass Communication Research Centre. Her main fields of interest are communication policy, international communication, political communications, and social impacts of new communication technology.

Minna Aslama is a doctoral candidate in communication studies at the University of Helsinki. Her focus is on television studies. She has authored several articles for Finnish and international publications, topics of which range from market and policy analyses to reality television.

Ralph Negrine is Professor of Political Communication at the University of Sheffield. His specialist areas of interest are in political communication, media policy and general communication theory. His research interests lie mainly in the communication of politics, and media policy, although he has also published in the filed of research methods. His books include *Television and the Press Since 1945* (1999), and *The Communication of Politics* (1996). He is co-editor (with Christina Holtz-Bacha, Paolo Mancini and Stylianos Papathanassopoulos) of a volume on the 'professionalization' of political communication in Europe (Intellect, 2006).

Trine Syvertsen is professor of media studies in the Department of Media and Communication and Sub Dean of the Faculty of Arts, University of Oslo. Her research interests include television programming, public broadcasting and media policy. She has published several books and articles in Nordic and international journals. She is currently co-chairing the collaborative research project *Participation and play in converging media.*

Dr. Stylianos Papathanassopoulos is a Professor in Media Organisation and Policy at the Faculty of Communication and Media Studies at the National and Kapodistrian University of Athens. He has written extensively on media developments in Europe and Greece and especially on television issues. His research interests are on European communications and new media policies as well as political communication. His publications can be found in various academic journals. His most recent books are: *Television in the 21st century,* 2005 and *Media and Politics: the case of Southern Europe.* Athens: Kastaniotis, 2004.

Gianpietro Mazzoleni, is professor of Sociology of Communication at the University of Milano. His research interests focus on mass communication, political communication and media policies. He served as chair of the Euromedia Research Group (1997–2005) and is chair of the Political Communication Division of the International Communication Association (2004–2006). He is member of the editorial boards of *The European Journal of Communication*, and of *Political Communication*. His most recent publications include: *The Politics of Representation: Election Campaigning and Proportional Representation* (with J. Roper & C. Holtz-Bacha) and *The Media in Europe* (edited with M. Kelly & D. McQuail).

Winfried Schulz, born in Berlin, holds the Chair in Mass Communication and Political Science at the University of Erlangen-Nuremberg (Germany) since 1983. He is member of the editorial boards of Javnost – The Public, Journal of Communication, Medienpsychologie and ComPol – Comunicazione Politica. His publications and his continuing research focus on political communication, mass media audiences and effects, news analysis, media policy and media performance.

Index

Page numbers in italics denote information in Tables not already referred to in the text.

service journalism 10–11, 18 *see also* journalism
Slovakia, PSB 144, 145, 147, *187*
social diversity 27, 89 *see also* diversity
society
    global civil 201–2
    information 127, 198
    knowledge 129
    and media 225–7
    and PSB 118–19
    see also civil society
South East Europe Media Organisation (SEEMO) 220
Spain
    audience shares *187*
    PSB (RTVE) 117
        content 143, 147, 180, 181, *182, 184*
        funding, 132, 151, *152*, 153, 155–6, *157*
        policies 189
        regulation 148–9
        television 148–9, 171
special interest channels 76 *see also* channels
spin-offs 13–14
Stability Pact for South Eastern Europe 214–15
stagnation 42–3
State Broadcasting Treaty, Germany 74–5, 76
SVT *see* Sweden, PSB
Sweden
    audience reach 147
    audience shares *187*
    PSB (SVT) 185
        content 145, 147, 173, 180
        funding *152*, 153, 154
        policies 170, 189
        regulation *190*
        remits 142, 144, 145, 147
system dissimilarity 70–2
system diversity 70 *see also* diversity

T
tabloidisation 11, 17–19 *see also* newspapers
television
    advertising 72, 216
    Belgium 43, 60–5
    competition 61–2, 64, 65, 70–1, 74, 77–8, 79, 80–1, 93–4
    and digital technology 14
    diversity 65, 70–2, 75–7, 79, 82–3, 84, 88, 93–4, 103–4
    enhanced 173, 174
    Finland 65, 70–2, 174
    Flanders 61–2, 64, 80, 171, 174, 176
    France *171–2, 184*
    Germany 72–9, 80–1, 93–4

Hungary 172
Netherlands 43, 82–6, 88, 93–4, 103–6
Norway *171*
performance criteria 57, 62–4, 104–6
Portugal 148, 149
privatisation 10
programme quotas 17–18
Spain 148–9, 171
see also commercial television; digital television
thematic or target channels 14, 131, 173–4 *see also* channels
transmission time 145
trilateralism 206
truth, and diversity 25–6

U
UNESCO 197–8, 229
United Kingdom (UK)
    audience shares 153, *187*
    Communications Act 2003 92
    diversity 92
    programme output 181, *182*, 184–5
    PSB (BBC) 117, 124–5, 153, 161
        content 131–2, 143, 146, 181, *182*, 184–5, 186
        and digitalisation 161
        funding 132, *152*, 154, *157*, 161, 189
        and new media 169–70, 173–6
        policies 154, 189
        remits 129–30, 142, 144, 149, 154. 189
    regulation 91–3, 148–9, 189, 190–1
universality 174, 188

V
viewing figures
    Belgium 57, 62, 64
    Finland 65
    Flanders 57, 60–2, 64
    Germany 73, 79
    Netherlands 86, 104–6
    see also audience; market share
VRT *see* Flanders, PSB

W
World Electronic Media Forum 198
World Summit on the Information Society (WSIS) 2003 197–8
WSIS *see* World Summit on the Information Society

Y
YLE *see* Finland, PSB